# Get Prepared Now!

## WHY A GREAT CRISIS IS COMING & HOW YOU CAN SURVIVE IT

ISBN: 150522599X
ISBN 13: 9781505225990

# PREFACE

Economic instability, continued drought, threats to global food production, increased weather changes, pandemic, and vulnerable national power grids has spurred the interest of many in the nation and across the globe to prepare for the uncertain times that lie ahead.

*Get Prepared Now!* walks the reader through step-by-step budget friendly chapters on water gathering, storage and purification, food storage, hygiene, alternative cooking, heating and lighting, emergency medical supplies, safety and bartering designed to get the reader prepared in record time with concrete life-saving solutions.

For some, the question is whether it is *right* to prepare, and Michael Snyder of the Economic Collapse Blog does an excellent job of addressing this issue with a Christian viewpoint that will bring comfort to many readers struggling over their decision.

Barbara Fix, author of *Survival: Prepare Before Disaster Strikes* tackles preparedness with proven, common sense tactics our forefathers practiced to survive a lifestyle without the modern conveniences most take for granted today.

If you're struggling over whether or not to relocate from a densely populated area, or how to prepare for grid-down, or what and how to store for long-term survival, *Get Prepared Now!* is an excellent place to start.

# Get Prepared Now!

## WHY A GREAT CRISIS IS COMING & HOW YOU CAN SURVIVE IT

*Section One*
*by Michael Snyder*

# CONTENTS--SECTION ONE
by
Michael Snyder

# INTRODUCTION
by Michael Snyder

The first presidential election that I have any memory of was in 1980. When Ronald Reagan was elected by a landslide, I remember being absolutely convinced that much better days were ahead for America. And for a while, it did seem like things were getting better. I was the son of a U.S. Navy officer, and I attended high school in a suburb of Washington D.C. during the late 1980s. As a family, we considered ourselves to be "middle class", and virtually everyone around me appeared to be in the "middle class" as well. Almost every family that I knew had a nice home, had a couple of vehicles and could afford to get nice things for their kids. Life certainly wasn't perfect, but I didn't know anyone that was truly poor. And there was this assumption that things would always be getting better and better because we lived in the greatest country on the planet. At that time, nobody could really imagine that really hard times would come to the United States someday.

When I graduated from high school, I wanted to get a business degree. After all, I was part of the "greed is good" generation. As a young person, I joked with my family that I would go into business, build a massive home, and then build a giant fence around it to keep them out. Like so many at that time, I got caught up in the notion that money was the key to more happiness in life. So I went away to the University of Virginia, and I ended up earning a degree from the much acclaimed McIntire School of Commerce.

But then a funny thing happened. I graduated during the midst of a terrible recession. Very few of my friends were able to find good jobs, and I was in the same boat.

This was quite a shock to me. I had been promised that if I worked really hard and got good grades that there would be a reward for me at the end of the rainbow.

Instead, I found myself working at Sears immediately after graduation.

At first, I thought that the problem must be with me.

I thought that I must not have worked hard enough or must not have applied myself to searching for a job hard enough.

But the truth was that there were millions of others out there just like me.

Well, the U.S. economy "recovered" as the nineties rolled along and everyone was pretty much convinced that things had gotten back to "normal". Personally, I made the decision to go to law school as the nineties rolled to a close. I needed to get my life back on track, and I figured that a lucrative new career was the way to go.

So I attended the University of Florida law school and I ended up earning two degrees while I was there. But once again, I graduated about the time that a great recession hit the United States. Only a handful of my fellow graduates were able to land good jobs, but almost all of us graduated with high levels of student loan debt.

I ended up in Washington D.C., and I was eventually able to spend an extended period of time with a major law firm where I mostly worked on a case involving Fannie Mae. It was actually dreadfully boring work, and I didn't particularly enjoy it.

But it did pay the bills.

I was just a working Joe getting up every morning and dragging myself to the Metro station. I would take the Metro down into the heart of the city right on K Street. In essence, I was working "in the belly of the beast". There was so much corruption going on all around me, but like most working Americans I was just happy to have a job.

Over time, though, I became increasingly concerned about the direction that this country was headed.

I wanted to do something to try to make a difference.

But what could I do?

I was just another schmoe trying to make a living however I could.

I was just another cog in a machine over which I seemingly had no control.

How in the world could I ever make an impact?

Well, eventually I decided to try my hand at writing. I had heard of "blogging", but I had never really explored it. But I figured that I might as well try to make my voice be heard somehow.

So I started writing. And at first very, very few people took notice of my work. But I kept at it, and I slowly began to build a following.

Then in December 2009 I started The Economic Collapse Blog. It really touched a nerve, because at the time millions of Americans were losing their jobs and millions of Americans were losing their homes and most of them really didn't understand why all of this was happening. Most of them just knew at a gut level that they were not getting the truth from our politicians and from the mainstream media, and many of them were seeking out alternative sources of information on the Internet.

When I created the Economic Collapse Blog, I decided to take a much different approach than others who write about these things. Most people who write about economics write at a level that is "way up in the clouds". In other words, they write at a level that the vast majority of people simply cannot understand.

I didn't want to be like that. So I tried very hard to write for "the man on the street". I used lots of charts and graphs and lists, and I tried to explain things in a way that virtually everyone should be able to grasp.

And the website really took off. Today, the Economic Collapse Blog averages somewhere around 1.2 million page impressions a month. I have written more than 1,100 articles about our coming economic problems, and they are shared on dozens of major websites all over the globe.

In the first major section of this book, I am going to briefly go over some of the reasons why I believe that a great economic crisis is coming. But it is not enough just to intellectually know about these things. One of the reasons why I sound the alarm so loudly about the coming storm is so that people will get prepared.

That is what the second major section of this book is going to be about. Personally, I am not a huge expert on things like canning and water storage, but I have teamed up with someone that has great knowledge about a whole host of these types of things. Her name is Barbara Fix, and she is a respected prepping expert.

This book is entitled "Get Prepared Now!" for a reason. We believe that a time of great trouble is coming for the United States. And we believe that the time to get prepared for what is ahead is right now.

To be honest, we should have probably gotten this book out sooner. There will be some that get this book too late. But I do believe that there will also be many that will be greatly helped by it.

I am certainly not perfect and neither is Barbara. We are just doing our best to sound the alarm and to help people get prepared. Hopefully you will be greatly encouraged and greatly blessed by what we have to share. It is my prayer that God will take our limited words and will use them for His purposes.

And even though I have been writing for so many years, there are times that I still feel that words fail me.

I wish that I could adequately impress upon you the certainty of what is coming.

I wish that I could adequately impress upon you the urgency of getting prepared.

The most difficult times in the history of the United States are almost upon us, and most Americans will be completely blindsided by them.

It is my hope that this book will wake a few more people up while there is still time.

# Chapter 1

## IS IT "ANTI-FAITH" TO GET PREPARED?

Is it "anti-faith" for a Christian to prepare for the hard times that are coming? A while back, someone that had come across one of my articles actually accused me of being "anti-faith" because I am encouraging people to do what they can to get prepared for the coming economic collapse. This individual believed that I was peddling worry and fear, and he insisted that what I was teaching people was not Biblical.

I was alarmed when I got this email, because the last thing I want to do is to steer people the wrong way. So I started thinking about this quite a bit, and I began asking myself some really hard questions. Does being a "prepper" show a lack of faith in God? Should good Christians reject prepping altogether?

In the email that I received, the individual that was accusing me used Matthew chapter 6 as evidence that what I was telling people to do was wrong. The following is what Matthew chapter 6 says from verse 25 to verse 32…

*25 Therefore I say unto you, Take no thought for your life, what ye shall eat, or what ye shall drink; nor yet for your body, what ye shall put on. Is not the life more than meat, and the body than raiment?*

*26 Behold the fowls of the air: for they sow not, neither do they reap, nor gather into barns; yet your heavenly Father feedeth them. Are ye not much better than they?*

*27 Which of you by taking thought can add one cubit unto his stature?*

*28 And why take ye thought for raiment? Consider the lilies of the field, how they grow; they toil not, neither do they spin:*

*29 And yet I say unto you, That even Solomon in all his glory was not arrayed like one of these.*

*30 Wherefore, if God so clothe the grass of the field, which today is, and tomorrow is cast into the oven, shall he not much more clothe you, O ye of little faith?*

*31 Therefore take no thought, saying, What shall we eat? or, What shall we drink? or, Wherewithal shall we be clothed?*

*32 (For after all these things do the Gentiles seek:) for your heavenly Father knoweth that ye have need of all these things.*

Jesus uses some pretty strong language in those verses. Obviously we are not to be filled with worry about our material needs. But do these verses rule out preparing for hard times? Do they actually say that we are not to plan for the future at all?

Those that read my articles on a regular basis know that I am a Christian and that I am very open about that fact. And I am also someone that places a very high value on faith. The Scriptures tell us that "all things are possible" for those that believe, and that is something that I take very seriously. Without God, none of us has any hope. In fact, without God I would probably be dead by now. But with God on our side, there are literally no limits as to what is possible.

Without a doubt, the Scriptures repeatedly command us to have faith. But does faith mean that we sit on our couches watching television while we wait for God to do everything for us?

If that was true, why would any of us ever go to work?

We could just sit back and wait for God to miraculously "provide" by putting money into our bank accounts for us.

Why would any of us ever fill up our vehicles with gasoline?

We would just sit back and wait for God to miraculously "provide" by putting gas into our gas tanks.

The truth is that faith is not about sitting on your couch and waiting for God to do everything for you. Rather, faith is about being obedient and taking action on what God has directed you to do.

Yes, without a doubt God can do mind blowing supernatural things that require absolutely no participation on our part. I know, because it has happened to me. But the vast majority of the time, God works with us and through us. He requires us to take steps of faith and obedience, and in the process He leads us, He guides us, He blesses us and He opens doors for us.

The story of Noah is a perfect example of this. Some have referred to Noah as the very first "prepper" in the Bible. God could have kept Noah and his family safe from the flood by transporting them to some sort of very comfortable "heavenly waiting area" and then brought them back to earth when everything was dry, but He didn't do that. Instead, God warned Noah about what was coming and ordered him to build a boat.

So did Noah just sit back and wait for God to do everything for Him? No, he exercised his faith by taking action. He believed the warning that God has given him and he built a giant boat. In Hebrews 11:7, Noah is commended for his radical faith which produced radical action...

*7 By faith Noah, being warned of God of things not seen as yet, moved with fear, prepared an ark to the saving of his house; by which he condemned the world, and became heir of the righteousness which is by faith.*

Faith almost always involves action. God wants to see if we are going to believe Him and do what He has instructed us to do.

And the amount of faith that Noah exhibited was absolutely staggering. The boat that he and his family constructed was approximately the size of a World War II aircraft carrier. It took many years to build it and to collect the massive amount of food and supplies that his family and all of the animals would need to survive the flood.

I don't know of any "prepper" today that could boast about taking more radical "preparations" than Noah did. If someone did the same thing today, that person would be considered absolutely insane.

And surely Noah must have grown very weary of all of the mocking that he received as he endlessly warned everyone else about what was coming month after month, year after year.

In the end, nobody outside of his own family listened to him, but Noah's prepping did pay off.

He and his family were saved, and everyone else drowned.

So what would have happened if Noah had not built that boat?

He and his family would have drowned with all of the rest of them.

Noah's faith did not mean sitting back and waiting for God to do something for him. Rather, his faith meant stepping up and being obedient to what God was telling him to do.

Unfortunately, there are lots of Christians out there today that are 100 percent against preparing for what is ahead, even though many of them will admit that a great economic collapse is coming.

In fact, the individual that accused me of being "anti-faith" is a perfect example of this. The following is an excerpt from the message that this person emailed to me...

*"Now, although I agree with you about the things you write about the corruption of the financial system, and that there will be a collapse, yet I do not agree with you in promoting people to be self-sufficient contrary to the Lord's teaching. If you truly have God then no provision needs to be made at all for yourself, just trust in God's providence alone."*

This individual actually agrees with me that an economic collapse is coming, but he insists that we should do absolutely nothing to prepare for it.

Is that really what God would have us do?

In Genesis chapter 41, God gave Pharaoh a very disturbing dream. It was so disturbing that Pharaoh desperately searched for anyone that could explain it to him.

Ultimately, God revealed the meaning of the dream to Joseph, and this enabled Joseph to rise to a position of great prominence in the land of Egypt.

God showed Joseph that there would be seven years of good harvests followed by seven years of crippling drought. In fact, God showed Joseph that the seven years of famine would be "very grievous".

So did Joseph advise Pharaoh to just sit back and wait for God to miraculously provide?

No. Instead Joseph advised Pharaoh to start taking immediate action to prepare for what was ahead, and Pharaoh decided to put Joseph in charge of making those preparations.

What Joseph did next was absolutely unprecedented. Joseph engaged in an "emergency food storage project" unlike anything that the world had ever seen up until that point. By heeding God's warning and taking action, he ultimately ended up saving the nation of Egypt and his entire family.

Some people believe that preparing for hard times means that you are "fearful", but I don't see it that way at all.

Rather, I am convinced that there is hope in understanding what is happening and that there is hope in getting prepared.

The people that are sticking their heads in the sand right now and ignoring the warnings are the ones that are going to get absolutely blindsided by what is coming. Many of them will give in to despair when they realize that they are completely unprepared for what is happening to them.

I think that all of us would benefit greatly by taking advantage of the wisdom found in Proverbs 6:6-11...

*6 Go to the ant, thou sluggard; consider her ways, and be wise:*

*7 Which having no guide, overseer, or ruler,*

*8 Provideth her meat in the summer, and gathereth her food in the harvest.*

*9 How long wilt thou sleep, O sluggard? when wilt thou arise out of thy sleep?*

*10 Yet a little sleep, a little slumber, a little folding of the hands to sleep:*

*11 So shall thy poverty come as one that travelleth, and thy want as an armed man.*

*12 But he answered and said, Verily I say unto you, I know you not.*

The Scriptures teach us that if we just sit back and do nothing and refuse to work, poverty will overtake us like a bandit.

So no, we are absolutely not supposed to be filled with worry and fear about our material needs, but we are not supposed to sit back and do nothing about them either. We are instructed to work hard and to trust God. As we take steps of obedience, He will bless us and provide for us.

If you just blindly believe that "everything will be okay" when all of the evidence is pointing to the contrary, you are just being foolish.

You don't prepare for a storm when it hits. At that point it is too late. Rather, you prepare while the storm is still off in the distance.

Throughout the Scriptures, those that "prepare" are commended. For example, just check out the following parable of Jesus that we find in Matthew chapter 25...

*1 Then shall the kingdom of heaven be likened unto ten virgins, which took their lamps, and went forth to meet the bridegroom.*

*2 And five of them were wise, and five were foolish.*

*3 They that were foolish took their lamps, and took no oil with them:*

*4 But the wise took oil in their vessels with their lamps.*

*5 While the bridegroom tarried, they all slumbered and slept.*

*6 And at midnight there was a cry made, Behold, the bridegroom cometh; go ye out to meet him.*

*7 Then all those virgins arose, and trimmed their lamps.*

*8 And the foolish said unto the wise, Give us of your oil; for our lamps are gone out.*

*9 But the wise answered, saying, Not so; lest there be not enough for us and you: but go ye rather to them that sell, and buy for yourselves.*

*10 And while they went to buy, the bridegroom came; and they that were ready went in with him to the marriage: and the door was shut.*

*11 Afterward came also the other virgins, saying, Lord, Lord, open to us.*

*12 But he answered and said, Verily I say unto you, I know you not.*

Do you want to be like the wise virgins or the foolish virgins?

The answer is obvious.

Yes, we never want to become obsessed with material things. We need to keep our priorities in order and focus on the things that are really important.

But that doesn't mean that we can all just sit on our couches, eat chips, and wait for God to do everything for us.

The following are some more Scriptures that show the importance that the Bible places on being prepared…

Proverbs 27:12

*"A prudent man foreseeth the evil, and hideth himself; but the simple pass on, and are punished."*

Proverbs 21:20

*"There is treasure to be desired and oil in the dwelling of the wise; but a foolish man spendeth it up."*

Ecclesiastes 10:18

*"By much slothfulness the building decayeth; and through idleness of the hands the house droppeth through."*

Proverbs 28:19

*"He that tilleth his land shall have plenty of bread: but he that followeth after vain persons shall have poverty enough."*

1 Timothy 5:8

*"But if any provide not for his own, and specially for those of his own house, he hath denied the faith, and is worse than an infidel."*

Proverbs 22:3

*"A prudent man foreseeth the evil, and hideth himself: but the simple pass on, and are punished."*

In my opinion, we have been warned about the coming economic collapse in a multitude of different ways. Later on in this book, I am going to share some of the reasons why I believe that a devastating economic crisis is on the way.

On the Economic Collapse Blog, I have written hundreds of articles and shared thousands upon thousands of facts and statistics that make it very clear that a horrific economic collapse is coming. I study these things constantly, and so to me it seems glaringly obvious that we should all be getting prepared. Unfortunately, most Americans have very little understanding of economics, and most people in our society rely on the mainstream media to tell them what to think about what is going on in the world. So most people have absolutely no idea what is on the horizon.

I am really trying to do my best to warn people about what is coming from my little spot "on the wall". In the Scriptures, those that are aware that a threat is coming are responsible for warning others about it. The following is a short excerpt from Ezekiel chapter 33...

*2 Son of man, speak to the children of thy people, and say unto them, When I bring the sword upon a land, if the people of the land take a man of their coasts, and set him for their watchman:*

*3 If when he seeth the sword come upon the land, he blow the trumpet, and warn the people;*

*4 Then whosoever heareth the sound of the trumpet, and taketh not warning; if the sword come, and take him away, his blood shall be upon his own head.*

*5 He heard the sound of the trumpet, and took not warning; his blood shall be upon him. But he that taketh warning shall deliver his soul.*

*6 But if the watchman see the sword come, and blow not the trumpet, and the people be not warned; if the sword come, and take any person from among them, he is taken away in his iniquity; but his blood will I require at the watchman's hand.*

In this book you are going to hear some very hard things.

The goal is not to fill you with worry and fear.

Rather, the goal is to get you to understand what is coming so that you can have hope of making it through the coming storm.

When you are done with this book, please pass it on to your family and friends. My hope is that people will use this book as a tool. We need to warn others about what is ahead and help them get prepared while there is still time.

Yes, very, very painful economic times are coming.

Those that heed the warnings and diligently prepare will have a good chance of weathering the nightmare that is rapidly approaching.

I honestly don't know what those that have made absolutely no preparations are going to do.

# Chapter 2

## AN ECONOMIC COLLAPSE?

Why should Americans be concerned about a coming economic collapse?

As the publisher of The Economic Collapse Blog (http://theeconomiccollapseblog.com/) that is a question that I get asked all the time. On that website, I have authored more than 1000 articles that explain in excruciating detail precisely why a great economic collapse is coming. In this chapter, I will try to summarize some of the main points. If you are interested in learning more about these issues after reading this chapter, I would encourage you to dig into the articles on my website.

First of all, I want to define what I mean by "economic collapse". Many people that write about "the coming economic collapse" hype it up like some sort of big Hollywood event. They imagine that it will unfold over the course of a week or a month and then it will be all over and we will rebuild.

Unfortunately, things are not so simple.

To me, our "economic collapse" is something that has been going on for many years, that is happening right now, and that will greatly accelerate in the future. It is a steady, systematic decline that will be punctuated by moments of great crisis.

What happened in 2008 was one of the first "waves" of our economic collapse, but it certainly did not destroy our economy completely. There will be more "waves" to come, and some of them will be far worse than what we experienced back in 2008.

So the "economic collapse" is not something that I put a specific date on. I believe that things are going to get progressively worse and that our current economic system is going to ultimately collapse completely.

But it is going to take time.

The primary reason why our economy is in the process of collapsing is debt. We have been living way, way above our means for a very long time. In fact, we have been doing this for so long that most of us no longer have any idea what "normal" actually is.

Right now, we are living in the terminal phase of the greatest debt bubble in human history. 40 years ago, the U.S. national debt was about a half trillion dollars. Today, it has crossed the 17 trillion dollar mark. By the time you read this book, it may be crossing the 18 trillion dollar mark. What we are doing to ourselves as a nation is absolutely insane.

And our debt growth has greatly accelerated in recent years. It is hard to believe, but we are actually on pace to accumulate more new debt during the presidency of Barack Obama than we did under all of the other presidents in U.S. history combined.

We are stealing about a hundred million dollars from our children and our grandchildren every single hour of every single day. This goes on week after week, month after month, year after year and most Americans do not seem to care.

We are literally destroying the future to make things more pleasant for ourselves. If our founding fathers could see us today they would be absolutely sickened by us.

Sadly, most Americans have just come to accept that being 17 trillion dollars in debt is "normal". The implications of such an enormous debt do not seem to register with most people.

When you are talking about a trillion dollars, you are talking about an amount of money that is almost unimaginable. The following are a couple of illustrations that I use to try to explain to people just how large a trillion dollars is…

If you were alive when Jesus Christ was born and you spent one million dollars every single day since that point, you still would not have spent one trillion dollars by now.

If right this moment you went out and started spending one dollar every single second, it would take you more than 31,000 years to spend one trillion dollars.

But of course it is not just the federal government that is piling up debt.

40 years ago, the total amount of all debt in our financial system (all government debt, all business debt and all consumer debt) was about 2 trillion dollars. Today, it is more than 56 trillion dollars. That means that the total amount of debt in this country has gotten more than 28 times larger during that time.

It has been the greatest debt binge of all time, and this is why we have been able to enjoy such a massively inflated standard of living for the past several decades.

But as anyone that has ever run up huge amounts of credit card debt knows, eventually the party comes to an end. A great day of reckoning is fast approaching, and when it arrives the party will be over.

Meanwhile, our economic infrastructure is being absolutely gutted and our economic power is steadily diminishing.

Most Americans don't realize this, but the U.S. economy is not nearly as important to the rest of the globe as it once was. According to the World Bank, U.S. GDP accounted for 31.8 percent of all global economic activity in 2001. That number dropped to 21.6 percent in 2011.

That isn't just a decline.

That is a collapse.

Other measurements of economic power show a similar drop. For instance, the United States was once ranked #1 in the world in GDP per capita. Today we have slipped all the way to #14.

A big reason for this is that politicians from both political parties have stood aside and done nothing as tens of thousands of businesses and millions of jobs have been shipped out of the country.

It is hard to believe, but more than 56,000 manufacturing facilities have been permanently shut down in the United States since 2001, and we are losing about half a million jobs to China every single year.

Just since the turn of the century things have changed dramatically. Back in the year 2000, about 17 million Americans were employed in manufacturing. Today, only about 12 million Americans are employed in manufacturing.

Once upon a time, our gleaming factories helped to support a booming middle class unlike anything the world had ever seen before. But now our formerly great manufacturing cities are being transformed into rotting, decaying hellholes all around us, and nobody seems to know how to stop it.

It is hard to believe, but the city of Detroit actually once had the highest per capita income in the entire nation, but now it is a dying, bankrupt city with 70,000 abandoned buildings.

And we are even losing when it comes to high-tech manufacturing. Back in 1998, the United States had 25 percent of the world's high-tech export market and China had just 10 percent. Today, China's high-tech exports are double the size of U.S. high-tech exports.

As a result of the systematic gutting of our economic infrastructure, there simply are not nearly enough jobs for everyone anymore.

Once upon a time, it seemed like anyone that was honest and that was willing to work hard could go out and get a decent paying job.

Back in 1950, more than 80 percent of all men in the United States had a job. Today, less than 65 percent of all men in the United States have a job.

And the quality of the jobs in this country continues to decline very rapidly as well.

Right now, only 47 percent of all U.S. adults have a full-time job, and one out of every ten jobs is being filled by a temp agency.

Many people know that the largest employer in the United States is Wal-Mart, but did you know that the second largest employer in this nation is actually a temp agency? It sounds crazy, but Kelly Services actually hires more people than anyone else except for Wal-Mart at this point.

But part-time jobs and temp jobs are not the kind of "breadwinner jobs" that the middle class needs to support their families.

As you read this, one out of every four American workers has a job that pays ten dollars an hour or less, and the percentage of low paying jobs in our economy continues to grow.

In fact, 40 percent of all U.S. workers are now making less than what a full-time minimum wage worker made back in 1968 after you account for inflation.

So it should not be a shock to learn that incomes in the U.S. are actually going down. In fact, according to the U.S. Census Bureau, median household income in the United States has fallen for five years in a row.

The middle class is being systematically shredded, and as a result poverty is absolutely exploding.

According to the latest numbers from the U.S. Census Bureau, the number of people receiving means-tested welfare benefits is greater than the number of full-time employees in the United States.

What is happening to us?

How can we have fallen so far?

Government dependents already outnumber full-time workers and the next major wave of the economic collapse has not even hit us yet.

And when you throw in those getting Social Security and Medicare, the numbers are absolutely staggering. According to the most recent numbers from the U.S. Census Bureau, 49.2

percent of all Americans are receiving benefits from at least one government program each month.

The mainstream media continues to insist that we are in the midst of an "economic recovery", but anyone with half a brain can see that is a lie.

While Barack Obama has been in office, the number of Americans on food stamps has grown from 32 million to 47 million.

At this point, the number of Americans on food stamps exceeds the entire population of Spain.

There is a massive amount of economic suffering out there in America today, and it just keeps getting worse.

Brand new numbers that have just been released show that the number of public school students in this country that are homeless is at an all-time record high. Currently, 1.2 million students that attend public schools in America are homeless. That number has risen by 72 percent since the start of the last recession.

Are you starting to get the picture?

We desperately need solutions, but instead our politicians continue to do the exact same things that got us into this mess in the first place.

Unfortunately, things are going to get a whole lot worse than they are now. Today, our entire economic system is based on credit. Just about every major purchase involves going into debt, and without a steady flow of credit economic activity in this country would dry up very rapidly.

The banks are at the core of this system of debt. In particular, there are six "too big to fail" banks that dominate the entire industry. They were at the heart of the problems that we experienced back in 2008, and they have become even more reckless since then. In this next chapter, I am going to explain why those big banks are also going to be at the epicenter of the next major wave of the economic collapse.

# Chapter 3

## OUR INCREDIBLY FRAGILE FINANCIAL SYSTEM

Most Americans have no idea that our banking system is more vulnerable today than it has ever been before. Over the past couple of decades, Wall Street has been transformed into the biggest casino in the history of the planet, and at this point it is a house of cards that could come tumbling down at any time.

Sadly, most Americans don't even realize what caused the last major financial crisis back in 2008. If you ask most Americans what happened back then, most of them will mumble something about "subprime mortgages" or banks that were "too big to fail" without giving you a clear, coherent answer.

And there are many Americans that have almost completely forgotten what happened during the last financial crisis. 2008 may as well be ancient history for them.

Most people don't take the time to study these things. Most people are just very busy living their daily lives, trusting that the government has fixed the problems that plagued the system back then.

Unfortunately, that is not the case at all. In fact, none of the underlying problems that caused the last financial crisis have been addressed in a meaningful way.

For example, the problem of having "too big to fail" banks has not been solved. In fact, the "too big to fail" banks are now bigger than ever before.

Over the past five years, the six largest banks in the United States (JPMorgan Chase, Bank of America, Citigroup, Wells Fargo, Goldman Sachs and Morgan Stanley) have collectively gotten 37 percent larger.

Meanwhile, 1,400 smaller banks have quietly disappeared from the U.S. banking industry.

What this means is that the health of JPMorgan Chase, Bank of America, Citigroup, Wells Fargo, Goldman Sachs and Morgan Stanley is now more critical to the U.S. economy than ever before.

If they were "too big to fail" back in 2008, then now they must be "too colossal to collapse".

What we are witnessing is a consolidation of the banking industry that is absolutely unprecedented. Hundreds of smaller banks have been swallowed up by these behemoths, and millions of Americans are finding that they have to deal with these banking giants whether they like it or not.

Without these banks, we do not have an economy. The six largest banks control 67 percent of all U.S. banking assets, and Bank of America accounted for about a third of all business loans all by itself last year.

Overall, the five largest banks account for 42 percent of all loans of all types in the United States. This gives these banks an enormous amount of control over our economy.

Our entire system is based on credit, and these giant banks are at the very core of our system of credit. If these banks were to collapse, the flow of credit would be crippled and a brutal economic depression would be guaranteed.

And it is hard to really convey in words just how massive these big banks have become.

For example, JPMorgan Chase is roughly the size of the entire British economy all by itself.

Overall, the four largest banks have more than a million employees combined.

That is staggering.

And certainly there are lots of Americans that don't like these big banks very much, but at this point we have become so dependent on them that we could not survive their downfall.

It is kind of like a cancer that has invaded the body of a patient so completely that it would be impossible for doctors to kill the cancer without killing the patient.

Because these banks have gotten 37 percent larger over the past five years, that means that we are now far more vulnerable to a collapse of those banks in 2014 than we were in 2008.

And unfortunately, those banks continue to become even more reckless with their money and our money with each passing year.

As you read this, there are five U.S. banks that each have total exposure to derivatives that is well in excess of 40 TRILLION dollars. This is something that I have written about extensively in the past, but for this book I went and found the very latest official government numbers on the amount of exposure that these banks have to derivatives. I think that you will agree that these numbers are absolutely eye-popping...

**JPMorgan Chase**
Total Assets: $2,476,986,000,000 (about 2.5 trillion dollars)
Total Exposure To Derivatives: $67,951,190,000,000 (more than 67 trillion dollars)

**Citibank**
Total Assets: $1,894,736,000,000 (almost 1.9 trillion dollars)
Total Exposure To Derivatives: $59,944,502,000,000 (nearly 60 trillion dollars)

**Goldman Sachs**
Total Assets: $915,705,000,000 (less than a trillion dollars)
Total Exposure To Derivatives: $54,564,516,000,000 (more than 54 trillion dollars)

**Bank Of America**
Total Assets: $2,152,533,000,000 (a bit more than 2.1 trillion dollars)
Total Exposure To Derivatives: $54,457,605,000,000 (more than 54 trillion dollars)

**Morgan Stanley**
Total Assets: $831,381,000,000 (less than a trillion dollars)
Total Exposure To Derivatives: $44,946,153,000,000 (more than 44 trillion dollars)

When we are talking about 40 trillion dollars, we are talking about an amount of money that is almost unimaginable. Unlike stocks and bonds, these derivatives do not represent "investments" in anything. They can be incredibly complex, but essentially derivatives are just paper wagers about something that will happen in the future. In essence, derivatives trading is not that much different from betting on baseball or football games. Trading in derivatives is basically just a form of legalized gambling, and the "too big to fail" banks have transformed Wall Street into the largest casino in the history of the planet. When this derivatives bubble finally bursts (and as surely as I am writing this it will), the pain that it will cause the global economy will be greater than words can describe.

Are you starting to understand just how serious this all is?

And the biggest chunk of the derivatives contracts that these big banks are holding is made up of interest rate derivatives contracts.

According to the Bank for International Settlements, the global financial system overall has a total of 441 TRILLION dollars in exposure to interest rate derivatives.

Usually interest rates stay fairly stable, so normally all of this exposure does not create a major problem.

But if rapidly rising interest rates suddenly caused trillions of dollars of those bets to start going bad, we could potentially see several of the "too big to fail" banks collapse in rapid succession.

An example might be helpful here.

Imagine if you owned a life insurance company, and you issued very large life insurance policies for millions upon millions of people and then all of them suddenly died at the same time.

The life insurance company would go bankrupt because there would be no way to pay off all of those policies.

That is the kind of crisis that we could be looking at if we see a huge spike in interest rates. Suddenly trillions upon trillions of dollars worth of interest rate contracts would go bad and some of the largest banks in American would be insolvent.

So what would happen then?

Would the federal government and the Federal Reserve somehow come up with trillions of dollars (or potentially even tens of trillions of dollars) to bail them out?

Would the federal government and the Federal Reserve allow them to fail this time?

Nobody knows exactly how all of this would play out. But without a doubt a major derivatives crisis would cause a worldwide financial panic far worse than what we experienced back in 2008. Once this house of cards falls, there won't be enough money available in the entire world to fix it.

Wall Street has been transformed into the largest and wildest casino the world has ever seen, and at some point all of this reckless gambling is going to end very, very badly.

I hope that you are getting prepared.

# Chapter 4

## THE DEATH OF THE DOLLAR?

For years, countless pundits have endlessly proclaimed that "the death of the dollar" is imminent. But it has not happened. So why should we keep waiting for it to happen when all of the previous predictions of doom have failed? What is going to make things different this time?

Right now, the U.S. dollar is the de facto reserve currency of the planet. Most global trade is conducted in U.S. dollars, and almost all oil is sold for U.S. dollars. More than 60 percent of all global foreign exchange reserves are held in U.S. dollars, and far more U.S. dollars are actually used outside of the United States than inside of it. As will be described below, this has given the United States some tremendous economic advantages, and most Americans have no idea how much their current standard of living depends on the dollar remaining the reserve currency of the world. Unfortunately, thanks to reckless money printing by the Federal Reserve and the reckless accumulation of debt by the federal government, the status of the dollar as the reserve currency of the world is now in great jeopardy.

The fact that the rest of the world uses our currency to trade with one another means that demand for U.S. dollars is far higher than it otherwise would be. And for many years major exporting nations such as China and Japan have been systematically suppressing the value of their own currencies and artificially inflating the value of the U.S. dollar in an attempt to increase their exports.

Because of this, American consumers have been able to buy imported goods very, very cheaply.

For example, have you ever gone into a dollar store and wondered how anyone could possibly make a profit by making those products and selling them for just one dollar?

Well, the truth is that when you flip those products over you will find that almost all of them have been made outside of the United States. In fact, the words "made in China" are probably the most common words found in your entire household if you are anything like the typical American.

Thanks to the massively unbalanced trade that we have had with the rest of the world, tens of thousands of our businesses, millions of our jobs and trillions of our dollars have left this country and gone over to the other side of the planet in recent years. Since 1975, we have run a total trade deficit of more than 8 trillion dollars with the rest of the globe, and this has fundamentally transformed the U.S. economy. Our economic infrastructure has been absolutely gutted, and formerly great manufacturing cities such as Detroit are now rotting, decaying hellholes.

But now another major shift is happening, which is going to change things once again.

Alarmed by all of the quantitative easing that the Federal Reserve has been doing and by the reckless accumulation of debt by the U.S. government, China has announced that it is going to quit stockpiling more U.S. dollars.

What that means is that the value of the Chinese yuan is going to rise and the value of the U.S. dollar is going to go down.

It isn't going to happen overnight, but soon you will find that your dollar does not go as far as it once did, and all of that cheap stuff that you are used to buying at Wal-Mart and the dollar store is going to become a lot more expensive.

In addition, as nations such as China start to move away from stockpiling U.S. dollars, we are also going to see demand for U.S. debt go down.

Instead of just sitting on all of the cash that they accumulate through their trading activities, major exporting nations such as China and Saudi Arabia have traditionally reinvested much of that cash into low risk securities that can be rapidly turned back into dollars if necessary. For a very long time, U.S. Treasury bonds have been considered to be the perfect way to do this. This has created tremendous demand for U.S. government debt and has helped keep interest rates super low. So every year, massive amounts of money that gets sent out of the country ends up being loaned back to the U.S. Treasury at super low interest rates.

And it has been a very good thing for the U.S. economy that the federal government has been able to borrow money so cheaply, because the interest rate on 10 year U.S. Treasuries affects thousands upon thousands of other interest rates throughout our financial system. For example, as the rate on 10 year U.S. Treasuries has risen in recent months, so have the rates on U.S. home mortgages. And if demand for U.S. government debt continues to go down, mortgage rates will continue to rise. That will be very bad for the housing industry and the real estate market.

Our entire way of life in the United States depends upon the game that I described above continuing. We must have the rest of the world use our currency and loan it back to us at ultra-low interest rates. At this point we have painted ourselves into a corner by accumulating so much debt. We simply cannot afford to have interest rates rise significantly.

For example, if the average rate of interest on U.S. government debt rose to just 6 percent (and it has been much higher than that at various times in our history), we would be paying more than a trillion dollars a year just in interest on the national debt.

This is why what the Federal Reserve has been doing is so dangerous. They have been recklessly creating hundreds of billions of dollars out of thin air and using it to buy up government debt and mortgage-backed securities. They call it "quantitative easing", but the rest of the world is watching this and they are becoming increasingly alarmed that the Fed is running a giant scam and that the U.S. financial system is becoming increasingly unstable.

If the U.S. federal government is just going to continue to borrow trillions of dollars that it never intends to repay, and if the Federal Reserve is just going to continue to wildly spend hundreds of billions of dollars that it creates out of thin air, then why should the rest of the planet continue to participate in such a charade?

At some point, the rest of the world may decide that what is best for them is to stop using our unstable currency and to stop lending us trillions of dollars at ultra-low interest rates.

When that happens, it will be absolutely disastrous for us.

As most Americans have heard, we are heavily dependent on foreign nations such as China lending us money. Right now, China owns approximately 1.3 trillion dollars of our debt.

China accounts for more global trade than anyone else does, and they also own more of our debt than any other nation does. If China starts dumping our dollars and our debt, much of the rest of the planet would likely follow suit and we would be in for a world of hurt.

That is why it was so alarming when China recently announced that they are going to quit stockpiling more U.S. dollars. For a long time China has been warning us to quit recklessly printing so much money, and now China is starting to make moves that will make them more independent from us financially.

If the Fed does not bring quantitative easing to a complete stop soon, other nations may start doing the same thing.

So the Fed knows that they are on borrowed time. Faith in the U.S. financial system is declining very fast.

But if the Federal Reserve does completely end quantitative easing, our financial markets will crash and we could very well experience a worse financial crisis than what we went through back in 2008.

Essentially, the Federal Reserve is stuck between a rock and a hard place, and with each passing day the rest of the world loses even more patience with our financial system.

In the end, the world will eventually stop playing our game someday and the U.S. dollar will die.

It might not happen today, it might not happen tomorrow, and it might not even happen next year, but it is coming.

I hope that you are getting prepared.

# Chapter 5

## FINANCIAL PREPARATION

---

One of the most common questions that I have been asked over the past several years is this: "What should I do with my money?"

Once people understand that a great economic crisis is coming, they want to know what to do with the money that they have accumulated. And the truth is that there are no easy answers. Just like with all other aspects of preparation, financial preparation is going to look different for each person.

Unfortunately, most Americans are not prepared at all for the great financial tidal wave that is coming. Just consider the following statistics...

- 76 percent of all Americans are living paycheck to paycheck.
-46 percent of all Americans have less than $800 in savings.
-27 percent of all Americans do not have even a single penny saved up.
-Less than one out of every four Americans has enough money stored away to cover six months of expenses.

When economic disaster strikes, most people are going to be totally wiped out.
Don't let that happen to you.
The following are a few ways that you can get financially prepared for what is ahead...

## #1 Build An Emergency Fund

Do you remember what happened when the financial system almost collapsed back in 2008? Millions of Americans suddenly lost their jobs, and because many of them were living paycheck to paycheck, many of them also got behind on their mortgages and lost their homes. You don't want to lose everything that you have worked for during this next major economic downturn. It is imperative that you have an emergency fund. It should be enough to cover all of your expenses for at least six months, but I would encourage you to have an emergency fund that is even larger than that.

## #2 Don't Put All Of Your Eggs Into One Basket

If the wealth confiscation that we witnessed in Cyprus taught us anything, it is that we should not put all of our eggs in one basket. If all of your money is in one single bank account, it would be easy to wipe out. But if you have your money scattered around a number of different places it will give you a little bit more security.

## #3 Keep Some Cash At Home

This goes along with the previous point. While it is not wise to keep all of your money at home, you do want to keep some cash on hand. If there is an extended bank holiday or if a giant burst from the sun causes the ATM machines to go down, you want to be able to have enough cash to buy the things that your family needs. Just ask the people of Cyprus how crippling a bank holiday can be. One way to keep your cash secure at home is by storing it in a concealed safe.

## #4 Reduce Your Expenses

Now is not the time to be buying lots of new toys and racking up lots of bills. When the next great economic crisis strikes, you want your financial profile to be "lean and mean". And the truth is that we all have room to reduce our expenses. We all spend money on things that we do not really need. If you learn to live simpler now, you will be able to save up some money and you will be able to adjust to the times that are coming much more easily.

## #5 Get Out Of Debt

A lot of people seem to assume that an economic collapse will wipe out all debts, but that will probably not be the case. In fact, if you are in a tremendous amount of debt you will be very vulnerable if the economy collapses and you are not able to find a job. Just ask the people who were overextended and lost their jobs during the last recession. So please get out of debt. Many debt collectors are becoming increasingly ruthless. In many areas of the country they are now routinely putting debtors into prison. You do not want to be a slave to debt when the next wave of the economic collapse strikes.

## #6 Consider Reducing Your Exposure To The Financial Markets

You do not want to have your life savings exposed in the stock market when it crashes. Just ask anyone that watched a 401K account shrivel up during the crash of 2008. And in recent months we have definitely seen the stock market soar to absolutely insane heights.

At this point, stock prices do not have any relationship to economic reality whatsoever. For example, just consider Twitter. This is a seven-year-old company that has never made a profit and that lost more than a hundred million dollars in 2013. Yet despite all of that, at one point in late 2013 it was worth more than 40 billion dollars according to the stock market.

When this stock market bubble bursts, it is going to be exceedingly painful. You don't want to be holding stocks when that happens.

## #7 Once You Have Done The Basics, Start Acquiring Gold And Silver

Some people start buying lots of gold and silver before doing any of the basic things that I just mentioned. That is a mistake.

However, once you have done the basics, accumulating gold and silver is a great way to protect your wealth.

In the long-term, the U.S. dollar is going to lose a tremendous amount of value and inflation is going to absolutely skyrocket. That is one reason why so many people are investing very heavily in gold, silver and other precious metals.

However, in the short-term and mid-term we are going to witness tremendous volatility in the financial markets. Prices for gold and silver are going to go up and down wildly over the next few years. If you do invest in gold and silver, you have got to be able to handle the ride. If you do not think that you can handle the wild swings that are going to happen, then perhaps you should stay on the sidelines.

Most people who write about these things tend to focus on gold, but I actually like silver even better for long-term investment for a couple of reasons.

First of all, silver and gold come out of the ground at about a 10 to 1 ratio. But in recent years the price of gold has normally been more than 60 times the price of silver. At some point an adjustment is coming.

Secondly, silver is used in thousands upon thousands of high tech products. That is not the case with gold. Over the coming years this is going to help push the price of silver up.

But without a doubt, the future of both gold and silver is very bright.

Unfortunately, most Americans do not own any gold and silver. In fact, it has been estimated that less than 10 percent of the U.S. population owns any gold or silver for investment purposes.

## #8 Start A Side Business

If you do not have much money, a great way to increase your income is by starting a side business. And it does not take a lot of money - there are many side businesses that you can start for next to nothing. And starting a side business will allow you to become less dependent on your job. In this economic environment, a job could disappear at literally any time.

This is going to mean less time in front of the television, but this is not the time to be fooling around. This is a time to get serious about preparing for the future. Anything that you can do to become independent of the system is a good thing.

## #9 Move Away From The Big Cities If Possible

For many people, this is simply not possible. Many Americans are still completely and totally dependent on their jobs. But if you are able, now is a good time to move away from the big cities. When the next major economic downturn strikes, there will be rioting, looting and a dramatic rise in crime in the major cities. If you are able to move to a more rural area you will probably be in much better shape.

## #10 Have A Back-Up Plan And Be Flexible

Mike Tyson once said the following...

"Everyone has a plan until they get punched in the mouth."

No plan ever unfolds perfectly. When your plan is disrupted, what will you do?

It will be imperative for all of us to have a back-up plan and to be flexible during the years ahead.

# Chapter 6

## SHOULD YOU RELOCATE?

---

This chapter is primarily for those that live in the United States. But if you live in another country there will be some principles that apply to you as well. One of the most common types of questions that I get is about relocation. People want to know where the "good places to live" are.

And in these troubled times, it is certainly understandable that many people want to try to insulate themselves and their families from what is coming. Our economy is on the verge of collapse, natural disasters are becoming more frequent and more intense, the U.S. population is becoming angrier and more frustrated by the day, our government has become incredibly oppressive and controlling, war could break out at any time and evidence that society is breaking down is all around us. As our world becomes increasingly unstable, many families are considering moving somewhere else. But what areas are best and what areas should be avoided? Is there really a "best place to live" in America? Well, the truth is that each family is facing a different set of circumstances. If you have a great support system where you live, it can be really tough to pick up and move 3000 miles away from that support system. If you have a great job where you live now, it can be really tough to move some place where there may be no job at all for you. And please keep in mind that relocating to another part of the country can be exceedingly expensive. All of these are very important considerations.

But without a doubt there are some areas of the country that will be far better off than others in the event of a major economic collapse. This chapter will take a look at each of the 50 U.S. states and will list some of the pros and cons for moving to each one.

Not all of the factors listed below will be important to you, and a few have even been thrown in for humor. But if you are thinking of moving in the near future hopefully this list will give you some food for thought.

And please keep in mind that this list simply represents my opinions. Other people see things very differently. For example, the other day I saw that Gallup ranked North Dakota as the "happiest state" in the nation, and West Virginia was ranked as the worst state. My rankings reach different conclusions. In the end, you have to make the choice that is right for you.

A few years ago when my wife and I were living near Washington D.C. we knew that we wanted a change and we went through this kind of a process. We literally evaluated areas from coast to coast. In the end, we found a place that is absolutely perfect for us. But different things are important to different people.

If I gave your particular state a low rating in this list, please don't think that I am trashing the entire state or all of the people who live there.

For example, there are some absolutely wonderful people that live in the state of California, and there are some areas of California that I would not mind visiting at all. But for the times that are coming I am convinced that it is going to be a really bad place to live.

Not that I have all the answers either. Hopefully this chapter can get some debates started, and hopefully those debates will help people that are thinking of moving to another state to be more informed.

The following are some pros and cons for all 50 states....

## Alabama

Pros: warm weather, southern hospitality, relatively low population density

Cons: hurricanes, tornadoes, crime, not enough jobs, multiple nuclear power plants, rampant poverty
Overall Rating: C+

## Alaska
Pros: great fishing, lots of empty space, low population density, great for rugged individualists
Cons: very high cost of living, earthquakes, volcanoes, extremely cold, short growing season, too much snow, potentially cut off from supplies from the lower 48 states during an emergency situation
Overall Rating: B

## Arizona
Pros: warm weather
Cons: illegal immigration, wildfires, return of dust bowl conditions, not enough jobs, not enough rain, multiple nuclear power plants, crime, gang violence, Phoenix
Overall Rating: D+

## Arkansas
Pros: southern hospitality, warm weather, Ozark National Forest
Cons: tornadoes, Clintons, New Madrid fault zone, multiple nuclear power plants, crime, rampant poverty
Overall Rating: C+

## California
Pros: Disneyland, warm weather, Malibu
Cons: extreme drought, high taxes, Jerry Brown, massive earthquake threat, mudslides, wildfires, gang violence, crime, traffic, rampant poverty, hostile political environment, ridiculous regulations, bad schools, political correctness, illegal immigration, not enough jobs, air pollution, multiple nuclear power plants, possible tsunami threat along the coast, Los Angeles, San Francisco, Oakland, Stockton, Sacramento, huge drug

problem, high population density, the state government is broke
Overall Rating: F

## Colorado
Pros: Rocky Mountains, Colorado Springs
Cons: wildfires, illegal immigration, short growing season, not enough rain, too much snow, huge drug problem
Overall Rating: B-

## Connecticut
Pros: beautiful homes
Cons: high taxes, hostile political environment, ridiculous regulations, political correctness, short growing season, multiple nuclear power plants, high population density
Overall Rating: C-

## Delaware
Pros: good fishing
Cons: Joe Biden, political correctness, ridiculous regulations, hostile political environment, crime, high population density
Overall Rating: D

## Florida
Pros: University of Florida Gators, oranges, low taxes, southern hospitality, Disneyworld, Gainesville, warm weather, beautiful beaches, Daytona
Cons: hurricanes, most of the state is barely above sea level, high population density, not enough jobs, multiple nuclear power plants, crime, gang violence, illegal immigration
Overall Rating: C

## Georgia
Pros: peaches, southern hospitality, warm weather

Cons: not enough jobs, multiple nuclear power plants, crime, gang violence, flesh eating disease, Atlanta
Overall Rating: B-

## Hawaii
Pros: awesome beaches, warm weather, great vacation destination
Cons: vulnerable to tsunamis, very high cost of living, volcanoes, traffic, high population density, high taxes
Overall Rating: C-

## Idaho
Pros: awesome people live there, great potatoes, low population density, high concentration of liberty-minded individuals, low crime, Sandpoint, Coeur d'Alene, north Idaho has plenty of water compared to the rest of the interior West, beautiful scenery
Cons: cold in the winter, wildfires, short growing season, not enough jobs
Overall Rating: A

## Illinois
Pros: once you get away from Chicago things are not quite so bad
Cons: Barack Obama, drought, New Madrid fault zone, high population density, political correctness, ridiculous regulations, hostile political environment, crime, gang violence, Chicago, East St. Louis, not enough jobs, multiple nuclear power plants, mob robberies, the state government is drowning in debt
Overall Rating: D-

## Indiana
Pros: it is in better shape than Illinois, good farming, high Amish population
Cons: drought, tornadoes, the city of Gary, relatively high population density, near the New Madrid fault zone, a "rust belt" state
Overall Rating: C-

## Iowa
Pros: low population density, low crime, good farming
Cons: drought, tornadoes, cold in the winter, multiple nuclear power plants, too much snow, very flat
Overall Rating: B-

## Kansas
Pros: low population density, low crime, good farming
Cons: drought, tornadoes, return of dust bowl conditions, very flat
Overall Rating: B

## Kentucky
Pros: southern hospitality, great horses, Lexington
Cons: New Madrid fault zone, not enough jobs, rampant poverty, Louisville
Overall Rating: C

## Louisiana
Pros: southern hospitality, warm weather
Cons: hurricanes, New Orleans, not enough jobs, tornadoes, multiple nuclear power plants, oil spills, rising crime, gang violence, rampant poverty
Overall Rating: D

## Maine
Pros: low population density, low crime, polite people
Cons: extremely cold, short growing season, political correctness, ridiculous regulations, hostile political environment, too much snow
Overall Rating: B-

## Maryland
Pros: the Washington Redskins play there, the western part of the state

Cons: Baltimore, borders Washington D.C., high population density, really bad traffic, political correctness, ridiculous regulations, hostile political environment, multiple nuclear power plants, crime, gang violence
Overall Rating: C-

## Massachusetts
Pros: beautiful homes
Cons: high taxes, political correctness, ridiculous regulations, hostile political environment, high population density, short growing season, almost everything is illegal in Massachusetts
Overall Rating: D+

## Michigan
Pros: once you get away from Detroit and Flint things get better, some of the extremely rural areas are actually pretty good
Cons: Detroit, Flint, Dearborn, extremely cold, short growing season, political correctness, ridiculous regulations, hostile political environment, not enough jobs, multiple nuclear power plants, too much snow, a "rust belt" state
Overall Rating: D

## Minnesota
Pros: land of 10,000 lakes
Cons: extremely cold, short growing season, multiple nuclear power plants, too much snow, hostile political environment, high taxes
Overall Rating: C

## Mississippi
Pros: southern hospitality, relatively low population density, warm weather
Cons: hurricanes, tornadoes, not enough jobs, rampant poverty, crime
Overall Rating: C+

## Missouri
Pros: good farming, Branson
Cons: drought, tornadoes, New Madrid fault zone, not enough jobs, crime
Overall Rating: C

## Montana
Pros: low population density, low taxes, high concentration of liberty-minded individuals, Missoula, Kalispell
Cons: extremely cold in the winter, wildfires, short growing season, not enough rain, near Yellowstone super volcano, rampant poverty, too much snow
Overall Rating: B+

## Nebraska
Pros: low population density, good farming
Cons: tornadoes, drought, multiple nuclear power plants, cold in the winter, very flat
Overall Rating: B

## Nevada
Pros: low population density, lots of empty space, low taxes, warm weather
Cons: extreme drought, hostile political environment, Harry Reid, Las Vegas, Reno, not enough water, not enough rain, wildfires, hard to grow food, not enough jobs, crime, gang violence, huge drug problem, Yucca Mountain
Overall Rating: D+

## New Hampshire
Pros: low crime, beautiful homes
Cons: extremely cold, short growing season, political correctness, ridiculous regulations, hostile political environment, too much snow
Overall Rating: C+

## New Jersey
Pros: anyone got something?
Cons: high population density, Camden, Newark, not enough jobs, multiple nuclear power plants, Atlantic City, crime, gang violence
Overall Rating: D-

## New Mexico
Pros: low population density, warm weather
Cons: illegal immigration, extreme drought, wildfires, return of dust bowl conditions, not enough jobs, not enough rain, crime, gang violence, huge drug problem
Overall Rating: D

## New York
Pros: the entire state is not like New York City
Cons: New York City, high taxes, cold in the winter, extremely high population density, political correctness, ridiculous regulations, hostile political environment, not enough jobs, multiple nuclear power plants, the "too big to fail" banks
Overall Rating: D

## North Carolina
Pros: southern hospitality, warm weather, Great Smoky Mountains National Park
Cons: hurricanes, not enough jobs, multiple nuclear power plants
Overall Rating: B+

## North Dakota
Pros: low crime, lots of oil-related jobs, low population density
Cons: extremely cold, short growing season, too much snow
Overall Rating: B+

## Ohio

Pros: the Cincinnati Reds, the Pro Football Hall of Fame, high Amish population

Cons: not enough jobs, cold in the winter, multiple nuclear power plants, high population density, Toledo, Cleveland, a "rust belt" state

Overall Rating: C

## Oklahoma

Pros: warm weather, good farming

Cons: drought, tornadoes, wildfires, return of dust bowl conditions, not enough rain, crime, Oklahoma City, rampant poverty

Overall Rating: C+

## Oregon

Pros: tremendous natural beauty

Cons: high taxes, Portland, political correctness, ridiculous regulations, hostile political environment, not enough jobs, huge drug problem, possible tsunami threat along the coast

Overall Rating: C-

## Pennsylvania

Pros: high Amish population

Cons: high population density, Philadelphia, Pittsburgh, not enough jobs, multiple nuclear power plants, a "rust belt" state

Overall Rating: C

## Rhode Island

Pros: so small that most people don't notice their problems

Cons: the state is flat broke, short growing season, political correctness, ridiculous regulations, hostile political environment, not enough jobs, high population density

Overall Rating: D+

## South Carolina
Pros: southern hospitality, warm weather, Myrtle Beach
Cons: hurricanes, not enough jobs, multiple nuclear power plants, crime, gang violence, rampant poverty
Overall Rating: B

## South Dakota
Pros: low population density, fun tourist traps, the Badlands, Mount Rushmore
Cons: extremely cold, short growing season, very flat, too much snow
Overall Rating: B

## Tennessee
Pros: Nashville, Michael W. Smith, southern hospitality, warm weather, Gatlinburg
Cons: Memphis, New Madrid fault zone, multiple nuclear power plants, crime, gang violence, rampant poverty
Overall Rating: B

## Texas
Pros: low taxes, warm weather, Austin
Cons: extreme drought, illegal immigration, tornadoes, wildfires, West Nile Virus, the Dallas Cowboys, return of dust bowl conditions, speed traps, not enough rain, multiple nuclear power plants, rising crime
Overall Rating: B

## Utah
Pros: beautiful mountains, low crime, low population density
Cons: cold in the winter, wildfires, Salt Lake City, short growing season, not enough rain, illegal to collect rain
Overall Rating: B-

## Vermont
Pros: low crime, beautiful homes
Cons: cold in the winter, hostile political environment, ridiculous regulations, short growing season, political correctness, not enough jobs, too much snow
Overall Rating: C+

## Virginia
Pros: the University of Virginia, southern hospitality, Charlottesville
Cons: borders Washington D.C., high population density, multiple nuclear power plants, Richmond, really bad traffic in northern Virginia
Overall Rating: B-

## Washington
Pros: the eastern half of the state is quite nice and much different from the coast, the Seattle Seahawks
Cons: way too much rain along the coast, volcanoes, wildfires, hostile political environment, ridiculous regulations, political correctness, not enough jobs, possible tsunami threat along the coast, Seattle
Overall Rating: C

## West Virginia
Pros: beautiful mountains
Cons: not enough jobs, rampant poverty, rising crime
Overall Rating: C

## Wisconsin
Pros: cheese, the Green Bay Packers
Cons: extremely cold, short growing season, multiple nuclear power plants, too much snow
Overall Rating: B-

## Wyoming

Pros: low population density, lots of empty space, very low taxes
Cons: extremely cold, too windy, too flat, wildfires, short growing season, not enough rain, Yellowstone super volcano
Overall Rating: B-

Once again, this list simply represents my opinions. Other people see things very differently.

In the end, if you do choose to move, you have got to pick the place that you believe will be best for you and your family.

And the most important thing to do before making any decision like this is to seek God in prayer.

Ultimately, he knows what is best for you and your family far better than anyone else does.

# Chapter 7

## MOVING OUT OF THE COUNTRY

---

As things continue to get progressively worse in the United States, is moving to another country an option that you should consider?

That is a question that a lot of ordinary Americans are asking these days. Personally, I have friends that have left the United States for good and never plan to come back. I also have friends that have chosen to remain in the United States and plan to be here until they die no matter what happens.

In the end, everyone needs to make the choice that they feel is right for them and for their family.

But without a doubt, the number of people that are making the hard decision to leave America permanently is growing. Just consider the following statistics...

-The number of Americans that renounced their citizenship was 221 percent higher in 2013 than it was in 2012.

-According to the U.S. State Department, 6.3 million Americans are either working or studying overseas. That is the highest number that has ever been recorded.

-According to one recent survey, "the percentage of Americans aged 25 to 34 actively planning to relocate outside the U.S. has quintupled in just two years, from less than 1 percent to 5.1 percent."

Dreams of moving on to "greener pastures" can be very appealing, but the truth is that making such a move is rarely easy – especially for those unaccustomed to living in a foreign land.

If you do decide to move out of the United States, there are some hard questions that you should ask yourself first. The following are ten that I would suggest...

**Do You Speak The Language? If Not, How Will You Function?**
If you do not speak the language of the country that you are moving to, that can be a huge problem. Just going to the store and buying some food will become a challenge. Every interaction that you have with anyone in that society will be strained, and your ability to integrate into the culture around you will be greatly limited.

**How Will You Make A Living?**
Unless you are independently wealthy, you will need to make money. In a foreign nation, it may be very difficult for you to find a job - especially one that pays as much as you are accustomed to making in the United States. It is important to have a plan for how you will survive financially in your new country before saying goodbye to the U.S. forever.

**Will You Be Okay Without Your Family And Friends?**
Being thousands of miles away from all of your family and friends can be extremely difficult. Will you be okay without them? And it can be difficult to survive in a foreign culture without any kind of a support system. Sometimes the people that most successfully move out of the country are those that do it as part of a larger group.

**Have You Factored In Weather Patterns And Geological Instability?**
As the globe becomes increasingly unstable, weather patterns and natural disasters are going to become a bigger factor in deciding where to live. For example, India recently suffered through the worst drought that it had experienced in nearly 50 years. It would be very difficult to thrive in the middle of such an environment.

Many of those that are encouraging people to "escape from America" are pointing to Chile as an ideal place to relocate to. But there are thousands of significant earthquakes in Chile each year, and the entire nation lies directly along the "Ring of Fire" which is becoming increasingly unstable. That is something to keep in mind.

## What Will You Do For Medical Care?

If you or someone in your family had a serious medical problem in the United States, you would know what to do. Yes, our health care system is incredibly messed up, but at least you would know that you could get the care that you needed if an emergency arose. Would the same be true in a foreign nation?

## Are You Moving Into A High Crime Area?

Yes, crime is definitely on the rise in the United States. But in some of the most popular areas where preppers are relocating to, crime is even worse. Mexico and certain areas of Central America are two examples of this. And in many foreign nations, the police are far more corrupt than they generally are in the United States.

In addition, many other nations have far stricter gun laws than the United States does, so your ability to defend your family may be greatly restricted.

So will your family truly be safe in the nation that you plan to take them to?

## Are You Prepared For "Culture Shock"?

Moving to another country can be like moving to a different planet. After all, they don't call it "culture shock" for nothing.

If you do move to another country, you may quickly find that thousands of little things that you once took for granted in the U.S. are now very different.

And there is a very good chance that many of the "amenities" that you are accustomed to in the U.S. will not be available in a foreign nation and that your standard of living will go down.

So if you are thinking of moving somewhere else, you may want to visit first just to get an idea of what life would be like if you made the move.

## What Freedoms and Liberties Will You Lose By Moving?

Yes, our liberties and our freedoms are being rapidly eroded in the United States. But in many other nations around the world things are actually much worse. You may find that there is no such thing as "freedom of speech" or "freedom of religion" in the country that you have decided to relocate to.

## Is There A Possibility That The Country You Plan To Escape To Could Be Involved In A War At Some Point?

We are moving into a time of great geopolitical instability. If you move right into the middle of a future war zone, you might really regret it. If you do plan to move, try to find a country that is likely to avoid war for the foreseeable future.

## When The Global Economy Collapses, Will You And Your Family Be Okay For Food?

What good will it be to leave the United States if you and your family run out of food?

Today, we are on the verge of a major global food crisis. Global food reserves are at their lowest level in nearly 40 years, and shifting global weather patterns are certainly not helping things.

And the global elite are rapidly getting more control over the global food supply. Today, between 75 and 90 percent of all international trade in grain is controlled by just four gigantic multinational food corporations.

All of these are things that you should consider carefully when deciding whether or not to move to another country.

These decisions can be absolutely heart-wrenching, and they should not be made lightly.

Above everything else, the key is to pray. Ultimately, God knows what each one of us should do, and He has promised to lead and guide those that will earnestly seek after Him.

# Chapter 8

## THE NIGHT THE LIGHTS GO OUT

What would you and your family do if the power grid went down for weeks, months or even longer?

Most people assume that such a scenario could never happen, but as you are about to read, many experts are now warning that our power grid is extremely vulnerable. And if the power grid does go down for an extended period of time, all of our lives will change in the blink of an eye. Our society is extremely dependent on technology, and if we were to suddenly have all of that technology taken away, our society would plunge into chaos very rapidly.

According to the Federal Energy Regulatory Commission's latest report, all that it would take to plunge the entire nation into darkness for more than a year would be to knock out a transformer manufacturer and just 9 key electrical substations. The reality of the matter is that our power grid is in desperate need of updating, and there is very little physical security at some of these substations. If terrorists, saboteurs, or special operations forces wanted to take down our power grid, it would not be very difficult.

When I read the following statement from the Federal Energy Regulatory Commission's latest report, I was absolutely stunned...

*"Destroy nine interconnection substations and a transformer manufacturer and the entire United States grid would be down for at least 18 months, probably longer."*

Could that possibly be true?

Remember, this is what the federal government is telling us.

So what would you and your family do without power for 18 months?

How would you possibly survive?

Most people don't think about what life would be like without electrical power.  The list below, which comes from one of my previous articles, will hopefully start to give you an idea of what we could potentially be facing in an extended grid down scenario…

*-There would be no heat for your home.*
*-Water would no longer be pumped into most homes.*
*-Your computer would not work.*
*-There would be no Internet.*
*-Your phones would not work.*
*-There would be no television.*
*-There would be no radio.*
*-ATM machines would be shut down.*
*-There would be no banking.*
*-Your debit cards and credit cards would not work.*
*-Without electricity, most gas stations would not be functioning.*
*-Most people would be unable to do their jobs without electricity and employment would collapse.*
*-Commerce would be brought to a standstill.*
*-Hospitals would not be able to function normally.*
*-You would quickly start running out of medicine.*
*-All refrigeration would shut down and frozen foods in our homes and supermarkets would start to go bad.*

Are you starting to get the picture?

If you want to get an idea of how quickly society would descend into utter chaos, just watch the documentary "American Blackout" some time.  It will chill you to your bones.

The truth is that we live in an unprecedented time. We have become extremely dependent on technology, and that technology could be stripped away from us in an instant.

If a group of agents working for a foreign government or a terrorist organization wanted to bring us to our knees, they could do it.

In fact, there have actually been recent attacks on some of our power stations. For example, it was reported in the Wall Street Journal that a team of snipers shot up an electrical substation in Silicon Valley, California in 2013. They were able to destroy 17 transformers in just 19 minutes before quietly escaping.

According to Jon Wellinghoff, the chairman of the Federal Energy Regulatory Commission at the time, it was "the most significant incident of domestic terrorism involving the grid that has ever occurred" in the United States.

Have you heard about that attack before reading this?

Most Americans don't know anything about it.

But it should have been very big news.

At the scene, authorities found "more than 100 fingerprint-free shell casings", and little piles of rocks "that appeared to have been left by an advance scout to tell the attackers where to get the best shots."

So what happens someday when the bad guys decide to conduct a coordinated attack against our power grid with heavy weapons?

It could happen.

And of course that is far from the only scenario that could cause our power grid to collapse.

Most people have absolutely no idea that the Earth barely missed being fried by a massive EMP burst from the sun in 2012 and in 2013. And earlier in 2014 there was another huge solar storm which would have caused tremendous damage if it had been directed at our planet. If any of those storms would have directly hit us, the result would have been catastrophic. Electrical transformers would have burst into flames, power grids would have gone down and much of our technology would have been fried. In essence, life as we know it would have ceased to exist – at least for a time. These kinds of solar storms have hit the Earth many times before, and experts tell us that it is inevitable that it will happen again. The most famous one happened in 1859, and was known as the Carrington Event. But other than the telegraph, humanity had very little dependence on technology at the time. If another Carrington Event happened today, it would be a complete and utter nightmare. A study by Lloyd's of London has concluded that it would have taken a $2,600,000,000,000 chunk out of the global economy, and it would take up to a decade to repair the damage. Unfortunately, scientists insist that it is going to happen at some point. The only question is when.

So what is going to happen when one of these massive electromagnetic blasts finally hits us?

Well, basically it will be a technological Armageddon. The following is a brief excerpt from one of my previous articles...

*An electromagnetic pulse can range from a minor inconvenience to a civilization-killing event. It just depends on how powerful it is. But in the worst case scenario, we could be facing a situation where our electrical grids have been fried, there is no heat for our homes, our computers don't work, the Internet does not work, our cell phones do not work, there are no more banking records, nobody can use credit cards anymore, hospitals are unable to function, nobody can pump gas, and supermarkets cannot operate because there is no power and no refrigeration. Basically, we would witness the complete and total collapse of the economy. According to a government commission that looked into these things, approximately two-thirds of the U.S. population would die from starvation, disease and societal chaos within one year of a massive EMP attack. It would be a disaster unlike anything we have ever seen before in U.S. history.*

Without any electrical power, our society would descend into a state of chaos very rapidly.

Today, our lives have been made very comfortable by technology.

But that technology could be stripped away from us in a single moment.

We should be thankful for the good things that we have, and we should not take for granted that we will always have them.

All it would take is one giant burst from the sun, and everything would change.

So what should people be doing to prepare for such a scenario?

You need to be thinking about how you can provide power for your home that is independent of the electrical grid.

Many people are installing generators, but most of them run on propane or gas. So being able to run them for an extended period of time is going to be dependent on your ability to get more propane or gas.

Other alternative forms of energy such as solar, wind and geothermal energy are great, but they can be very expensive to set up.

In the end, you are going to have to make the choice that you think is right for your own family.

And in addition to food and water, you should also be stockpiling things that you will need in the event of a grid down scenario.

Personally, I think that it is good to have a stash of cash at home so that you will be able to buy necessities for your family during such a crisis. And if you take medicine, you will want to have enough to get you through until you can see a doctor again. Basically, you will want to have extra supplies of anything that you can't live without.

A grid down scenario is one of the toughest things to get prepared for. But it is imperative that we do so. Because we are so dependent on technology, life without power would be extremely challenging for most people and the thin veneer of civilization that we all take for granted would disappear very quickly.

Those that are prepared will at least have a chance of making it through such a crisis.

# Chapter 9

## THE FEDERAL RESERVE: THE HEART OF OUR ECONOMIC PROBLEMS

Since I started the Economic Collapse Blog back in 2009, I have written more than 1000 articles on the economy. A lot of people have wanted to know how we ended up in such a giant mess, and I have had a lot of time to reflect on that question.

In essence, the primary reason why we are drowning in debt as a society is because our financial system was set up to be a debt-based system in the first place.

Most people don't realize this, but when more money is created in our system, more debt is also created.

For example, imagine that you take $100 that your employer has paid you and put it in the bank. The bank would not just hold that money and wait for you to come back for it. Instead, the bank would loan out most of that money.

So instead of keeping your $100 stashed away, the bank would perhaps loan out $90 to someone else. Now there would be $190 floating around, and in the process $90 of "new money" would have been created.

At the heart of this debt-based system is the Federal Reserve. A little more than 100 years ago, this "central bank" was designed to create a gigantic debt spiral from which the United States could never possibly escape. As you will see in this chapter, the way that the system was designed was that whenever the Federal Reserve put more money into circulation the federal government would go into more debt. And the more the federal government goes into debt, the more money it has to drain from the taxpayers.

Since the Federal Reserve was created, there have been 18 recessions or depressions, the value of the U.S. dollar has declined by 98 percent, and the U.S. national debt has gotten more than 5000 times larger.

And yet most people today still think that it is a good system.

The following is a list of 100 reasons why the Federal Reserve should be shut down from one of my previous articles. I think that you will see why an increasing number of Americans are so upset about this insidious debt-based financial system...

#1 We like to think that we have a government "of the people, by the people, for the people", but the truth is that an unelected, unaccountable group of central planners has far more power over our economy than anyone else in our society does.

#2 The Federal Reserve is actually "independent" of the government. In fact, the Federal Reserve has argued vehemently in federal court that it is "not an agency" of the federal government and therefore not subject to the Freedom of Information Act.

#3 The Federal Reserve openly admits that the 12 regional Federal Reserve banks are organized "much like private corporations".

#4 The regional Federal Reserve banks issue shares of stock to the "member banks" that own them.

#5 100% of the shareholders of the Federal Reserve are private banks. The U.S. government owns zero shares.

#6 The Federal Reserve is not an agency of the federal government, but it has been given power to regulate our banks and financial institutions. This should not be happening.

#7 According to Article I, Section 8 of the U.S. Constitution, the U.S. Congress is the one that is supposed to have the authority to "coin Money, regulate the Value thereof, and of foreign Coin, and fix the Standard of Weights and Measures". So why is the Federal Reserve doing it?

#8 If you look at a "U.S. dollar", it actually says "Federal Reserve note" at the top. In the financial world, a "note" is an instrument of debt.

#9 In 1963, President John F. Kennedy issued Executive Order 11110 which authorized the U.S. Treasury to issue "United States notes" which were created by the U.S. government directly and not by the Federal Reserve. He was assassinated shortly thereafter.

#10 Many of the debt-free United States notes issued under President Kennedy are still in circulation today.

#11 The Federal Reserve determines what levels some of the most important interest rates in our system are going to be set at. In a free market system, the free market would determine those interest rates.

#12 The Federal Reserve has become so powerful that it is now known as "the fourth branch of government".

#13 The greatest period of economic growth in U.S. history was when there was no central bank.

#14 The Federal Reserve was designed to be a perpetual debt machine. The bankers that designed it intended to trap the U.S. government in a perpetual debt spiral from which it could never possibly escape. Since the Federal Reserve was established 100 years ago, the U.S. national debt has gotten more than 5000 times larger.

#15 A permanent federal income tax was established the exact same year that the Federal Reserve was created. This was not a coincidence. In order to pay for all of the government debt that the Federal Reserve would create, a federal income tax was necessary. The whole idea was to transfer wealth from our pockets to the federal government and from the federal government to the bankers.

#16 The period prior to 1913 (when there was no income tax) was the greatest period of economic growth in U.S. history.

#17 Today, the U.S. tax code is about 13 miles long.

#18 From the time that the Federal Reserve was created until now, the U.S. dollar has lost 98 percent of its value.

#19 From the time that President Nixon took us off the gold standard until now, the U.S. dollar has lost 83 percent of its value.

#20 During the 100 years before the Federal Reserve was created, the U.S. economy rarely had any problems with inflation. But since the Federal Reserve was established, the U.S. economy has experienced constant and never ending inflation.

#21 In the century before the Federal Reserve was created, the average annual rate of inflation was about half a percent. In the century since the Federal Reserve was created, the average annual rate of inflation has been about 3.5 percent.

#22 The Federal Reserve has stripped the middle class of trillions of dollars of wealth through the hidden tax of inflation.

#23 The size of M1 has nearly doubled since 2008 thanks to the reckless money printing that the Federal Reserve has been doing.

#24 The Federal Reserve has been starting to behave like the Weimar Republic, and we all remember how that ended.

#25 The Federal Reserve has been consistently lying to us about the level of inflation in our economy. If the inflation rate was still calculated the same way that it was back when Jimmy Carter was president, the official rate of inflation would be somewhere between 8 and 10 percent today.

#26 Since the Federal Reserve was created, there have been 18 distinct recessions or depressions: 1918, 1920, 1923, 1926, 1929, 1937, 1945, 1949, 1953, 1958, 1960, 1969, 1973, 1980, 1981, 1990, 2001, 2008.

#27 Within 20 years of the creation of the Federal Reserve, the U.S. economy was plunged into the Great Depression.

#28 The Federal Reserve created the conditions that caused the stock market crash of 1929, and even Ben Bernanke admits that the response by the Fed to that crisis made the Great Depression even worse than it should have been.

#29 The "easy money" policies of former Fed Chairman Alan Greenspan set the stage for the great financial crisis of 2008.

#30 Without the Federal Reserve, the "subprime mortgage melt-down" would probably never have happened.

#31 If you can believe it, there have been 10 different economic recessions since 1950. The Federal Reserve created the "dotcom bubble", the Federal Reserve created the "housing bubble" and now it has created the largest bond bubble in the history of the planet.

#32 According to an official government report, the Federal Reserve made 16.1 trillion dollars in secret loans to the big banks during the last financial crisis. The following is a list of loan recipients that was taken directly from page 131 of that report...

Citigroup - $2.513 trillion
Morgan Stanley - $2.041 trillion
Merrill Lynch - $1.949 trillion
Bank of America - $1.344 trillion
Barclays PLC - $868 billion
Bear Sterns - $853 billion
Goldman Sachs - $814 billion
Royal Bank of Scotland - $541 billion
JP Morgan Chase - $391 billion
Deutsche Bank - $354 billion
UBS - $287 billion
Credit Suisse - $262 billion
Lehman Brothers - $183 billion
Bank of Scotland - $181 billion
BNP Paribas - $175 billion
Wells Fargo - $159 billion
Dexia - $159 billion
Wachovia - $142 billion
Dresdner Bank - $135 billion
Societe Generale - $124 billion
"All Other Borrowers" - $2.639 trillion

#33 The Federal Reserve also paid those big banks $659.4 million in "fees" to help "administer" those secret loans.

#34 During the last financial crisis, big European banks were allowed to borrow an "unlimited" amount of money from the Federal Reserve at ultra-low interest rates.

#35 The "easy money" policies of Federal Reserve Chairman Ben Bernanke have created the largest financial bubble this nation has ever seen, and this has set the stage for the great financial crisis that we are rapidly approaching.

#36 Since late 2008, the size of the Federal Reserve balance sheet has grown from less than a trillion dollars to more than 4 trillion dollars. This is complete and utter insanity.

#37 During the quantitative easing era, the value of the financial securities that the Fed has accumulated is greater than the total amount of publicly held debt that the U.S. government accumulated from the presidency of George Washington through the end of the presidency of Bill Clinton.

#38 Overall, the Federal Reserve now holds more than 32 percent of all 10 year equivalents, and that percentage is rising by about 0.3 percent each week.

#39 Quantitative easing creates financial bubbles, and when quantitative easing ends those bubbles tend to deflate rapidly.

#40 Most of the new money created by quantitative easing has ended up in the hands of the very wealthy.

#41 According to a prominent Federal Reserve insider, quantitative easing has been one giant "subsidy" for Wall Street banks.

#42 As one CNBC article recently stated, we are seeing absolutely rampant inflation in "stocks and bonds and art and Ferraris".

#43 Donald Trump once made the following statement about quantitative easing: "People like me will benefit from this."

#44 Most people have never heard about this, but a very interesting study conducted for the Bank of England shows that quantitative easing actually increases the gap between the wealthy and the poor.

#45 The gap between the top one percent and the rest of the country is now the greatest that it has been since the 1920s.

#46 The mainstream media has sold quantitative easing to the American public as an "economic stimulus program", but the truth is that the percentage of Americans that have a job has actually gone down since quantitative easing first began.

#47 The Federal Reserve is supposed to be able to guide the nation toward "full employment", but the reality of the matter is that an all-time record 102 million working age Americans do not have a job right now. That number has risen by about 27 million since the year 2000.

#48 For years, the projections of economic growth by the Federal Reserve have consistently overstated the strength of the U.S. economy. But every single time, the mainstream media continues to report that these numbers are "reliable" even though all they actually represent is wishful thinking.

#49 The Federal Reserve system fuels the growth of government, and the growth of government fuels the growth of the Federal Reserve system. Since 1970, federal spending has grown nearly 12 times as rapidly as median household income has.

#50 The Federal Reserve is supposed to look out for the health of all U.S. banks, but the truth is that they only seem to be concerned about the big ones. In 1985, there were more than 18,000 banks in the United States. Today, there are only 6,891 left.

**#51** The six largest banks in the United States (JPMorgan Chase, Bank of America, Citigroup, Wells Fargo, Goldman Sachs and Morgan Stanley) have collectively gotten 37 percent larger over the past five years.

**#52** The U.S. banking system has 14.4 trillion dollars in total assets. The six largest banks now account for 67 percent of those assets and all of the other banks account for only 33 percent of those assets.

**#53** The five largest banks now account for 42 percent of all loans in the United States.

**#54** We were told that the purpose of quantitative easing is to help "stimulate the economy", but today the Federal Reserve is actually paying the big banks not to lend out 1.8 trillion dollars in "excess reserves" that they have parked at the Fed.

**#55** The Federal Reserve has allowed an absolutely gigantic derivatives bubble to inflate which could destroy our financial system at any moment. Right now, four of the "too big to fail" banks each have total exposure to derivatives that is well in excess of 40 trillion dollars.

**#56** The total exposure that Goldman Sachs has to derivatives contracts is more than 381 times greater than their total assets.

**#57** Former Federal Reserve Chairman Ben Bernanke had a track record of failure that would make the Chicago Cubs look good. He assured us over and over that there would not be a recession in 2008, and subsequently we experience the worst economic downturn since the Great Depression.

**#58** The secret November 1910 gathering at Jekyll Island, Georgia during which the plan for the Federal Reserve was hatched was attended by U.S. Senator Nelson W. Aldrich, Assistant Secretary of the Treasury Department A.P. Andrews and a whole host of representatives from the upper crust of the Wall Street banking establishment.

#59 The Federal Reserve was created by the big Wall Street banks and for the benefit of the big Wall Street banks.

#60 In 1913, Congress was promised that if the Federal Reserve Act was passed that it would eliminate the business cycle.

#61 There has never been a true comprehensive audit of the Federal Reserve since it was created back in 1913.

#62 The Federal Reserve system has been described as "the biggest Ponzi scheme in the history of the world".

#63 The following comes directly from the Fed's official mission statement: "To provide the nation with a safer, more flexible, and more stable monetary and financial system." Without a doubt, the Federal Reserve has failed in those tasks dramatically.

#64 The Fed decides what the target rate of inflation should be, what the target rate of unemployment should be and what the size of the money supply is going to be. This is quite similar to the "central planning" that goes on in communist nations, but very few people in our government seem upset by this.

#65 A couple of years ago, Federal Reserve officials walked into one bank in Oklahoma and demanded that they take down all the Bible verses and all the Christmas buttons that the bank had been displaying.

#66 The Federal Reserve has taken some other very frightening steps in recent years. For example, back in 2011 the Federal Reserve announced plans to identify "key bloggers" and to monitor "billions of conversations" about the Fed on Facebook, Twitter, forums and blogs. Someone at the Fed will almost certainly end up reading this chapter.

#67 Thanks to this endless debt spiral that we are trapped in, a massive amount of money is transferred out of our pockets and into the pockets of the ultra-wealthy each year. Incredibly, the U.S. government spent more than 415 billion dollars just on interest on the national debt in 2013.

#68 In September, the average rate of interest on the government's marketable debt was 1.981 percent. In January 2000, the average rate of interest on the government's marketable debt was 6.620 percent. If we got back to that level today, we would be paying more than a trillion dollars a year just in interest on the national debt and it would collapse our entire financial system.

#69 The American people are being killed by compound interest but most of them don't even understand what it is. Albert Einstein once made the following statement about compound interest...

*"Compound interest is the eighth wonder of the world. He who understands it, earns it ... he who doesn't ... pays it."*

#70 Most Americans have absolutely no idea where money comes from. The truth is that the Federal Reserve just creates it out of thin air. The following is how I have previously described how money is normally created by the Fed in our system...

*When the U.S. government decides that it wants to spend another billion dollars that it does not have, it does not print up a billion dollars.*

*Rather, the U.S. government creates a bunch of U.S. Treasury bonds (debt) and takes them over to the Federal Reserve.*

*The Federal Reserve creates a billion dollars out of thin air and exchanges them for the U.S. Treasury bonds.*

#71 What does the Federal Reserve do with those U.S. Treasury bonds? They end up getting auctioned off to the highest bidder. But this entire process actually creates more debt than it does money...

*The U.S. Treasury bonds that the Federal Reserve receives in exchange for the money it has created out of nothing are auctioned off through the Federal Reserve system.*

*But wait.*

*There is a problem.*

*Because the U.S. government must pay interest on the Treasury bonds, the amount of debt that has been created by this transaction is greater than the amount of money that has been created.*

*So where will the U.S. government get the money to pay that debt?*

*Well, the theory is that we can get money to circulate through the economy really, really fast and tax it at a high enough rate that the government will be able to collect enough taxes to pay the debt.*

*But that never actually happens, does it?*

*And the creators of the Federal Reserve understood this as well. They understood that the U.S. government would not have enough money to both run the government and service the national debt. They knew that the U.S. government would have to keep borrowing even more money in an attempt to keep up with the game.*

#72 Of course the U.S. government could actually create money and spend it directly into the economy without the Federal Reserve being involved at all. But then we wouldn't be 17 trillion dollars in debt and that wouldn't serve the interests of the bankers at all.

#73 The following is what Thomas Edison once had to say about our absolutely insane debt-based financial system...

*That is to say, under the old way any time we wish to add to the national wealth we are compelled to add to the national debt.*

*Now, that is what Henry Ford wants to prevent. He thinks it is stupid, and so do I, that for the loan of $30,000,000 of their own money the people of the United States should be compelled to pay $66,000,000 — that is what it amounts to, with interest. People who will not turn a shovelful of dirt nor contribute a pound of material will collect more money from the United States than will the people who supply the material and do the work. That is the terrible thing about interest. In all our great bond issues the interest is always greater than the principal. All of the great public works cost more than twice the actual cost, on that account. Under the present system of doing business we simply add 120 to 150 per cent, to the stated cost.*

*But here is the point: If our nation can issue a dollar bond, it can issue a dollar bill. The element that makes the bond good makes the bill good.*

#74 The United States now has the largest national debt in the history of the world, and we are stealing more than 100 million dollars from our children and our grandchildren every single hour of every single day in a desperate attempt to keep the debt spiral going.

#75 Thomas Jefferson once stated that if he could add just one more amendment to the U.S. Constitution it would be a ban on all government borrowing....

*I wish it were possible to obtain a single amendment to our Constitution. I would be willing to depend on that alone for the reduction of the administration of our government to the genuine principles of its Constitution; I mean an additional article, taking from the federal government the power of borrowing.*

#76 At this moment, the U.S. national debt is sitting at more than 17 trillion dollars. If we had followed the advice of Thomas Jefferson, it would be sitting at zero.

#77 When the Federal Reserve was first established, the U.S. national debt was sitting at about 2.9 billion dollars. On average, we have been adding more than that to the national debt every single day since Barack Obama has been in the White House.

#78 We are on pace to accumulate more new debt under the 8 years of the Obama administration than we did under all of the other presidents in all of U.S. history combined.

#79 If all of the new debt that has been accumulated since John Boehner became Speaker of the House had been given directly to the American people instead, every household in America would have been able to buy a new truck.

#80 Between 2008 and 2012, U.S. government debt grew by 60.7 percent, but U.S. GDP only grew by a total of about 8.5 percent during that entire time period.

#81 Since 2007, the U.S. debt to GDP ratio has increased from 66.6 percent to 101.6 percent.

#82 According to the U.S. Treasury, foreigners hold approximately 5.6 trillion dollars of our debt.

#83 The amount of U.S. government debt held by foreigners is about 5 times larger than it was just a decade ago.

#84 If the U.S. national debt was reduced to a stack of one dollar bills it would circle the earth at the equator 45 times.

#85 If Bill Gates gave every single penny of his entire fortune to the U.S. government, it would only cover the U.S. budget deficit for 15 days.

#86 Sometimes we forget just how much money a trillion dollars is. If you were alive when Jesus Christ was born and you spent one million dollars every single day since that point, you still would not have spent one trillion dollars by now.

#87 If right this moment you went out and started spending one dollar every single second, it would take you more than 31,000 years to spend one trillion dollars.

#88 In addition to all of our debt, the U.S. government has also accumulated more than 200 trillion dollars in unfunded liabilities. So where in the world will all of that money come from?

#89 The greatest damage that quantitative easing has been causing to our economy is the fact that it is destroying worldwide faith in the U.S. dollar and in U.S. debt. If the rest of the world stops using our dollars and stops buying our debt, we are going to be in a massive amount of trouble.

#90 Over the past several years, the Federal Reserve has been monetizing a staggering amount of U.S. government debt even though Ben Bernanke once promised that he would never do this.

#91 China recently announced that they are going to quit stockpiling more U.S. dollars. If the Federal Reserve was not recklessly printing money, this would probably not have happened.

#92 Most Americans have no idea that one of our most famous presidents was absolutely obsessed with getting rid of central banking in the United States. The following is a February 1834 quote by President Andrew Jackson about the evils of central banking....

*I too have been a close observer of the doings of the Bank of the United States. I have had men watching you for a long time, and am convinced that you have used the funds of the bank to speculate in the breadstuffs of the country. When you won, you divided the profits amongst you, and when you lost, you charged it to the Bank. You tell me that if I take the deposits from the Bank and annul its charter I shall ruin ten thousand families. That may be true, gentlemen, but that is your sin! Should I let you go on, you will ruin fifty thousand families, and that would be my sin! You are a den of vipers and thieves. I have determined to rout you out and, by the Eternal, (bringing his fist down on the table) I will rout you out.*

#93 There are plenty of possible alternative financial systems, but at this point all 187 nations that belong to the IMF have a central bank. Are we supposed to believe that this is just some sort of a bizarre coincidence?

#94 The capstone of the global central banking system is an organization known as the Bank for International Settlements. The following is how I described this organization in one of my previous articles...

*An immensely powerful international organization that most people have never even heard of secretly controls the money supply of the entire globe. It is called the Bank for International Settlements, and it is the central bank of central banks. It is located in Basel, Switzerland, but it also has branches in Hong Kong and Mexico City. It is essentially an unelected, unaccountable central bank of the world that has complete immunity from taxation and from national laws. Even Wikipedia admits that "it is not accountable to any single national government." The Bank for International Settlements was used to launder money for the Nazis during World War II, but these days the main purpose of the BIS is to guide and direct the centrally-planned global financial system. Today, 58 global central banks belong to the BIS, and it has far more power over how the U.S. economy (or any other economy for that matter) will perform over the course of the next year than any politician does. Every two months, the central bankers of the world gather in Basel for another "Global Economy Meeting". During those meetings, decisions are made which affect every man, woman and child on the planet, and yet none of us have any say in what goes on. The Bank for International Settlements is an organization that was founded by the global elite and it operates for the benefit of the global elite, and it is intended to be one of the key cornerstones of the emerging one world economic system.*

#95 The borrower is the servant of the lender, and the Federal Reserve has turned all of us into debt slaves.

#96 Debt is a form of social control, and the global elite use all of this debt to dominate all the rest of us. 40 years ago, the total amount of debt in our system (all government debt, all business debt, all consumer debt, etc.) was sitting at about 2 trillion dollars. Today, the grand total exceeds 56 trillion dollars.

#97 Unless something dramatic is done, our children and our grandchildren will be debt slaves for their entire lives as they service our debts and pay for our mistakes.

#98 Now that you know this information, you are responsible for doing something about it.

#99 Congress has the power to shut down the Federal Reserve any time that they would like. But right now most of our politicians fully endorse the current system, and nothing is ever going to happen until the American people start demanding change.

#100 The design of the Federal Reserve system was flawed from the very beginning. If something is not done very rapidly, it is inevitable that our entire financial system is going to suffer an absolutely nightmarish collapse.

# Chapter 10

## THE COMING GLOBAL FOOD CRISIS

Today, most Americans have absolutely no idea that we are on the verge of an absolutely devastating global food crisis. Yes, prices are going up, but we can still walk into extremely well-stocked supermarkets and fill up our carts with as much food as we would like. To most people, it is inconceivable that we could ever be facing a day when there is not enough food to go around.

But such a day is not too far away. In 2012, the world had consumed more food than it had produced for six of the last eleven years. And now, as you will read about in this chapter, crippling diseases and unprecedented drought are having a dramatic effect on global food production. As you read this, global food reserves are at their lowest level in about 40 years, and if current trends continue, it is inevitable that a major league crisis will soon be here.

For example, a horrifying bacterial disease known as "early mortality syndrome" is crippling the shrimping industry all over Asia right now. This disease has an extremely high mortality rate. In fact, it has been reported that it kills approximately nine out of every ten shrimp that it infects. This is causing huge price increases for shrimp all over the planet. According to the U.S. Bureau of Labor Statistics, the price of shrimp has jumped an astounding 61 percent compared to a year ago.

The price of pork is also moving upward aggressively thanks to a disease which has already killed about 10 percent of all of the pigs in the entire country. It is known as the porcine epidemic diarrhea virus, and in less than a year it has spread to 30 states and has killed approximately 7 million pigs.

By the time you read this, those numbers will probably be significantly higher.

U.S. pork production was down by as much as 10 percent in 2014, and Americans paid 20 percent more for pork by the end of the year.

The price of beef has also moved to unprecedented heights. Thanks to the crippling drought that never seems to end in the western half of the nation, the size of the U.S. cattle herd has been declining for seven years in a row, and it is now the smallest that is has been since 1951.

Over the past year, the price of ground chuck beef is up 5.9 percent. It would have been worse, but ranchers have been slaughtering lots of cattle in order to thin their herds in a desperate attempt to get through this drought. If this drought does not end soon, the price of beef is going to go much, much higher.

As prices for shrimp, pork and beef have risen, many consumers have been eating more chicken. But the price of chicken is rising rapidly as well.

In fact, the price of chicken breast is up 12.4 percent over the past 12 months.

Perhaps you are thinking that since you don't eat meat or since you plan to eat less meat that you and your family will not be greatly affected by this.

Well, unless the multi-year drought in California ends soon, prices for fruits and vegetables are going to be skyrocketing as well.

Right now, the state of California is enduring the worst drought in the recorded history of the state. As Dust Bowl conditions return, there are some scientists that are warning that we could potentially be facing "a century-long megadrought".

And considering how much the rest of the nation relies on the agricultural production coming out of the state of California, that is more than just a little bit alarming.

You see, the percentage of our produce that is grown in California has become quite large. Just consider the following numbers...

-99 percent of the artichokes

-44 percent of asparagus

-two-thirds of carrots

-half of bell peppers

-89 percent of cauliflower

-94 percent of broccoli

-95 percent of celery

-90 percent of the leaf lettuce

-83 percent of Romaine lettuce

-83 percent of fresh spinach

-a third of the fresh tomatoes

-86 percent of lemons

-90 percent of avocados

-84 percent of peaches

-88 percent of fresh strawberries

-97 percent of fresh plums

So what happens if the key agricultural areas of California can't produce those fruits and vegetables for us any longer?

You guessed it – we will be in a massive amount of trouble.

In addition, terrible plagues have been hitting some of our key staples such as oranges and bananas.

For example, have you ever heard of citrus greening disease? Probably not, but it has already gotten so bad that it is being projected that Florida's orange harvest will be the smallest in 30 years.

Have you heard of TR4? Probably not, but it has become such a nightmare that some analysts believe that it could eventually wipe out the entire global supply of the type of bananas that Americans eat.

Let's talk about citrus greening disease first.

Citrus greening disease has been a steadily growing problem that has reached epidemic levels this year. Because of this disease, the U.S. Department of Agriculture is projecting that orange production in the U.S. this year will be down 18 percent compared to last year.

As the supply goes down, the cost of fresh oranges and the cost of orange juice is going to go up substantially.

Another horrifying disease is threatening the global supply of bananas. In fact, some experts are projecting that the kind of bananas that we eat today could eventually be totally wiped out by the TR4 fungus.

Let's hope that does not happen, but we would be foolish to ignore the warnings.

Now is the time to get prepared.

And already, hunger is growing like a cancer in this nation.

A decade ago the number of American women that had jobs outnumbered the number of American women on food stamps by more than a 2 to 1 margin. But now, the number of American women on food stamps actually exceeds the number of American women that have jobs.

With each passing day, more Americans are struggling to feed themselves.

As I write this, 49 million Americans are facing food insecurity.

By the time that you read this, that number will probably be even higher.

And this is not just happening in the United States. Hunger is a growing problem all over the planet.

Right now, approximately 1 billion people throughout the world go to bed hungry each night. And every 3.6 seconds, someone starves to death, and three-quarters of those that starve to death are children under the age of 5.

Sadly, this is just the beginning. As diseases, plagues and drought continue to cripple global food production, global food supplies are going to get even tighter.

So please do not be apathetic. There is a reason why this book has such a dramatic title.

Now is the time to get prepared. If you keep putting it off for another day, eventually it will be too late.

# *Chapter 11*

## THE COMING PANDEMIC — WILL IT BE EBOLA?

Scientists tell us that it is only a matter of time before another great pandemic comes along and kills millions of us.

So will that next great pandemic be the Ebola virus?

I wish that I knew the answer to that question.

What we do know is that this is already the worst Ebola outbreak in recorded history by a very wide margin.

What we do know is that the number of cases and the number of deaths is growing at an exponential rate.

And what is frightening is that the official numbers greatly understate the true scope of this crisis. In fact, the World Health Organization has just come out with a statement in which it said that "the numbers of reported cases and deaths vastly underestimate the magnitude of the outbreak".

So what are the real numbers?

Experts tell us that the death rate for Ebola can be up to 90 percent, but during this current outbreak it is just a little bit more than 50 percent.

Conventional medicine does not have a cure for Ebola, so that means that if you rely on conventional medicine once you get Ebola you are probably going to die.

And what makes Ebola so dangerous is that you can be carrying it around for up to three weeks before you ever know that you have it. In fact, one doctor that has been working on the front lines fighting this disease says that Ebola victims can "look quite fit and healthy and can be walking around until shortly before their deaths".

In addition, Ebola can remain in the systems of recovering victims for up to seven weeks.

So anyone carrying this disease can spread it around for a long period of time.

Yes, we have had Ebola outbreaks before, but this one seems very different.

What got my attention was when they started announcing that health workers fighting this virus on the front lines were contracting Ebola. Keep in mind that these workers are dressed head to toe in suits that are specifically designed to prevent the spread of the virus. So how is this happening? I could understand a handful of "mistakes" by health workers, but this is unlike anything that we have ever seen in the history of infectious diseases. These health workers take extraordinary precautions to keep from getting the virus. If it is spreading so easily to them, what chance is the general population going to have?

Up to this point, more than 200 health workers have been infected. That is an absolutely staggering number.

Could it be possible that this strain of Ebola spreads more easily than other strains?

The mainstream media is telling us that we have very little to worry about and that Ebola is not an "airborne disease", but the hard science seems to suggest otherwise.

For example, a study conducted in 2012 proved that Ebola could be transmitted between pigs and monkeys that were in separate cages and that never made physical contact with one another.

So what would it look like if there was an Ebola outbreak in the United States?

If a pandemic were to erupt, the very limited number of hospital labs and isolation units that we currently have would be rapidly overwhelmed. Yes, we may be able to provide "state of the art care" for a handful of people, but if thousands (or millions) of Americans get the virus you can forget about it. Our health industry is already stretched incredibly thin, and we simply do not have the resources to handle a tsunami of high risk Ebola patients.

As panic spread, our society would start to shut down. In areas where there were confirmed cases of Ebola, it is inevitable that schools would be closed and large gatherings of people such as concerts and sporting events would be canceled. In addition, due to fear of catching the virus foot traffic at grocery stores and shopping malls would drop off dramatically. If the panic lasted for multiple months, our economy would essentially grind to a halt. Most economic activity still involves face to face interaction, and if people are afraid that if they go out in public they might catch a disease that will kill them, it would create an economic disaster of unprecedented proportions.

And what happens if strict travel restrictions (to prevent the spread of the disease) or plain old fear cause massive interruptions in our transportation system? Almost all economic activity involves moving something from one location to another, and if we are not able to move stuff around because of an Ebola pandemic, that would create nightmarish problems almost immediately.

A major transportation disruption would not just result in an economic downturn. Many Americans would start running out of food and basic supplies very rapidly. Without the ability to constantly resupply at the grocery store, a lot of people would start giving in to fear in just a matter of days.

And needless to say, a full-blown Ebola outbreak would wreak havoc on our financial system. The stock market would almost certainly collapse and we would witness a credit crunch that would be absolutely unprecedented. Nobody would want to lend to anybody in the midst of an Ebola pandemic. The flow of money through our system would come to a screeching halt, and we would be facing an economic nightmare that would make 2008 look like a Sunday picnic.

So how can we get prepared for an event such as this?

Basically, you will want to be prepared to stay at home as much as possible.

That means that you will need enough food and supplies to last for at least a couple of months, and it could potentially be a lot longer than that.

Just think about it. If Ebola is spreading, you certainly would not want to go to places such as grocery stores that large numbers of people circulate through every day. But if you do not have any food, eventually you would be forced to leave your home. And that decision could end up costing you dearly.

And during a major pandemic, any suspicion that you have gotten sick could get you forcibly separated from your family for an extended period of time.

If the worst Ebola outbreak in recorded history reaches the United States, federal law already permits "the apprehension and examination of any individual reasonably believed to be infected with a communicable disease". These individuals can be "detained for such time and in such manner as may be reasonably necessary". In other words, the federal government already has the authority to round people up against their will, take them to detention facilities and hold them there for as long as they feel it is "reasonably necessary".

In addition, Barack Obama recently signed an executive order that gives the federal government authority to round up and detain anyone that shows symptoms of "diseases that are associated with fever and signs and symptoms of pneumonia or other respiratory illness, are capable of being transmitted from person to person, and that either are causing, or have the potential to cause, a pandemic, or, upon infection, are highly likely to cause mortality or serious morbidity if not properly controlled."

So the legal framework for apprehending large numbers of Americans and housing them in temporary holding centers, tent cities, sports stadiums, old military bases and FEMA camps is already there.

All it is going to take is for these provisions to be activated is for a deadly virus to start spreading.

Will it be Ebola?

Let's hope not.

Personally, I am hoping for the best, but I am also preparing for the worst.

## *Chapter 12*

## A WARNING AGAINST APATHY

Have you ever heard of "normalcy bias"?

Basically the idea is that people tend to underestimate the possibility that a disaster will occur because they have never seen it happen before.

And as a result, they do not get prepared.

I fear that this is something that I am witnessing on a grand scale right now.

Back in 2009, 2010 and 2011 large numbers of Americans joined the "prepper movement". In fact, at one point it was estimated that there were two million preppers in the United States alone.

But then something happened.

People started to get comfortable again.

People started to forget about what happened back in 2008.

People started to become convinced that our leaders actually know what they are doing and actually fixed whatever caused our problems the last time.

Of course that is not true at all. In fact, as I have covered earlier in this book, our underlying financial problems have gotten much worse since 2008.

But a full-blown economic collapse has not happened yet, and many are now wondering if it will ever happen.

Instead of using this temporary bubble of debt-fueled false prosperity to prepare like never before, many Americans have given up on preparation entirely.

According to the people that I talk to, sales of emergency food and supplies are way down across the entire industry. A lot of people have simply lost interest. And I believe that this is a tragic, tragic mistake.

Anyone with half a brain should be able to see that the ingredients for a perfect storm are brewing.

The global financial system is a massive unsustainable Ponzi scheme based on ever-increasing amounts of debt. In fact, global government debt levels have risen by 40 percent just since 2008. And the big banks are being more reckless than they have ever been before. If you still have any doubt that an economic collapse is coming, please visit The Economic Collapse Blog where I have published more than 1000 articles that explain the reasons why we are heading for a horrific economic implosion in excruciating detail.

Geopolitical tensions are rising to levels that we have not seen in ages. Conflicts in Israel, Ukraine and Iraq threaten to plunge us into World War III at any time.

As I write this, we are in the midst of the worst Ebola outbreak in recorded history, and it is still growing at an exponential rate. If that outbreak reached the United States, it could collapse our economy all by itself.

The number of earthquakes and the number of volcano eruptions around the planet continue to increase. This is particularly true along the Ring of Fire. Meanwhile, our weather continues to get crazier and crazier and the epic multi-year drought in the western half of the United States is causing massive problems for farmers and ranchers.

I could go on and on, but hopefully you get the point.

Our financial system is so vulnerable that all it is going to take is one major "Black Swan event" to collapse the whole thing.

In the years ahead, I believe that there is going to be great turmoil in the financial markets.

In the years ahead, I believe that we are going to see large numbers of very important financial institutions completely fail.

In the years ahead, I believe that credit markets are going to freeze up and it is going to become very difficult for anyone to get a loan for just about anything.

In the years ahead, I believe that we are going to see unemployment and home foreclosures soar far higher than we have ever seen before.

In the years ahead, I believe that we are going to see rioting, looting and civil unrest in the streets of America.

In the years ahead, I believe that we are going to see a massive crime wave as people become increasingly desperate.

In the years ahead, I believe that we are going to see flash mobs looting rich neighborhoods.

In the years ahead, I believe that the government will feel forced to declare martial law in at least some of our major cities in an attempt to restore order.

In the years ahead, I believe that we are going to see food prices soar to ridiculous levels. At some point we could even see armed guards on food trucks.

In the years ahead, I believe that confidence in the federal government will almost completely disappear.

After years of careful study and investigation, these are the conclusions that I have reached.

I am an analytical person that tries to examine everything using logic and reason. And the cold, hard facts tell me that America is headed for trouble.

So my wife and I have been using this period of relative calm to prepare like never before. Sometimes people look at us a little funny because we are buying so much stuff at the grocery store.

But that is okay.

There is a time for everything, and right now it is a time to get prepared.

Please – get prepared now, while you still can.

# *Chapter 13*

## RECOMMENDED PREPPING WEBSITES

When it comes to prepping, there are literally millions of variables. Prepping is going to look a little bit different for every family, and no book on prepping could possibly cover every technique and every contingency. The good news is that there is literally almost an endless supply of free information available about prepping on the Internet. If you are new to prepping, you can find almost everything that you need to know online. Preppers tend to be very generous people, and they also tend to really enjoy sharing what they have learned with others.

What follows is a list of 50 of the best prepper websites, blogs and forums on the Internet. This is not a ranking from best to worst. Rather, this is a list of websites, blogs and forums that are very popular with preppers and that contain excellent free information about prepping. If you have a question about prepping, you can almost certainly find the answer to that question on one of these sites. And these sites are also great for finding other preppers to network with. I think that you will agree that these sites are literally a gold mine of resources and information...

1. Survival Blog (http://survivalblog.com/)
2. American Preppers Network (http://americanpreppersnetwork.com/)
3. The Survival Mom (http://thesurvivalmom.com/)
4. SHTFPlan.com (http://www.shtfplan.com/)

5. Survival 4 Christians (http://survival4christians.blogspot.com/)
6. Urban Survival (http://urbansurvival.com/blog/)
7. Backdoor Survival (http://www.backdoorsurvival.com/)
8. Off Grid Survival (http://offgridsurvival.com/)
9. Modern Survival Online (http://modernsurvivalonline.com/)
10. The Survivalist Blog (http://www.thesurvivalistblog.net/)
11. The Suburban Prepper (http://www.suburbanprepper.com/)
12. The Great Northern Prepper (http://www.greatnorthern-prepper.com/)
13. Prepper Website (http://www.prepperwebsite.com/)
14. The Survival Podcast (http://www.thesurvivalpodcast.com/)
15. Doom And Bloom (http://www.doomandbloom.net/)
16. Provident Living Today (http://www.provident-living-today.com/index.html)
17. The Prepper Journal (http://www.theprepperjournal.com/)
18. Prepared Christian (http://preparedchristian.net/)
19. SHTFblog.com (http://www.shtfblog.com/)
20. Survival Cache (http://survivalcache.com/)
21. Modern Survival Blog (http://modernsurvivalblog.com/)
22. Rural Revolution (http://www.rural-revolution.com/)
23. Preparedness Advice Blog (http://www.preparednessadvice.com/)
24. Prep-Blog.com (http://www.prep-blog.com/)
25. The Organic Prepper (http://www.theorganicprepper.ca/)
26. TEOTWAWKI Blog (http://teotwawkiblog.blogspot.com/)
27. Survival Sherpa (http://survivalsherpa.wordpress.com/)
28. The Apartment Prepper (http://apartmentprepper.com/)
29. How To Survive It (http://howtosurviveit.com/)
30. The Berkey Guy Blog (http://www.directive21.com/blog/)
31. The Home For Survival (http://www.thehomeforsurvival.com/)
32. My Family Survival Plan (http://www.myfamilysurvivalplan.com/)
33. Prepography (http://prepography.com/)
34. Prepper Resources (http://www.prepper-resources.com/)

35. SHTF School (http://shtfschool.com/)
36. Canadian Preppers Network (http://www.canadianpreppersnetwork.com/)
37. Maximum Survival (http://maximumsurvival.net/)
38. Survivor Jane (http://www.survivorjane.com/)
39. Prepping To Survive (http://preppingtosurvive.com/)
40. The Prepper Project (http://thepprojectproject.com/)
41. SGTReport (http://sgtreport.com/)
42. Off The Grid News (http://www.offthegridnews.com/)
43. Prepared For That (http://preparedforthat.com/)
44. Survival Magazine (http://www.survivalmagazine.org/)
45. Seasoned Citizen Prepper (http://seasonedcitizenprepper.com/)
46. Prepper Forums (http://www.prepperforums.net/)
47. Survivalist Boards (http://www.survivalistboards.com/)
48. The Doomsday Moose (http://www.doomsdaymoose.com/)
49. The Prepared Ninja (http://www.thepreparedninja.com/)
50. Common Sense Homesteading (http://www.commonsense-home.com/)

# Get Prepared Now!

WHY A GREAT CRISIS IS COMING & HOW YOU CAN SURVIVE IT

*Section Two*
*by Barbara Fix*

ISBN: 150522599X
ISBN 13: 9781505225990

# CONTENTS--SECTION TWO
## by
## Barbara Fix

# INTRODUCTION
## by Barbara Fix

Long before having my first preparedness book published and well before 2008 brought the dominoes crashing down, I was preparing for the economic crisis I felt was coming. Friends and family who witnessed my basement begin to fill with food storage and preparedness must-haves scratched their heads and asked, "But you're a Christian. Aren't we told that the Lord will provide? So why are you filling your shelves with food storage?" It's now years later and as the writer of hundreds of preparedness and gardening articles under the pen name Survival Diva, that same question is still being asked.

I trust that Michael's words helped clarify the reasons why we should prepare, and what the Lord has to say about the wisdom of preparedness.

The truth is, the camo-wearing survivalists hiding in bunkers portrayed on Doomsday Preppers is not representative of the average prepper. Most have regular jobs and regular lives who have decided to get prepared in the wake of economic concerns, skyrocketing food prices, and the number and severity of natural disasters. Already the economic tsunami has reached Europe, spurring demonstrations and riots in reaction to impossibly high unemployment and anger over austerity measures that include an extended retirement age, steep tax increases, deep cuts to welfare programs, cuts to public sector jobs and salaries, and a reduction of unemployment benefits.

Here in America the demographics point to an increased interest in self-sufficiency. The National Garden Association reports that since 2008 the increase in garden sales totals in the billions. Elsewhere, water catchment systems have increased in popularity and wood-burning stove usage has skyrocketed in response to punishingly high energy costs. It's estimated that there are over 2 million preppers in the U.S., but that number is pure conjecture as people quietly put aside essentials. My guess is the actual number could be much higher.

Over the past decade I have heard from multitudes of Christians who received the Lord's call to prepare. For some, it led to a move. For others, it involved a journey into preparedness to protect their loved ones, and still for others, their journey was centered on community involvement, so should a disaster strike, they will better be able to help their neighbors.

For those who are new to prepping, getting started is the most difficult part of preparedness, for it can bring more questions than answers; should I store bulk food and canned goods or MRE's? What type of preparedness goods will I need to make it through a crisis, and what about water storage and gardening and preserving the overflow from a garden? What do people pack in those 72-hour emergency kits I keep hearing about? What type of medical supplies should I put aside? And, possibly the most often asked question during these trying economic times; how can I afford to prepare, and if I find a way to prepare, what about helping others?

These questions will be addressed for your specific circumstances, taking your budget, lifestyle and ability into consideration.

*Get Prepared Now!* is a collaborative effort that explains why now is the time to prepare and breaks down how to become self-sufficient in manageable steps, chapter by chapter, so that you will be ready for whatever may come without fear and without going into debt.

In fact, you may be surprised to discover that by following the budget-conscience tips in the following chapters, and by buying

for your situation, basic preparedness is not as financially pro-
hibitive as it may seem.

Self-sufficiency often starts with self discipline. For me that
meant staying out of department and antique stores–at one time,
Nordstrom salespeople knew me by name! For others, it may
mean postponing that Hawaiian vacation, or waiting on high-
ticket items like a super-sized TV until you have put aside the
essentials. If you are on a tight budget and have decided to make
preparedness a priority, movie nights and dinners out may need
to be postponed until food storage and basic preparedness items
have been put aside.

The good news is prepping isn't a lifetime commitment.
Rather, it represents a short-term investment in your and your
loved ones survival.

One of the more difficult aspects of preparedness may be
convincing those closest to you of the need to prepare. I'm still
trying to convince a few friends and family members, while they
try to entice me back to the Nordstrom's rack. If this becomes
your reality, know that you are not alone. Through prayer, and
by encouraging your loved ones to do their own research on current economic, political and weather trends, your loved ones will
likely decide to join you!

Whenever I'm asked, "But what if nothing ever happens?
What if you bought all of the food and supplies for nothing?" My
answer is simple. Since I began preparing, the beans and rice and
other bulk goods I purchased have already doubled or tripled in
price. The cost of supplies like toilet paper and medical supplies
have gone up as well. The beans and rice and other bulk food
tucked safely away for long-term storage will last for 30 years. In
the meantime, the food and toilet paper and medical supplies
that represent self-sufficiency were far cheaper when they were
purchased than they are today and much cheaper than they will
be tomorrow. Should you find yourself having to explain your
reasons for wanting to be prepared, these facts alone may help
tip the scales in favor of preparedness.

In January of 2010 while writing *Survival: Prepare Before Disaster Strikes*, a 7.0 earthquake struck Haiti, killing hundreds of thousands of souls and displacing some 1.5 million people. Since then, the number and intensity of earthquakes has been growing, and crop-decimating drought has already affected U.S. growers and ranchers, leading to out of control food prices. Hurricanes and tornadoes are occurring with more intensity, and flooding and mudslides have become an ever-growing danger.

On the economic front, we only have to listen to the warnings of Michael Snyder and others who believe the U.S. is on the precipice of an economic collapse that may eclipse the hardships experienced during the Great Depression.

The fact is, the challenges we are facing today needn't leave us cowering in fear. We can mitigate the affects of financial hardship and natural disasters through prayer and by preparing ahead for emergencies.

## Living What I Write

On a personal note to readers of *Get Prepared Now!* I live what I write from a wilderness cabin in the frigid north, but the principles of self-sufficiency were learned as a child in an off-grid cabin in Alaska. There, water was collected from the lake that faced this remote cabin, or was hauled in from town. Power came from a generator, although oil lamps and Coleman lanterns sufficed for times when the fuel ran out. The cabin was heated by a wood stove and cooking and refrigeration was powered by a large propane tank that stood sentry amongst the birch trees that dotted the property.

Bathing was done in a sauna, heated by a small pot-bellied stove. In summer, jumping in the lake in bathing suits with a bar of soap was another option.

There was one aspect of living off-grid that I never did get used to, and that was the infamous outhouse. As outhouses go, it wasn't all that bad–especially after my mother changed out the toilet seat from a traditional one that tended to freeze skin to its surface (Alaska winters can deliver -40 degree days, or worse) for a thick sheet of Styrofoam. I'll admit that the sanitary properties of Styrofoam is not ideal, but at least it didn't grab the cold. But what really set this outhouse apart was the treacherous hike it took to get there. The trail was peppered with devils club, a large leafy weed that can grow from seven to eight feet tall with sharp, lethal thorns that were inches long on the underside of the leaves. Even so, devils club wasn't the worst of it. Moose roamed the area, and as far as they were concerned, *we* were the interlopers inhabiting this beautiful wilderness setting. Moose may look like lumbering, slow-witted animals, but they can charge at 35 miles an hour. And, unlike bear, their charge doesn't require getting too near their young for them to decide you need to be driven from their territory. I once spoke with a well-known Alaskan wildlife photographer who shared that she wasn't afraid to camp alongside Grizzly bears to take the amazing photographs she was so famous for. It was moose she didn't trust. I agree with her!

Today I live on acreage that hugs the side of a mountain with a back-up plan for self-sufficiency similar to what existed at the Alaskan cabin years ago. For now, I enjoy satellite TV and Internet, a phone, electricity, and a well that delivers water to the cabin. I'm thrilled to have a working bathroom, but an outhouse sits a reasonable distance away from the main cabin. So far, I have spotted only one moose on this property, and the cow's size, so far south of Alaska, was thankfully much smaller, but I respect her strength and speed and give her a wide berth on the occasions I have seen her on the property, always with a calf in tow.

There is a large den of coyotes only a few hundred feet from my property that lick their lips at the thought of free-range chickens. Most mornings, typically around 4:00 am, they wake me with their yips as they greet the dawn. A bobcat occasionally makes itself at home under the cabin on cold winter nights, and I'm told several cougar live in the vicinity. Although I've never spotted one, I have seen evidence of their kills of white-tail deer that are thick in this unpopulated region. Black bear roam freely here, and after a summer of hearing, but not seeing a black bear that camped itself against a steep slope on the property, it left a calling card–a nose print against my sliding glass doors that measured five feet tall. I purchased a shot gun which I hope to never have to use.

Soon after the bear incident I heard about a neighbor who had opened the door to air out her cabin of cooking odors and was visited by a black bear. It ambled into her cabin to investigate the irresistible smell of dinner simmering on her stove top. She took a broom to shoo it outdoors, I'm told. I will be forever awed by her bravery. Had it been me, I would have crawled through a window to cocoon myself behind the door of my SUV that would have been tearing down the driveway in nothing flat.

I should clarify that I am not a die-hard homesteader. My days usually consist of writing—an enjoyable way to make a living while surrounded by wilderness–and my idea of fun doesn't include chopping wood or hauling water . . .at least not until the time comes when it's necessary and my immediate family join me. At that point, we will be sharing the chores that would otherwise be impossible for one person to accomplish—a subject we'll be diving into in Chapter 2, *Keeping It Simple & Must-Have Skills*.

Living so far from civilization is not a prerequisite for self-sufficiency, however. You can become self-sufficient from just about anywhere with only a few exceptions, which will be addressed as we move forward with this section of the book that is devoted to the how-to of preparedness.

# Chapter 1

## ARE YOU PREPARED?

Brandon Nolan had a long list of errands to run if he had any hope of surprising his wife, Sarah. He had already said goodbye to their twelve year old daughter and ten year old twin sons on their rush to catch the school bus. Now it was time to head to the bank, and then the florists, and eventually he'd need to stop by the bookstore to pick up the novel he'd ordered. It was the latest in a series, written by Sarah's favorite author. He'd booked dinner reservations at their favorite restaurant on Vashon Island weeks ago and unless they missed the ferry crossing from downtown Seattle, they would be celebrating their fifteenth anniversary over a candlelight dinner of Dungeness crab.

The traffic was light and Brandon's thoughts traveled to the article he'd finished the previous night. The piece was about the economy, a subject he was considered an expert on. The truth was, though he had earned a doctorate of economics at MIT and had called the 2007/2008 collapse just before Lehman Brother's started the domino's falling, he remained as clueless as everyone else. How the economy had remained seemingly solvent since the first sign of trouble was beyond comprehension. Of course, the term solvent was subjective. Although the banks may still have the trust of most, behind the scenes it was complete bedlam. Daily, Brandon expected to wake up to pandemonium on the stock market floor. That was where he expected the first cracks to appear . . . just before the dam broke and the banks imploded with the strain. Actually, the too big to fail banks had *already* failed. The Federal Reserve's flooding the market with newly printed currency and digitized bytes, was the only thing keeping them afloat. Yet, they continued to deny the derivatives addiction they'd developed. The 2008 debacle apparently hadn't taught them their lessons because as addicts, they continued to play the shell game, delving ever deeper into that black void. It would be their undoing. The only question that remained was *when* the bubble would burst, thus forcing them to answer to the public.

The drive to the small neighborhood bank he and Sarah used took only minutes. It was attached to a small strip mall that shared the parking lot with the areas neighborhood grocery store. It wasn't until Brandon reached the front door that he was jarred from his daydreams. It was locked, its interior an uninviting dark void. He searched for a notice, something to explain why on a Friday, the busiest day of the week, they were locked down as tight as Fort Knox. No notice was posted on the door, nor on either of the large plate glass windows that flanked it.

The bank's parking lot was nearly empty, but across the large expanse of asphalt, the grocery store was in complete gridlock. The customers he watched exiting the store were dragging overflowing grocery carts with them. In a few cases, more than one cart. As he approached the store's entrance on foot, Brandon could feel the atmosphere of fear telegraphing from the shopper's he passed. There were no polite nods, no smiles.

Typically, this was a place where neighbors stopped to visit one-another and catch up on their week. Today as Brandon passed through the electronic doors, he was greeted with people blindly wheeling their overflowing carts towards the checkout stands or out the exit doors. People in line were barely moving while disgruntled customers stood arguing with clerks who appeared to be every bit as frustrated as their customers.

Walking past the checkout stands, Brandon was confronted with a view of bare shelves. Only a handful of dented cans remained, some toppled on their sides, others left to litter the floor. A store employee was wheeling an abandoned cart down the aisle, sorting through its jumbled contents to place cans on their appropriate shelf, only for them to be snatched up by a passing shopper.

Empty-handed, Brandon walked to the crowded customer service line. Mike, the store manager, was a friend. If anyone would know what was going on, it would be him. He was the sort of guy people confided in, which meant that if Calder, the Chief of Police, or their newly elected Mayor had any inside information, they would probably have shared it with Mike.

Within minutes of standing in line, Brandon turned the corner from wishful thinking to facing head-on what was clearly written on everyone's face and the reason why the bank had bolted its doors. He was about to head for the front door when Mike exited his office, preoccupied with a stack of flyers he held in his hand. He slowed when he saw Brandon.

"We'll talk while I get these posted," Mike said in a neutral voice. He walked head down, wide shoulders relaxed, giving nothing away as he advanced to a cork board that took up nearly half of the wall space between the customer service desk and the public restrooms.

Brandon followed, reading the flyer that Mike tacked to the board. It was a notice informing customers that all purchases would be cash only.

"How bad is it?" Brandon asked.

"The stock market crashed. By crashed, I'm talking it was annihilated. They closed the trading floor. The banks reacted by locking their doors to avoid a bank run. Plus, electronic banking is down. We haven't been able to process charge card, ATM or EBT food card transactions for hours."

"Has the administration made an announcement?"

"Minutes ago. I just finished watching it in the office. They're promising the public it's a temporary glitch. I've got a bad feeling about this. When people get hungry, can't feed their families, and realize help isn't coming, things are gonna turn ugly," Mike said, nodding towards the long line of people standing at the customer service counter.

"Most are there to ask if we'll accept a credit card or a personal check. I've had to turn down customers who have been shopping with us for years, but corporate has decided to protect themselves, which means cash or nothing."

"Has corporate figured out how to stop the looting, then?" Brandon said.

"It's already started. We've had to stop people from making a run for it with full grocery carts when they realized electronic banking's down. I was told looting in the cities is already out of control. I'm guessing here in outlining areas, most people will put up with hunger until they grow desperate. That's when the looting will begin in earnest. The Chief came by, told me he called in his off-duty officers. Same with the fire department and the hospital. In the metropolitan areas, the police are already out in full force. The administration may not be saying it publicly, but they're expecting trouble on a level that's never been seen before unless this situation can be turned back around."

"We both know that's not going to happen. This time it's for keeps. The Fed's kept things going by lowering interest rates and printing money as fast as they could print it, but it's finally caught up with them," Brandon said.

"Will you leave for the cabin?" Sam asked.

"As soon as I pick up the kids from school and get Sarah at the office. I don't want her on the road by herself. What about you?" Brandon asked.

"We've put enough aside to get by, but if things get out of control, we'll head to Paula's folks. Their farm is isolated. We'll be okay. It won't be long before I'm forced to lock the store. The inventory's been picked clean and suppliers won't deliver until things are under control, and even then, they're insisting on cash. Our account is frozen, just like everyone else."

Brandon nodded his understanding and felt a mixture of relief and guilt wash over him. They were the lucky ones. They had the resources to protect their families. What about those who didn't through circumstances they had no control over? The cabin Mike referred to had been in the Nolan family for three generations. It was tucked away in the mountains, nearly 200 miles from Seattle's urban sprawl–hopefully far enough to stay clear of the worst of the backlash. Over the past few years, he and Sarah had managed to stock the cabin with over a year's worth of food and supplies. They'd installed a manual pump at the well, and with a little arm-twisting, Brandon had convinced Sarah to let him clear a portion of the south-facing old growth on the property for a large garden.

Brandon had taken a few other precautions when the telltale signs of economic implosion grew to uncomfortable levels, especially when big investors started selling off their stock portfolios in exchange for gold. He withdrew their savings from the bank and invested it in junk silver and silver rounds. They'd already seen a profit from their investment as rumors of the shaky stock market grew legs and the price of silver spiked.

Just last month they had spent the better part of a weekend purchasing bartering goods. Most of the items were inexpensive, purchased at Dollar Stores, but it would help fill any gaps in their preparations if the crash lasted as long as Brandon suspected it would. Crowding the last available space of the basement shelves were grosses of magnified reading glasses, bleach, salt, toothpaste, toothbrushes, shampoo, medical supplies, garden seed, matches, and batteries that people would need. Purchasing the barter items had spurred Sarah to add to their medical supplies. Now the large linen closet in the bathroom of the cabin was filled to overflowing. She'd also purchased oil lamps and enough lantern oil to keep a dozen lamps burning, 'round the clock for years, but she'd been adamant that cooking, and tasks, and family time required lighting and she wasn't about to sit in the dark waiting for the power to come back on. She had been right to invest in lighting. Their bank account was officially frozen, just like everyone else in the country. If the power company stayed afloat, there were no guarantees they wouldn't start hitting the off switch for nonpayment.

The previous summer they had ten cords of seasoned firewood delivered to fuel the old wood-burning cook and heat stoves that had sat in the cabin ever since Brandon could remember. The dilapidated chicken coop hadn't been repaired yet, but over the years, Brandon had hauled enough wood, nails and roofing material to the property to make necessary repairs and to build an outhouse that was probably against code, but necessary for survival. If their neighbor was true to his word, the chicken coop would be filled with chickens for eggs and meat in exchange for Brandon's help clearing more of the neighbor's land for a larger garden. They'd made the agreement several years ago when they discovered they shared an interest in preparing for the hard times they saw coming.

And now that time had come. There wouldn't be any bailout. The too big to fail banks were going down with a thud of insolvency as CEO's fled to their Swiss bank accounts.

Brandon said goodbye to Mike and walked back to his car. He would top off the tank, pick his children up at school, and Sarah at her downtown office. Their 72-hour emergency kits were stored in the back of the SUV and would cover them on the 200 mile drive to the cabin. There was an off-chance they would be able to return home once the inevitable unrest had settled down and people had found a way to work together to survive. But it was just as likely they would have to remain at the cabin for the duration. Only time would tell who had the fortitude to survive the hard times that lie ahead.

———

The reason for including this short vignette was to describe, in story form, what being prepared for an emergency entails. It takes a commitment to put aside food, water, and medical supplies and a back-up plan to cook, heat and light a home. In this scenario, it wasn't a natural disaster that took out the electrical grid, but if banks ever locked their doors and ATM's and point of sale terminals ceased to operate, being prepared to survive without cash by having necessities planned for ahead of time will see you through.

The following chapters will break down what to plan ahead for and why and assumes the worst-case scenario by encouraging you to prepare for a long-term crisis that brings an electrical outage that often accompanies a disaster, whether it's man-made, celestial, or is delivered by mother nature.

# Chapter 2

## KEEPING IT SIMPLE & MUST-HAVE SKILLS

Keeping it simple requires getting past the emotional road-blocks that get in the way of effective preparedness, to be able to admit that we cannot know how long an emergency may last and to willingly give up the expectation of a pampered 21st century lifestyle in exchange for one that values function over convenience.

The pioneers knew the meaning of self-sufficiency. They went to bed when it grew dark and woke up with the dawn. The tools and devices they used were manual with few moving parts and were not dependent upon fuel or electricity as they are today. They dug root cellars to preserve the overflow from the garden, rather than depending upon refrigerators. They kept chickens for meat and eggs, cows for milk, butter, and cheese, and when the cow stopped producing, for meat. Hogs were fed slops and were slaughtered to provide the family with bacon and ham. Wild game was cured, smoked, or made into jerky through dehydrating the meat.

Lighting was provided for with oil lamps and cooking was done in a fireplace, or for those who could afford the luxury, a wood-burning cook stove. Their homes were heated with wood, which meant the difficult chore of tree-felling and splitting the wood, which often involved the entire family.

Women gave birth at home with the help of a midwife and most medical emergencies were treated at home because of the distance that had to be crossed to reach a doctor. Herbs were used for medicinal purposes and sometimes made into tonics.

Laundry was washed by hand, wrung out, and hung to dry. A day in the life of a pioneer was long and no one counted calories or obsessed over the fat intake in their diets, yet most burned every calorie. Family members were expected to pitch in with all chores and there were no TV's or Play stations and no such thing as soccer moms.

If you've ever wondered what it will be like during a protracted crisis that takes down the electrical grid, when services, retailers, gas stations, grocery stores, doctor care and emergency services are unavailable, you only need to look at the life of a pioneer.

In today's world we will need to be prepared to defend ourselves against looters, for far too many Americans have grown soft and have come to expect a lifeline that will not arrive during a nationwide emergency. Few will have any clue how to survive living off the land, and fewer still will be prepared to preform the many chores that will be required for basic survival from sun up to sun down.

To survive day-to-day without the benefit of modern conveniences will require keeping things simple. Yet, a running theme I see with those who are interested in self-sufficiency, be they newbies or experienced, is the need to parlay today's standards into a long-term preparedness plan. This often leads peppers to modern conveniences such as a generator to run lights, a refrigerator, a washer and dryer, a stove, an electric pump for a well, or a chainsaw to collect firewood.

The problem with relying on something like a generator or a chainsaw is that in a long-term crisis, the fuel to run these conveniences will eventually be consumed and it isn't likely there will be any replenishing it.

When you begin a preparedness plan, it's best to start with the basics; manual tools that aren't dependent upon fuel to run or have parts that can break when those parts may be difficult or impossible to replace. An example is choosing a tree-felling ax to collect firewood, rather than choosing a chainsaw that requires storing replacement parts and chains and is dependent upon fuel to run.

Once you have all of the basics provided for, a generator or a chainsaw are great to have on hand. They will make tasks easier while fuel supplies last! But please, not before filling in the just-in-case basics.

Pioneers approached life pragmatically and were big believers in an heir and a spare. Instead of one ax, they had several, including the means to replace a broken handle. For all the can't-live-without-them items, there was a back-up, because redundancy was life itself, just as it will be if we ever find ourselves plunged into life without the conveniences we take for granted today.

The pioneers didn't have to be taught how to survive. Instead, they lived it every day. Today, there are reference books and training courses that can fill in what's been lost over the generations.

The following are subjects that can be referenced with a comprehensive book on the subject:

- Emergency Medical (Where There is no Doctor–highly recommended)
- Emergency Dental (Where There is no Dentist–also excellent)
- Curing Wild Game–if you plan to hunt or trap
- Home Canning– to preserve the overflow from the garden and wild game
- Wild Edible Foods–specific to your region
- Dehydrated Foods–to preserve fruits, vegetables and game
- Gardening–should include a section on seed-saving and be related to your climate zone
- Food Storage Related Cook Book

All of the suggested books can be purchased gently used and will prove to be worth their weight in gold! It never hurts to search the Internet for recipes that work well with food storage, but it's a good idea to download them and keep them in a three-ring binder because if the power goes down, so does your ability to access those recipes. Listed at the end of Chapter 6, *Alternative Cooking & Heating* are several preparedness-related websites where you will find a wealth of recipes that can be printed and included in a recipe binder.

Although, reference books are extremely important to have on hand, they can never take the place of hands-on experience. It is important to practice skills such as cooking with alternative cooking devices, gardening, preserving food, first aid, and wilderness survival, which is discussed at length throughout the next chapters on preparedness.

———

Links relating to chapter subjects are listed below to help you locate important information. At the time of publication, each of the links listed were verified to be operational.

Nuclear War Survival:
http://www.nukepills.com/docs/nuclear_war_survival_skills.pdf

Where There is no Doctor (Consider Donating):
http://www.hesperian.org/publications_download.php

Where There is No Dentist:
http://www.hesperian.org/publications_download.php

Where Women Have No Doctor:
http://www.hesperian.org/publications_download.php

# Chapter 3

## PRAY FOR THE BEST, PREPARE FOR THE WORST: TECHNOLOGY OVERLOAD

On July 23, 2012 a coronal mass ejection (CME) released two massive plasma clouds that narrowly missed earth. It was the most powerful solar storm on record in the past 150 years.

Upon releasing the sobering news two years later, NASA gave the following statement:

*"Analysts believe that a direct hit could cause widespread power blackouts, disabling everything that plugs into a wall socket. Most people wouldn't even be able to flush their toilet because urban water supplies largely rely on electric pumps".*

Steve Tracton of the Capital Weather Gang went to the heart of the matter in his insightful April 6, 2009 article, entitled *Do Solar Storms Threaten Life As We Know It?* The following is an excerpt:

*"Electric power grids, communications and navigation systems (including GPS), and satellites (including weather) could be damaged beyond repair for many years. The consequences could be devastating for commerce, transportation, agriculture and food stocks, fuel and water supplies, human heath and medical facilities, national security, and daily life in general."*

Think about the previous statement. Grid-Down has the potential to take out communications, banking and other financial institutions, the Internet, GPS, transportation, emergency ser-vices, food distribution, and utilities such as power, natural gas and water delivery, and sewer processing. It would lead to school closures, it has the potential to halt all forms of travel (includ-ing air travel), and it could easily force the closure of businesses, retailers and services–including gas stations that rarely have emergency back-up power. Basically, if the grid went down for more than a few days, the nagging inconvenience would soon escalate into full-blown panic.

More recently, on September 10, 2014 NASA warned of two powerful CME's that had the potential to disrupt radio, GPS, satellite and the power grid may be headed our way. Happily, it turned out to be a non-event, as, once again, it missed directly hitting earth.

People tend to ignore the possibility of a disruption of the power grid and the technologies we have grown so dependent upon. Add to this that most have never spent more than a few hours without power, flushing toilets, running water, grocery stores, and services, and you suddenly have the makings of the perfect storm should the grid ever go down for more than a few days. In truth, we live in a world dangling from a gossamer thread, where it would take surprisingly little for us to wake up one day to discover that thread has been broken and we are on our own to sort it out.

This is why a common theme you will see throughout most preparedness-related sites is advice on preparing for grid-down while our nation remains woefully unprepared to cope with the realities of life without modern conveniences.

The average American has a three-day food supply in their cupboards and little if any stored water. Yet, supplying every man, woman and child in the U.S. with just two meals a day would require distributing **622 million** meals each day. Such a task would be humanly impossible. Where would that many prepared meals come from, and how could it be transported in the face of grid-lock and road closures that usually accompanies a disaster? And what about the manpower it would take to distribute 622 million meals when most aid givers will be needed at home?

Municipalities and utility providers typically have emergency back-up power for only a few days time. After that, we will be on our own.

## The Vulnerability of Layered Technologies

Put simply, technology has become a quagmire of interdependence, each layer dependent upon the next; our fragile electrical grid, Satellites; GPS, and the nations alarming dependency upon computers, which themselves are vulnerable to sophisticated hackers and terrorists. Today most utilities employ SCADA (Supervisory Control Data Systems), which are sophisticated computer based systems designed to run unmanned. Recently, SCADA has come under attack for its vulnerability to cyberattack.

Additionally, today's advanced technology has left the U.S. vulnerable to coronal mass ejections (CME) from the sun and electromagnetic pulse weaponry (EMP)–either one of which has the potential to take down the power grid in concentrated or widespread areas.

You may have already heard about the 1859 Carrington Event that Michael discussed in the first section *Get Prepared Now*! The Carrington Event received little press back in1859 because the technological age was in its infancy and the small power stations that eventually delivered power to small sections of cities wasn't introduced until the 1880's.

Today, if a Carrington Event occurred, it would crash the grid . . . for years. The large, extra-high voltage (EHV) transformers that would need to be replaced in a worst case kill-shot from the sun, or a strategically deployed EMP, are made in South Korea and Germany and have an approximate wait time of three years. In grid-down, and assuming that the U.S. could get their hands on multiple EHV's (in a situation where South Korea and Germany may likewise be impacted, they are likely to take care of the home-front first), we would need to transport these monoliths (weighing hundreds of tons each) by sea, then by rail, and transfer them to a semi for transport to their final destination. That could be problematic when refineries that process the fuel needed to transport them may be crippled in a grid-down event.

There is also the matter of the vulnerability of GPS (Global Positioning Satellite), which the maritime industry and the railways depend upon for tracking and collision avoidance capabilities. Yet, GPS can be disrupted by a powerful CME or EMP.

Satellites are just as corruptible to a CME or EMP, and they are the glue that holds many systems crucial to every-day life together. Perhaps it will be that humpty-dumpty will not be able to be put back together again, or perhaps we will continue to dodge what many claim is inevitable.

Scientists believe that we are overdue for a kill shot from the sun. The U.S. government was concerned enough about the threat that CME's and EMP's pose to technology and the infrastructure of the nation to have commissioned several studies on the matter. The consensus of each study was chilling: the nation is indeed vulnerable, as are all nations that are dependent upon the power grid.

In fact it has already happened.

In 1989 the strongest geomagnetic storm in 50 years was caused by a CME, which disabled Hydro Quebec's electricity transmission system, leaving six million people in Quebec without power for nine hours. The storm disrupted radio signals, satellites, Geostationary Operational Environmental Satellite System (GOES) weather satellite communications, and interfered with a sensor on the Space Shuttle Discovery.

In 2003, a powerful geomagnetic storm, dubbed the "Halloween Storm," interfered with satellite communications and left Sweden without power for a brief period.

Between the threat of a CME taking down the grid, and an EMP attack while political tension tightens across the globe, it is prudent to plan head for an unexpected grid-down event.

Note: EMP is similar to an extremely powerful radio wave, and unless it is specifically concentrated (very unlikely), it will not harm humans or animals. Likewise, a CME will not physically harm humans or animals. It is the aftermath of an EMP or a CME that takes down the grid that can threaten humankind.

## Lighting

It goes without saying that if the grid goes down and you don't have alternative lighting, you will need to acclimate to getting up with the dawn and going to bed when it grows dark. However, if you stock up on solar lighting, long-burning emergency candles, flashlights (and batteries) and kerosene or oil lanterns, along with the fuel they require, you can provide for lighting.

When you think back to a storm that took down the power, it wasn't all that bad. You probably lit candles or fired up a lantern. Life slowed down, giving you a chance to reconnect as a family, maybe over a board game, or just to talk about every-day things. Grid-down won't be that much different as long as you've put aside back-up lighting. Without it, family life will suffer. You will need task lighting for cooking, reading, or to sit down to a board game. Because lighting is so important to day-to-day life, it's worth special attention and when it comes to lighting, back-up is key. Solar lighting that is not dependent upon fuel should be included in a preparedness plan so if your fuel storage runs out during a protracted crisis, you will still have the ability to light your home.

Plan ahead for a headlamp or lantern that will leave your hands free for tasks that must be preformed after dark.

## Water

It is important to locate a reliable source for water, and to have a way to transport it, and a method in which to purify it, *ahead of a crisis*. Chapter 4, *Water: Gathering, Storing & Purification* covers this in detail. In grid-down, water will not be delivered to your home once utilities have exhausted their emergency back-up power. Those with a water well will fare better as long as a manual water pump is available.

## Sewer

It is possible that toilets will not be able to be flushed and sinks and bathtubs will not drain once municipal sewer plants emergency power ceases to operate. In a worst case scenario, sewers may back up into homes, although it helps to live on a hill where gravity can help back-ups from occurring. Chapter 13, *Long-Term Survival* details items you will need for bathing, laundry and toilet facilities.

Sewage back-up into a home presents a health risk, but it's possible to plug a sewer line to avoid back-flow.

Visit *Disaster Survival Guide: How To Plug Your Sewer Line* for instructions:

http://www.disaster-survival-guide.com/emergency-utilities-shutoff/how-to-plug-your-sewer-line/

## Natural Gas

A common belief of most people, including many preppers, is that natural gas feeds into homes will be operable during a disaster. This is an incorrect assumption. Natural gas is delivered to the homeowner through compressor stations, most of which depend upon electricity to deliver natural gas. Additionally, providers have a system of automatic shut-off during an emergency for safety reasons. Compressor stations rely upon SCADA (Supervisory Control Data Systems), and as already mentioned, SCADA systems are vulnerable to cyberattack.

For these reasons it isn't wise to depend upon natural gas to heat your home, or run a gas range, or to fuel a natural gas generator.

## GPS Navigational Devices

Reliance upon GPS with a directional device such as a Garmin or an app from a smart phone should not be relied upon. During a particularly strong CME, it's not unusual for announcements from NASA to go out, warning of possible disruptions to GPS, radio and communications signals.

GPS was developed by the Department of Defense, and during a national emergency the use of GPS may be disallowed if public use poses a threat to nationally security. Purchasing a compass, street maps, and topographical maps will make travel easier in the midst of grid-down.

## Transportation

There are differing opinions on whether a strong CME or an EMP has the capability to disable a vehicle. An earlier government study that tested the effects of a CME on 37 cars and trucks reported that only one truck required repairs, but detractors of the study claim that as these vehicles were only subjected to 50 k V/m, lasting for only a millisecond, the test was not representative of the effects of what a strong EMP or a CME could deliver.

The biggest threat to vehicles is the sensitive solid state electronics that have been used in their manufacture since the late 1970s, which studies have shown may be disabled by a powerful CME or an EMP. Consider keeping an alternative form of transportation like a bicycle on hand that isn't dependent on fuel.

## Hardening (Protecting) Electronics from CME & EMP

Critical items like an emergency radio, 2-way radios, Ham Radio, LED flashlights, batteries and any other electronics you deem important for survival can be protected from CME or EMP by storing them in a Faraday Cage.

A Faraday cage can be made from something as simple as a galvanized garbage can. A Berhrens galvanized trash can with a locking lid is a popular choice for preppers wanting to protect sensitive electronics. They are available at some of the big-box hardware stores in 5-gallon and 10-gallon sizes.

To ensure that your electronics are protected, you can line the galvanized trash can with cardboard, and place valuable electronics in a separate cardboard box before adding them to the lined trash can. Be sure to add cardboard insulation on the bottom and top of the trash can as well.

Once the lid of the trash can is securely in place, you can make an even better seal by stuffing steel wool or aluminum foil under the edge of the lid and then secure the lid to the body of the trash can with aluminum tape.

———

Links relating to chapter subjects are listed below to help you locate important information. At the time of publication, each of the links listed were verified to be operational.

Government Study on Global Positioning System (GPS) Disruptions:
http://www.gao.gov/assets/660/658792.pdf

Government Study on Electromagnetic Pulse (EMP) Attack:
http://empcommission.org/docs/A2473-EMP_Commission-7MB.pdf

Commission to assess the threat to the U.S. from Electromagnetic Pulse Attack:
http://www.globalsecurity.org/wmd/library/congress/2004_r/04-07-22emp.pdf Report of the EMP

How To Plug A Sewer Line to Avoid Back-Up:
http://www.disaster-survival-guide.com/emergency-utilities-shutoff/how-to-plug-your-sewer-line/

# Chapter 4

## WATER: GATHERING, STORING & PURIFICATION

When it comes to water, always keep in mind the rule of three: Man can live without water for three days, food for three weeks and air for three minutes. Water collection, storage, and purification should go to the very top of your priority list.

A minimum requirement of water storage is 28 gallons a month per person. This provides for drinking, cooking, and cleanup water. To estimate your basic water needs for six months, we'll use the example of the water needs for a family of four:

Example: 4 (people) X 28 gallons of water per month X 6 months = 678 gallons of water, minimum.

This does not include the extra drinking water required for hot days and while working outdoors. And should you want to bathe rather than take sponge baths, or if you plan to garden, your water requirements will be much greater.

If you aren't familiar with gardening, the best way to estimate water needs is by reading gardening books written specifically for your climate zone, or you can get in touch with your local horticultural society, or a garden co-op.

In a perfect world, we would all be living on property with a well and a manual hand pump to draw water in case the power grid goes down. Most municipal water facilities only have a few days emergency back-up power to continue to deliver water to their customers. After that, anyone hooked to municipal water will be on their own.

Adaptability is key to survival, however one deal-breaker is living in a location without a dependable water source. If that is your situation, it is time to consider relocating. That's a harsh statement, I know, but my job is to help you get prepared for any emergency, and water is something you simply cannot live without.

The following states are experiencing drought to varying degrees. The percentages reflected are statistics from May, 2014: California (76.7%), Nevada (38.7%), New Mexico (33.3%), Kansas (48.1%), Arizona (7.7%), Oklahoma (50.1%), and Texas (39.9%). The current drought didn't happen overnight. California, the worst hit in the current drought, has experienced extreme drought for several years. It has become enough of a concern that many locations in California have restricted or have begun to monitor the watering of lawns, and have banned washing cars and hosing down sidewalks in an attempt to continue to provide drinking water to residents. Recently, some areas of California have begun to report dry wells as experts warn that this current drought is likely to continue, which will require officials to further restrict water usage to protect drinking water.

If you live in a state suffering from extreme drought, it is critical to stay abreast of the situation. If ever a location must transport drinking water, it should serve as a red flag with regard to survival. In a disaster that leads to a blackout, or roads are either blocked or suffer heavy grid-lock, it may become impossible to transport water to afflicted areas.

## Water Sources

Once you have located a water source, keep in mind that although it may *appear* to be drinkable, it still must be filtered through a quality water purifier or boiled before drinking or cooking with it–no exceptions! During an emergency that lasts weeks or months, sanitation will be non-existent and it's likely that refuse and disease will find its way into open waterways. A good quality water purifier like a Berkey, Katadyn or Sawyer are capable of removing most contaminants, but comparison shop before settling on a specific water purifier, and be sure to purchase extra replacement filters.

## Hauling Water

With regard to water collection, there are a couple of important considerations you should plan ahead for. The first one is the challenge of transporting water. A gallon of water weighs 8.34 pounds, which may on the surface seem like useless information . . . until you're forced to haul it. A typical 5-gallon water container weighs 41.7 pounds when filled, and a 7-gallon container weighs 58.38 pounds. Now, picture yourself hauling that weight on a regular basis, and you will see the wisdom of investing in a wheeled hand cart. It will make the task of transporting several filled water containers at a time much easier to do.

## Water Containers

Water containers themselves are another consideration. Over the years of writing about preparedness, I have heard people suggest storing water in old milk cartons. My advice? Don't do it! Milk cartons are biodegradable, designed to break down within six months due to landfill concerns. Many people store their water and food storage in the same location. Should the carton begin to leak, it has the potential to ruin any food storage it comes in contact with.

Be sure the water containers you choose are specifically designed for long-term storage. For ease of use, containers with a handle and a pour spout will make pouring water for drinking, cooking and general clean-up that much easier.

Note: Storing water in an indoor or heated space is a necessity in northern climates during winter months that deliver freezing temperatures. As water freezes, it expands, and will cause water containers to split. The same is true for water bladders and water barrels used for catchment systems.

## Safety

Few of us have experienced what it is like to be in the midst of a long-term crisis where people are scrambling to survive. Katrina is arguably the closest we have come as a nation to the social unrest a full-blown crisis may bring. The reports of looting and gang activity were as disheartening as the help that others offered one-another was uplifting. The fact is there will be those we must watch out for when venturing out, which includes times when you must collect water, especially for those who live in a city or a populated town.

Once you have located a dependable water source, practice walking to this source from as many alternate routes as possible, so should your location experience unrest, you increase the potential of getting in and out safely. Look for the most effective access points to collect the water so the time it takes to collect water can be reduced. If you plan on using a handcart, make sure to bring it along for practice runs. This will allow you to find the best access points in a real-world application.

## Water Purifiers

A quality water purifier is one of those must-have items that should go to the very top of your preparedness list. With one, you will be able to process even the water from a swimming pool or a stagnant pond into safe drinking water–but realize that filtering such water will shorten the life of the replacement filters. For specific information on this, contact the manufacturer, as this varies per manufacturer.

Throughout the chapters on preparedness, I intentionally promote budget-conscience purchases. The reason for this is to help get you ready as quickly as possible, without breaking the bank or going into debt. However, safe drinking water is essential for life. As such, a quality water purifying system is one area where you can't afford to scrimp.

There are portable models available for Berkey, Kathryn, Sawyer, as well as another popular brand, the LifeStraw. These personal-sized water purifiers have been designed to easily fit into a back pack or an emergency 72-hour kit, and are widely used by hikers and campers to safely purify lake, stream, and pond water. It is important to understand when preparing for a protracted emergency that portable hiker/camper water purifiers have relatively small capacity filters (anywhere from 110 gallons to 265 gallons), which means the replacement filters will need to be changed often in order to continue to have safe drinking and cooking water.

Make sure before purchasing any water purifier that it is capable of filtering pathogenic bacteria, parasites, herbicides, pesticides, organic solvents, VOC's and heavy metals such as cadmium, chromium, copper, led, mercury, aluminum, as well as nitrates. A quality water purifier will also remove cloudiness, silt and sediment along with foul tastes and odors.

Bacteria such as shigella, vibrio. escherichia coli and salmonella are undetectable by the human eye, but should your family drink untreated water that is contaminated with any of these bacterias, you take the chance of becoming ill at a time when illness must be avoided at all costs.

Viruses are another concern. Giardia, cryptosporidium and entameba cannot be seen by the naked eye, but they will certainly be felt by anyone drinking water containing any of these viruses! The symptoms of these microorganisms are nausea, vomiting, stomach cramps and diarrhea. It's important to take into consideration that others will be collecting water from the same source as you are, and the possibility of its becoming contaminated with refuse and worse exists–which brings us right back to the need for a quality water purifier.

The cost of a good water purifier depends upon the size of the unit you chose and the amount of water you expect to purify, as it dictates how many replacement filters you will need. With respect to water purification, it's always best to overestimate what you feel you will need. If you were to set up for six months of water purification and a crisis lasted years, this would present a problem.

When I began researching for a water purifier I searched for one that would filter out bacteria and viruses, plus it had to have the capability to filter out iron–water wells in my vicinity have a high concentration of iron, which has an unpleasant taste that I wanted to be sure would be filtered out. I needed a quality purifier that was large enough to process water for 23 people. Yes, a smaller one would do the same job, but would take more time filling it and there will be plenty of other chores to keep us all busy in a disaster. After extensive research, I chose a Berkey. I use it every day for clean drinking water and keep track of the water that's processed to make sure the replacement filters are changed when needed. The model I chose was the Imperial Berkey because of its size and the need to process large amounts of drinking and cooking water. Here is the equation I used:

28 gallons drinking and cooking water per person per month for 23 people;

28 gallons water X 23 people = 644 gallons of purified water needed pr month

Calculated for 24 months (to cover a worst-case scenario);

644 gallons water X 24 months =15,456 gallons of purified water needed for two years

Number of filters needed at a calculation of two filters processing 6,000 gallons of water before replacement;

6,000 / 15,456 gallons = three sets (6) replacement filters

Note: When estimating replacement filter needs, always check factory specifications. Berkey specifies that processing 6,000 gallons of water using a pair of replacement filters is based upon tap water. Silty water such as pond water or water that is processed from a swimming pool containing chlorine will require replacing filters sooner that the 6,000 gallon estimate because silt, sediments and chlorine forces the filters to work harder. They can be cleaned, but at some point they will need to be replaced.

Should your budget cringe at the cost of a quality water purifier, you will find instructions for boiling water for safe drinking and cooking later in this chapter.

Before we move on from the subject of water purification, two other water filtration methods need to be discussed which are reverse osmosis and distillation. While either one of these methods will get you safely through a crisis, the long-term affects of drinking water processed through either a reverse osmosis or a distillation method have been shown to have significant long-term health ramifications because each removes all of the beneficial minerals in water, and over time, can lead to degenerative disease such as osteoporosis. Conversely, a quality water purifier is designed to keep the beneficial minerals in purified water.

Warning: A water purifier cannot rid water of contaminants from nuclear fallout. To be clear, water itself cannot become contaminated from a nuclear event, but the particles that fall into a body of water *can* be (later in the chapter are instructions on filtering out fallout contaminants).

## Methods For Storing Water Long-Term

It is possible to store safe drinking water indefinitely. Be sure the water container has been thoroughly washed and has never contained harmful chemicals. As already discussed, avoid using old milk cartons, as they are specifically designed to break down due to landfill concerns. For those who are on a strict budget, consider using 2-liter pop bottles with the lids securely twisted closed once filled.

## Storing Water Using the Bleach Method

Make sure to use unscented chlorine bleach with a 5.25% sodium hypochlorite ratio that does **not** contain soap or phosphate additives.

* Use 1/8 teaspoon of chlorine bleach per each gallon of water.

## Storing Water Using the Ion Method

Ion is made of stabilized oxygen and is available online or at hunting, camping and preparedness supply stores.

* Use 20 drops of Ion per each gallon of water.

## Storing Water Using the Iodine Method

Iodine is another popular method to store water, long-term. Before using this method, it should be pointed out that some people have, or can develop, allergies to iodine, therefore the safest approach is to seek doctor approval before ingesting iodine.

* Use 12 drops of iodine per each gallon of water.

Note: If possible, change out water every six months. Treated water stored for longer than six months is still safe to drink, but it will taste better by pouring it back and forth from one container to another to re-oxygenate it.

## Safe Drinking, Cooking & Clean-Up Water Without a Water Purifier

In an emergency situation, there are four alternative methods that can be used to purify water without a water purifier. It's critical, however, to understand that none of these methods will make water safe after a nuclear event–refer to *Purifying Water After a Nuclear Event*.

## Boiling Method

There are differing views with regard to how long water must be boiled before riding water of harmful microorganisms. Some claim five minutes, others one minute, and yet others suggest that once water has come to a boil, it is safe to drink.

The correct answer is to boil water for a full minute before drinking or cooking with it . . . and remember, just because you may not be able to see anything harmful with the naked eye or by smell, always assume that water collected from an open water source is unsafe to drink before treating it.

## Chlorine Bleach Method

Just as with storing water long-term using the bleach method, you can add unscented chlorine bleach with 5.25% sodium hydro-chloride ratio that does **not** contain soap or phosphate additives to purify collected water.

However, when treating suspected contaminated water, the bleach dosage should be increased to 1/4 teaspoon of bleach per each gallon of water. After adding bleach to the water, let it stand for 1/2 hour before drinking or cooking with it.

## Purification Tablets

Purification tablets made of either chlorine or iodine are surprisingly affordable. They can be purchased online or at many sporting good stores. One tablet will usually purify water for drinking or cooking, but for cloudy water, it's best to double the recommended dosage.

## Sunlight Method

Filling a clear plastic bottle with water and exposing it to 10 full hours of sunlight (laying it down on a reflective surface such as tin foil) will purify water to 99.999 percent pure. This method will remove bacteria and parasites.

Important Note: You should filter cloudy water through a clean, absorbent cloth such as a towel before exposing the bottle to sunlight to enable UV rays to penetrate into the bottle. This method will not rid contaminated water of the effects of chemical pollutants. Bottle size should be no larger than 2-liters and made of food grade clear plastic (like that of a used, but clean water bottle). The following symbol below indicates it is safe to drink from:

## Distilling Water for Heavy Metals, Salt and Chemicals

The four methods just described will not remove heavy metals, salts and most chemicals. It requires either a quality water purifier or distilling it. Below are the instructions to distil water:

- Fill a pot halfway with water.
- Tie a cup to the handle of the pot's lid, then place the lid, cup side down above the water, making sure that the cup is not dangling in the water.
- Boil the water for 20 minutes. The cup will fill with the distilled water as condensed water drips from the lid into the cup.

## Fallout Purification

A nuclear event, whether concentrated in a relatively small area or widespread, changes the rules on water purification because as already mentioned in this chapter, neither a top-of-the line water purifier nor the boiling method will rid water of fallout contaminates.

Any open waterway should be considered contaminated in the aftermath of a nuclear event. Covered wells are typically considered relatively safe from fallout, but if you suspect contaminated groundwater may have seeped into a covered well, treat the water with the instructions below.

The effects of radiation is cumulative. Therefore, continued exposure to radiation will build up in the body and can become life-threatening.

The good news is purifying fallout-contaminated water only requires two clean 5-gallon buckets, heavy absorbent cloth such as a towel, and soil.

## Materials Needed

- Two five-gallon plastic buckets (food grade)
- Heavy, absorbent cloth such as a towel
- Soil (the heavier clay content, the better)

## Instructions

- Cut holes in the bottom of one of the buckets.
- Cut a towel, or another heavy, absorbent fabric a little larger than the circumference of the bucket.
- Collect soil dug at least six inches below the surface soil (this will ensure the soil collected is not contaminated) and fill the bucket with the holes you've cut with two inches of soil–keeping in mind the more clay, the better--garden areas are good collection spots.
- Place the cloth over the soil.
- To filter the water, simply pour water into the bucket with the holes, soil, and the heavy, absorbent cloth and allow the filtered water to empty into the second five-gallon bucket.

Warning: The soil and absorbent towel material must be changed out after 50 quarts of water has been processed through it, so it is critical to keep track of water usage.

## Water Wells

The majority of the U.S. population live in heavily populated urban areas, but if you are fortunate enough to own rural property with a well, there are a few things you should plan ahead for.

Wells deliver water to a home or cabin via an electric well pump, but most emergencies go hand-in-hand with electrical outages. Even an expected snow storm will take down tree limbs, and the power grid along with it. To pull water from a well during grid-down requires a manual hand pump. If you live in a climate zone that doesn't deliver below-freezing winter temperatures, this necessary device will only cost a fraction of what a frostless model costs, but either way, if you don't want to be standing at your well, frantic that you don't have access to the water just under your feet, start shopping for a manual water pump.

Not everyone is blessed with spring-fresh well water. If your well water needs to be run through a water filtration system to rid it of the usual culprits such as iron, manganese, or hydrogen sulfide, then investing in a quality water purifier now, ahead of a crisis, will allow you to process water you will want to drink.

Note: If budget constraints make purchasing a manual hand pump for a well difficult, check into Lehman's water collection cylinder. It's designed to fit down a well casing and collects a little under two gallons of water at a time by lowering it down by a rope. This method isn't as efficient as a manual hand pump, but for around $60.00, it will allow you to collect water from your well.

## Water Catchment System

You don't have to live in the country to set up a water catchment system. All it takes is a roof and diverting the rainwater run-off from gutters into containment barrels and permission to do so in certain cases where CC&R's (covenants, conditions & restrictions) may frown on them. Actually, this would be an interesting project, to see if water collection would be allowed for gardening in a townhouse or condo complex. Nothing ventured, nothing gained . . .

The good news is just one inch of rainfall can produce 600 gallons of water from an average sized roof. A water catchment system is inexpensive, especially when following the DIY instructions provided here, but first you will want to check with your state. Believe it or not, some states have decided rainwater collection is illegal, claiming the rain belongs to someone else, but so far, just who that someone else is remains unclear.

It wouldn't be surprising to see playhouses and sheds go up with roofs that connect to downspouts, and it's doubtful officials will be canvassing neighborhoods to issue code violations during a disaster. Even so, it would be wise to camouflage water catchment barrels, so you will not be telegraphing your preparedness to others.

## Materials Needed to Build a Water Catchment System

- 55-Gallon Food Grade Plastic Water Barrels
- Hole Saw
- Silicone
- Faucet
- 3/4 inch Female Adapter
- Window Screen

## Instructions

- Drill a one-inch hole to install a faucet at the bottom portion of a 55-gallon barrel (but leave enough clearance to place containers under the faucet for water collection).
- Spread silicone around the faucet threads.
- Insert the faucet into the one-inch hole you cut and secure it in place with a 3/4 inch PVC female adapter.
- At the top of the barrel, as close to the top as possible, cut a 2-inch hole. This is for overflow. Cover the two inch

hole with window screen cut a little larger than 2-inches and secure it in place with silicone sealant.

- With a jigsaw, cut a 6-inch water intake hole on the top of the barrel and protect it with window screen–this will keep debris out of the barrel.
- Place the barrel under the downspout to collect rainfall from the roof.

Note: Fill bathtubs and sinks with water at the start of a crisis to stretch your water supply and listen for broadcasts on your emergency radio (yes, you need one!) for alerts on possible water contamination before drinking or cooking with it.

———

Links relating to chapter subjects are listed below to help you locate important information. At the time of publication, each of the links listed were verified to be operational.

How to Drill Your Own Water Well:
http://www.drillyourownwell.com/

Roof Rainwater Containment Systems:
http://www.gardeners.com/Rain-Barrel-How-To/5497,
default,pg.html

Water Bladder Containment System:
http://store.interstateproducts.com/water_bladders.htm

Water Barrels & Storage Tanks:
http://www.plastic-mart.com/?gclid=CNyize6w86YCFQUSbAod
N3wNBg

http://www.bayteccontainers.com/waterbarrels.html

Manual Water Pumps:
http://www.survivalunlimited.com/deepwellpump.htm

http://www.oasispumps.com/pumps.html

Lehman's Galvanized Well Bucket ITEM# 550202:
http://www.lehmans.com/?partner_id=bcbgoog&gclid=CO6Cn
om386YCFQN7gwodp1utIA

# *Chapter 5*

## DETERMINING THE BEST TYPE OF
## FOOD STORAGE FOR YOUR CIRCUMSTANCES

Choosing the right type of food storage and alternative cooking method should take into consideration safety, ability, budget and living conditions.  By assessing your circumstances carefully, the final result will lead you in the right direction, whether your choice is bulk food, dehydrated or freeze-dried food, canned goods, or MRE's.  For some, a combination of more than one type of food storage may be the final choice due to the flexibility and convenience it offers.

### Avoid Stumbling Blocks

Indecision breeds confusion which can lead to giving up before even getting started.  One common stumbling block is determining the length of time to prepare for.  Should it be for three months, or six months, or one year?  If you find yourself stuck, unable to make a decision, don't let time lines be the determining factor.

As money becomes available for food storage and an alternative cooking method or two (it never hurts to have back-up!) your cupboards will begin to fill and the worry over being caught unprepared will dissipate.

Another stumbling block that may not become clear until *after* the onset of an emergency is the belief that things will remain relatively normal.  With such a mindset, it's not unusual for people to forget to prepare for a time when their electric or gas appliances may not work. Yet, emergencies, even short-term emergencies, almost always come with electrical outages. In fact, when you think about it, have you ever watched the five-o'clock news reporting on a serious storm front, or a hurricane, or tornado or a widespread crisis that *didn't* take down the power grid?

If a national emergency lasts for more than a few days, it is probable that power, natural gas, and water and sewer processing will be disrupted because these utilities only have up to a week of emergency back-up power. This reality is rarely shared with the public, but it's something we witnessed during Katrina and other disasters across the globe. The difference between a storm front that knocks out the power grid and a nationwide disaster is that with a storm, power is restored within a few hours, or days. In a national disaster, the situation could have long-lasting consequences and it's why it is imperative to plan ahead for alternative cooking and heating, which is discussed in detail in Chapter 6, *Alternative Cooking & Heating.*

## Fitting The Pieces Together

Preparedness is nothing short of a puzzle, where one piece of the puzzle fits into the other, and on to the next. Miss a piece of the puzzle, and the results will be less than stellar. As failure is *not* an option during a full-blown crisis, we'll be running through all the possible scenarios which will enable you to whittle down choices that will lead to success.

## Will You Be "Sheltering In Place" Or "Bugging Out"?

Is your plan to **shelter in place** (prepper terminology for standing your ground in your own home, come what may) or to **bug out** (prepper terminology for "head for the hills" or to a planned-ahead-for remote location when trouble arrives)? In the case of sheltering in place, bulk and canned foods, although heavy and harder to transport, will not necessarily be a negative. This type of food storage is the most versatile and the least expensive approach for long-term food storage. As long as bulk food is stored properly, which is addressed in Chapter 8, *Bulk Food Recommendations & Long-Term Storage,* it is a dependable way to solve your food storage needs.

For those who will be bugging out at the first sign of trouble, compact, lighter-weight food such as dehydrated and freeze-dried foods or MRE's may be the better choice. Be aware that MRE's are typically high in sodium, which is problematic for those who are on a low sodium diet. The high sodium content can cause constipation when MRE's are consumed day after day, therefore it is important to plan ahead for additional drinking water.

## Cooking Safety

It may be difficult to conceive of a time when just firing up a pot of beans brings neighbors and passerby's to your doorstep in droves, thus opening yourself and your loved ones to possible danger. If you're shaking your head in denial, bear with me . . .

Cooking smells coming from that pot of beans *will* waif through the air, and it will be a calling card of opportunity for anyone with an empty stomach. In a dense population, there will be multitudes of desperate people in search of food. Grocer's shelves will have been emptied, as is the case even during a short-term event like a winter storm.

Now times the problem of empty grocers shelves one-hundred-fold in the event of a long-term crisis. Grocers no longer stock back inventory. Those days have been traded for "Just In Time" inventory. This system of ordering stock daily frees up cash flow and is a workable plan . . . until the day comes when truckers are unable to make regular deliveries. The plain truth is that grocers have zero reserves. Therefore, in an emergency your survival and food security is tied directly to what you have stored for an emergency.

In the event of a widespread crisis, there are no guarantees that truckers will still be running. There may be road closures and electrical outages that render gas pumps inoperable. Martial Law may have been enacted, thus crippling transportation. An economic collapse could lead to banks freezing personal and corporate bank accounts to avoid a bank run, thus halting trucking and the ability for grocers to restock empty shelves.

Looting and social unrest will follow a widespread emergency, which means truckers may opt to stay off the roads and remain home to watch over their family's safety.

Those who live in densely populated areas must consider the safety of themselves and their family when it comes to use of alternative cooking methods and cooking odors. MRE's, canned food and freeze-dried food do not require more than heating and will not produce heavy cooking odors, making them a popular choice of many urban preppers.

## Ability

If you've never had an interest in cooking, trying to learn to cook from scratch with bulk food storage in the midst of a crisis will be difficult at best. Consider MRE's and canned food.

Health issues may also be a consideration. Although cooking from scratch with bulk food will provide nutritious meals at a lower cost than MRE's, it can be physically demanding as it requires standing for long periods of time. A solution may be to share the responsibility of cooking with other family or group members. If this is a possibility, it should be discussed and agreed upon before selecting bulk food storage as the lions share of a food storage plan.

Even for cooking aficionado's, there may be times when MRE's or canned food will become a necessary plan B, especially at the start of a crisis when your time must be spent getting everything in place, or during times of illness.

## Budget

These days, it isn't always easy to find room in a budget to put aside long-term food storage. Chapter 7, *Food Storage: Budget,*

*Food Storage Myths & Shelf Life* offers money saving tips so that you can get prepared as quickly as possible while avoiding costly mistakes. If your budget is tight, MRE's may not be the best approach due to the higher cost. Instead, you may decide to invest in canned goods and bulk food, or if you feel your situation may require relocating to a safer location, dehydrating your own food for easy portability and cost savings may be the best approach, which is addressed in Chapter 8, *Bulk Food Storage Recommendations & Long-Term Storage.*

# Chapter 6

## ALTERNATIVE COOKING & HEATING

I can't picture anything worse than to have a basement full of food storage with no way to cook it. But if you're depending on an electric or gas range to work during a crisis, you might find yourself in trouble.

The following is a breakdown of alternative cooking devices, their pros and cons, and when possible, their approximate costs. In many cases, it's possible to find used alternative cooking devices at garage sales, thrift stores, secondhand stores, craigslist, the Nickles Worth and the classified section of your local newspaper. Provided they are in good working order, it will save you much needed cash, so you can move on to the next thing on your priority list.

One last thing before getting started: it is imperative to have several fire extinguishers on hand in case of fire. Make sure that you open a window for ventilation whenever cooking with a wood-burning device or a camp stove. This will avoid a buildup of CO that you cannot smell, but can be deadly. Cooking indoors with an alternative cooking device should always include a working, battery-run CO detector and fire alarm.

### Gas & Charcoal Grills

Gas and charcoal grills should never be used indoors due to the unsafe level of carbon monoxide they produce. In a setting where the population is not so dense that their use will draw unwanted attention, this alternative outdoor cooking method is viable. Some BBQ's can be retrofitted for larger propane canisters than the typical 20 lb. size.

## Camp Stoves

Camp Stoves are versatile and inexpensive. Some models are designed to accept multiple fuel sources, which can solve the problem of having to store volatile fuel. Fuels such as propane, butane, kerosene, unleaded gas, and Coleman fuel (white gas) must be stored away from an open flame, such as that from a gas hot water heater, furnace or any other source of ignition, which generally requires storing fuel in an outbuilding.

If you live in a condo or apartment, where storing volatile fuel would pose a danger, look into camp stoves that run on alcohol, alcohol gel, or sterno.

Camp stoves are available in single or multiple burner models which are user-friendly when cooking for a family. Price ranges start at $20.00 and go up, depending upon the features you choose. If you plan to bake, look into a camp stove that has an oven, but expect to pay from $175 to $200. With all of a camp stoves pros, including their price, it is always a good idea to plan ahead for a back-up alternative cooking method such a solar oven, or open fire-pit cooking (stock plenty of matches!).

Note: Coleman makes ovens that are designed to sit on top of a camp stove burner that will provide a way to bake whatever you need. Expect to pay between $25.00 to $35.00, depending upon the model.

## Electric Ranges

In a widespread or nationwide disaster, it's almost a given that the grid will be impacted. Running an electric range during a crisis will likely involve the use of a generator which will place a substantial drain on fuel reserves at a time when finding replacement fuel will be difficult or impossible, and if found, it will cost dearly. For this reason it's best to add an alternative cooking device to your prep list that doesn't require generous amounts of fuel to run each day.

## Natural Gas Ranges

Natural Gas Ranges are wonderful as long as natural gas continues to be delivered to your home. The delivery of natural gas is dependent upon electrical power to send it down pipelines, and eventually into your home. Additionally, natural gas providers have a system in place that automatically shuts off the feed of natural gas to homes during a natural disaster for safety reasons. When planning ahead for an alternative cooking method, a natural gas range has far too many weak links to be considered a reliable back-up plan for cooking. The same applies to a natural gas furnace to heat a home during an extended emergency.

## Open Fire Pit

Open Fire Pit cooking is easier to accomplish with a cast iron dutch oven and cookware, and why as you investigate preparedness sites, you will notice they are mentioned time and time again. With a dutch oven and the hot coals of a fire pit you can cook the foods your family is accustomed to. Another convenience, well worth the $25.00 to $30.00 investment, is a cooking tripod. They are made to hold cookware over an open flame and can be adjusted up and down to control cooking temperatures.

Here is where a reflector oven will come in handy, for they are collapsible and are designed to bake goods by the reflective heat of a campfire. The price varies from $55.00 to $80.00, but if you're handy, you can go online for do-it-yourself instructions to make your own.

Note: Open fire pit cooking generates strong cooking odors and is not recommended for use in a densely populated location.

## Rocket Stoves

Rocket Stoves are a fairly new invention, made for versatility and built to be rugged. They will burn wood, charcoal or dry biomass (twigs, sticks and the like). They are heavy (up to 26 pounds depending upon the model) and most come with a cooking surface made of cast iron. Although the sheer weight of these workhorses doesn't make them backpack friendly, they offer a great solution for day-to-day cooking. What I love most about the design of this stove is it uses 60% less wood and emits 70% less smoke than an open fire pit does, and they are not dependent upon non-renewable fuel that may be impossible to replenish. The price of a Rocket Stove starts at around $100.00 and goes up from there.

## Wood-Burning Heat Stoves

The top surface of a wood-burning heat stove can be used to cook on. Cooking can also be done over hot coals in the fire-box. Cast iron cookware can withstand high temperatures and do not have plastic handles that most cookware has that would melt when exposed to extreme heat. If you already own a wood-burning heat stove, it's possible to have a water reservoir retro-fitted to supply hot water.

As with any wood-burning devise, a supply of seasoned fire-wood is necessary to have on hand, which should be kept out of sight from passerby's.

## Pellet Stoves

Pellet Stoves are not the best choice for heating a home or for alternative cooking because of the need to stockpile pellets. Some models are dependent upon electricity to dump the pellets every few minutes, which would be impossibly demanding to do manually while juggling the added chores that come with a crisis.

## Propane Ranges

Propane ranges are popular with those who own cabins or live off-grid. Look for a model that doesn't require electricity to run and consider purchasing or renting a large propane tank to allow for long-term cooking. However, it's always a good idea to have a back-up plan for the possibility of a crisis outlasting the propane you have available. A positive of a propane stove is they don't generate the heat that a fireplace, or wood-burning heat or cook stove does, making them user-friendly in summer. To save the budget, look into used propane ranges at an RV store or on craigslist, moving sales, or classified ads.

Propane heaters and refrigerators are alternatives preppers turn to as well, but a back-up that is not dependent upon propane fuel is highly advised to cover heating and refrigeration needs during a protracted crisis.

## Sheppard Stoves, Outfitter Stoves, Barrel Stoves, Cylinder Stoves & Tent Stoves

Sheppard, Outfitters, Barrel Stoves, Cylinder Stoves, or Tent Stoves will serve double-duty for both heating and cooking. They operate much like a wood heat stove and cooking can be done on the stove top or inside the firebox over hot coals. Cast iron cookware is a must-have to handle the high heat these stoves generate.

Some models are designed to collapse for easy transport, therefore when planning to purchase an alternative cooking device that will be installed later in your home or getaway cabin, a collapsible stove may be a good fit for your needs. Their price starts at around $50.00, but at that price point research them first for design flaws that may exist for in-home use, not the least of which is 2 1/2 inch chimney piping rather than the traditional 6 to 8 inches. Here is where due diligence is extremely important. Check the reviews of the model you are interested in and do a bit of research on the importance of an airtight stove (they retain valuable heat and will not leak smoke) before purchasing. Even after having said this, I believe these stoves are a perfect solution for anyone on a budget who needs an affordable way to cook and heat a home or cabin. They stand the height of a range and many models come with a side water reservoir for hot water. Look for a chimney oven that installs directly into the stove pipe if you plan to bake.

You will need a supply of seasoned firewood to fuel them which should be stored out of sight.

## Solar Ovens

Solar Ovens are the perfect answer for those who live in a warm climate zone and they will provide welcome relief for northerners who need a break from a hot kitchen during summertime. They can be used on decks or patios and do not generate the cooking odors many other alternative cooking methods do. One of the biggest benefits of a solar oven is that they are not dependent upon a fuel source.

The negatives of a solar oven is that they require sunlight to work properly and when placed in sunlight, the temperature can raise to a sizzling 400 degrees. It is difficult to control the temperature of a solar oven; however, they will cook an excellent pot of beans and rice!

Expect to pay around $100.00 for a basic solar oven, but if you're handy you can go online and research do-it-yourself instructions to build your own.

## Wood-Burning Cook Stoves

Wood-burning cook stoves are workhorses, plain and simple. They will allow you to cook and bake and home can as our forefathers did. They will also heat at least a portion of your home in winter when cordoning off the area nearby a wood-burning cook stove with floor to ceiling blankets to contain the heat for a comfortable living space. Some wood-burning cook stoves are available with a built-in water reservoir that supplies hot water. If you purchase a used wood-burning cook stove you can check into having a water reservoir retro-fitted by an expert.

One of the negatives of a wood-burning cook stove is the expense. A new stove can be purchased from $1,000.00 on up to $8,000.00, but if you're on a budget, used wood-burning cook stoves can be found for as little as $100.00. When buying used, make sure it's in working condition, as replacement parts are usually costly and can be difficult to find.

## Wood-Burning Fireplaces
Wood-Burning Fireplace cooking is a lost art, but cooking over hot coals with cast iron cookware is similar to cooking over an open fire. Baking can be done in a cast iron dutch oven. Fireplaces, although not as efficient as a fireplace insert or a wood-burning stove, will heat at least a portion of your home. To conserve heat, heavy blankets can be hung from floor to ceiling to provide a warm living space.

Cooking and heating with a fireplace requires a seasoned supply of firewood, which should be stored out of view of passersby.

Note: If you already have a fireplace, be sure to have the chimney checked for creosote build-up if you haven't done so already to avoid a chimney fire.

## Volcano Stoves
Volcano Stoves are built for outdoor use, designed for backpacking and camping and fold to a mere few inches. They can be purchased in a tri-fuel model that will burn charcoal, propane and wood, which is great for adaptability in an emergency and has earned them the respect of many outdoor enthusiasts and preppers. The cost of a volcano stove starts at around $140.00 and up, depending on whether you choose the tri-fuel model and purchase a propane adapter.

## Wood-Burning Fireplace Inserts
Wood-Burning Fireplace Inserts can increase the efficiency of a fireplace by 70%, which, when having to keep a home warm

without power, is nothing short of a blessing.  They have an opening door, much like a wood heat stove, making cooking over hot coals fairly simple.  The cost of a wood-burning fireplace insert varies depending upon the features chosen, but costs are generally between $1,000.00 and $2,500.00, plus the cost of installation.

———

Links relating to chapter subjects are listed below to help you locate important information.  At the time of publication, each of the links listed were verified to be operational.

Camping Equipment
http://www.cabelas.com

Cast Iron Cookware
http://www.lodgemfg.com/
http://www.ironpotsdepot.com/
http://www.agrisupply.com

Sheppard Stoves
http://www.walltentshop.com/CatStoves.html

Wood-Burning Fireplace Inserts & Wood Heat Stove
http://www.vermontcastings.com/

Wood Cook Stoves
http://www.woodstoves.net/cookstoves.htm

Propane Refrigerators and Ranges
http://www.adventurerv.net/major-appliances-oven-amp-range-c-24_86.html
http://www.pplmotorhomes.com/parts/rv-stoves-ovens-microwaves-parts-1.htm
http://www.lpappliances.com/

Solar Cookers
http://shop.solardirect.com/index.php?cPath=24_81&gclid=C
Jubtt3h9KYCFRRqgwodum2-HA
http://www.solarcooker-at-cantinawest.com/buy-a-solar-cooker.
html

Camp Ovens & Reflector Ovens
http://www.wisementrading.com/outdoorcooking/outdoor-
baking.htm
http://www.mainemade.com/members/profile.asp?ID=2541

Recommended Reading
http://solarcookers.org/basics/how.html

Do-It-Yourself Resources
http://solarcooking.org/plans/
http://www.builditsolar.com/Projects/Cooking/cooking.htm
http://www.kayak2go.com/reflectoroven.PDF

Recipes
http://boyslife.org/outdoors/outdoorarticles/12765/
great-reflector-oven-recipes/
http://whatscookingamerica.net/CastIronRecipes.htm
http://papadutch.home.comcast.net/~papadutch/
http://www.recipesfromscratch.com/dutch/index.htm
http://www.cookwiththesun.com/recipes.htm
http://www.solarovens.org/recipes/

# Chapter 7

## FOOD STORAGE: BUDGET, FOOD STORAGE MYTHS & SHELF LIFE

There are ways to cut your food storage costs in half, and with food prices spiraling out of control, cutting costs should be a top priority. Some of these budget-saving tips found in this chapter you may already be aware of, and others, possibly not. Just keep in mind; if your objective is to put aside what you will need and then get back to everyday life, these tips will get you there quicker, without breaking the bank.

It never hurts to have recipes set aside before doing any heavy-duty shopping. Preparedness-related cook books are available, but if you are on a budget, check online preparedness sites for recipes.

Make a list of what you will need for recipes (including spices) and take it with you when you go to the grocery store. Show no mercy. When something on your food storage list goes on sale, stock up and save.

Include treats that you you enjoy with your food storage plan. You may be put to the test during hard times, but that doesn't mean you have to face it without an occasional treat!

Fresh fruits, vegetables and meats are included in the following budget-busting tips, which require home canning or dehydrating to preserve it long-term. Neither home canning nor dehydrating is a prerequisite for successful food storage, but it can save you money. If you've never done either, why not grab an experienced friend or family member who has and give it a try?  If you discover you like preserving foods, it may be time to make an investment in canning supplies or a food dehydrator.

## Case Good Sales

You can save 50% or more during case sales.  If you've never heard of a case sale, they are annual or semi-annual bonanza's where you can save substantially on cases of canned fruits, vegetables, soups, sauces (including spaghetti sauce), mushrooms, peppers, stew, chili, canned fish, evaporated milk, and much more.

Case sales and holiday sales many times include sales on pasta's such as spaghetti noodles and macaroni as well as baking supplies like flour, sugar (brown sugar, granulated sugar, and powdered sugar), baking powder, baking soda, vinegar, cooking oil, and salt.  Also, watch for sales on paper products like toilet paper (there's no such thing as too much toilet paper), paper towels, paper plates and the like.  Although wholesale stores like Walmart and Costco may have every-day low prices, many times you can save an incredible amount of money when you buy in quantity during case sales and holiday sales at various grocery store chains.

Case sales are usually held in October, November, and February, but this isn't written in stone.  Check with the grocers in your area and write the dates down so you are able to budget accordingly.

## Seasonal & Monthly Grocery Sales

Grocery stores offer "loss leaders," which are items that are sold at a loss and advertised to pull in shoppers, which grocers antici-pate will lead to profitable sales on other regularly priced items.  Sale items vary, but a general guide of preparedness-related items that typically go on sale are listed here, broken down by month.

January caters to New Year's resolutions, and as such, you will find many diet-related items on sale.  In a crisis, diet food may not be your best friend.  Remember, you will be busy with chores day after day and you will burn calories! However, January is the month that vitamins and cold medicines go on sale, as well as condiments. For those who plan to home can or dehydrate foods, January is a good month to take advantage of sales on certain fruits and vegetables that will round out food storage.

Condiments: Mayonnaise, Sandwich Spreads, Salsa & Dips

Dairy: Cheese (refer to the shelf life section for tips on storing cheese, unrefrigerated, for years)

Fresh Fruit: Kiwi, Oranges, Pears, Grapefruit, Tangerines

Fresh Vegetables: Broccoli, Carrots, Cabbage, Cauliflower, Celery, Kale, Spinach, Chard, Collards

Grains: Quaker Oatmeal Products, Crackers

Medicine: Cold Medicine, Vitamins.

February is a traditional month for canned goods to go on sale--either as a case sale or individual canned goods, depending upon the grocer. The holidays have come and gone and food manufacturers and grocers need to get rid of any overflow, which gives you a golden opportunity to fill in your food storage.

Condiments: Syrup, Soy Sauce, Teriyaki Sauce

Canned Goods: Fruit, Vegetables, Fruit Pie Filling, Salmon, Tuna Fish, Chicken, Meats

Fresh Fruits: Raspberries, Strawberries

Fresh Vegetables: Potatoes, Broccoli, Carrots, Cauliflower, Celery, Kale, Chard, Spinach

Hot Cereals: Malt O Meal, Oatmeal

Treats/Comfort Food: Chocolate, Hershey's Syrup

<u>March</u> is not typically a good month to find sales on prepared-
ness-related foods, but if you keep a watch for coupon savings
and focus on buying in bulk for items such beans, oats, dry corn,
rolled oats, pasta and spices, you will be able to continue to fill
in your food storage at a savings. For those who will be home
canning or dehydrating, you will find sales on fresh fruit and
vegetables.

Fresh Fruit: Rhubarb, Strawberries, Oranges, Tangerines,
Lemons, Limes

Fresh Vegetables: Leeks, Broccoli, Carrots, Cabbage, Cauliflower,
Celery, Chard, Collards, Kale, Chard, Spinach, Mushrooms, Peas,
Green Onions

<u>April</u> delivers sales on spices, baking supplies, vegetables and
goodies, but comes in short on fruits for home canning or
dehydrating.

Baking & Cooking Supplies: Baking Extracts, Baking Powder,
Baking Soda, Brown Sugar, Chocolate Chips, Coconut, Cooking
Oil, Flour, Marshmallow, Spices, White Sugar, Powdered Sugar

Boxed/Packaged Goods: Boxed Baking Mixes, Brownie Mixes,
Cake Mixes

Canned Goods: Canned Ham

Dairy: Eggs, Butter (refer to the shelf life section, where you will
find tips on storing eggs unrefrigerated for months and a link
for home canning butter)

Fresh Fruit: Grapefruit, Rhubarb

Fresh Meat: Ham (look for canned ham if you will not be home canning)

Vegetables: Beets, Broccoli, Cabbage, Carrots, Mushrooms, Onions, Peas

Preparedness Goods: Rechargeable Batteries

<u>May</u> kicks off the barbecue season and you will find deals on most meats and poultry, including steak, hamburger and chicken. This is also a good time to stock up on condiments, paper plates, insect repellant and sunscreen.

Condiments: Salsa & Dips, Barbeque Sauce, Marinade Sauces

Fresh Fruit: Blackberries, Raspberries, Strawberries

Fresh Vegetables: Green Beans, Peas, Potatoes, Beets, Carrots, Onions

Preparedness Goods: Paper Plates, Plastic Utensils, Insect Repellant, Sunscreen

<u>June </u>is a great time to test your skills at preserving cheese and eggs and home canning butter while these items are on sale. Near the end of June grocers gear up for traditional Fourth of July barbecues, so keep a watch for sales on steak, hamburger, sausage and chicken, which for those who do their own home canning is great news. But a barbecue isn't a barbecue without mustard, mayonnaise, ketchup and other popular condiments, and you will find killer deals on these items. June is a great time to stock up on fresh fruit that can be home canned or dehydrated.

Condiments: Dips, Ketchup, Mustard, Mayonnaise, Barbecue Sauce, Pickles, Salad Dressing, Sweet Relish

Fresh Meats: Hamburger, Chicken, Steak, Sausage

Fresh Fruit: Apricots, Blackberries, Blueberries, Boysenberries, Cherries, Grapes, Nectarines, Peaches, Raspberries, Strawberries

Fresh Vegetables: Corn, Cucumber, Eggplant, Potatoes, Onions, Squash, Tomatoes

Preparedness Goods: Charcoal Briquettes

July is the month to make up for lost time if you didn't take advantage of the sales in June, as many of the same sale prices carry over into the early part of July. There are additional sales for school supplies, which you really do need to stock up on if you have children or grandchildren.

Condiments: Barbeque Sauce, Dips, Ketchup, Mayonnaise, Mustard, Pickles, Salad Dressing, Sweet Relish

Fresh Fruit: Blueberries, Figs, Grapes, Nectarines, Oranges, Pears, Peaches, Plums

Fresh Vegetables: Bell Peppers, Corn, Cucumber, Eggplant, Green Beans, Onions, Potatoes, Squash, Tomatoes

Fresh Meats: Chicken, Hamburger, Pork, Steak

Preparedness Goods: Binders, Charcoal Briquettes, Colored Markers, Colored Pencils, Crayons, Folders, Notebooks, Pencils, Pens, Printer Paper, Tape

<u>August</u> offers end-of-the-summer deals on preparedness must-haves and excellent savings on produce.

Fresh Fruit: Apples, Blackberries, Figs, Grapes, Peaches, Pears, Raspberries, Strawberries

Fresh Vegetables: Beans, Bell Peppers, Corn, Cucumber, Eggplant, Green Beans, Onion, Squash, Tomatoes

Preparedness Goods: Bleach, Hand Disinfectant

<u>September</u> offers another chance to save on school supplies and another opportunity to try home canning and food dehydration with end-of-the-growing-season fruits and vegetables.

Fresh Fruit: Apples, Grapes, Oranges, Pears, Pomegranate

Fresh Vegetables: Beans, Bell Peppers, Chili Peppers, Cucumber, Eggplant, Onion, Squash, Tomatoes

Preparedness Goods: Binders, Crayons, Colored Pencils, Colored Markers, Folders, Notebooks, Pencils, Pens, Printer Paper, Tape

<u>October</u> is National Seafood Month, so watch for sales on all types of fresh fish and crustaceans. October also offers sales on nuts, and if you home can, fresh pumpkin. The month of October is also the start of case sales, so hopefully you're able to find extra room in your budget to save a substantial amount on canned goods. This is also the month to stock up on pet food and other preparedness-related supplies which are listed below.

Baking Supplies: Chocolate Chips

Boxed/Packaged Goods: Candy

Canned Goods: Canned Tuna Fish, Crab, Herring, Sardines, Salmon, Shrimp, Oysters, Clams, Mackerel, Pumpkin

Dairy: Evaporated Milk

Fresh Fruit: Apples, Cranberries, Lemons, Pears, Pomegranate, Pumpkin

Seafood: Fresh Seafood of all kinds

Nuts: Almonds, Chestnuts

Fresh Vegetables: Arugula, Beets, Broccoli, Brussels Sprouts, Cabbage, Chard, Parsnip, Potatoes, Squash, Sweet Potatoes, Spinach, Turnips, Yams

Preparedness Goods: Batteries, Smoke Detectors, Carbon Monoxide Detectors, Fire Extinguishers, Dog Food

<u>November</u> is a difficult month for any dedicated prepper to get past without emptying their wallets, but if you plan ahead you can fill those holes in your food storage at great savings, especially for baking supplies, evaporated milk (check in the shelf life section why this is a good thing), many boxed and canned goods, and goodies that serve double-duty as comfort foods.

Baking Supplies: Flour, White Granulated Sugar, Brown Sugar, Powdered Sugar, Coconut, Chocolate Chips

Boxed/Packaged Goods: Candy, Gravy Mixes, Jello, Potatoes

Canned Goods: Broths, Cranberry Sauce, Fruits, Gravy, Pumpkin, Soups, Spaghetti Sauce, Vegetables

Dairy: Evaporated Milk, Sweet Condensed Milk

Fresh Fruit: Cranberries, Kiwi, Lemons, Oranges, Pears

Fresh Vegetables: Beets, Broccoli, Brussels Sprouts, Cabbage, Carrots, Celery, Cranberries, Potatoes, Squash, Yams

December delivers more holiday savings on canned goods and baking supplies, and if you can find room in your budget, you can save upwards of 50% on food storage items that come with the benefit of a long shelf life.

Baking Supplies: Flour, Sugar, Marshmallow

Boxed/Packaged Goods: Brownie Mixes, Cake Mixes, Gravy Mixes, Jello, Muffin Mixes, Potatoes

Canned Goods: Broth, Cranberry Sauce, Fruits, Ham, Soup, Spaghetti Sauce, Vegetables

Dairy: Butter, Condensed Milk

Fresh Fruit: Dates, Grapefruit, Kiwi, Kumquat, Lemon, Oranges, Pears

Fresh Meat: Ham

Fresh Vegetables: Bok Choy, Broccoli, Brussels Sprouts, Cabbage, Carrots, Cauliflower, Celery, Kale, Rutabaga, Spinach, Squash, Sweet Potatoes, Turnips, Yams

## Food Storage Myths & Shelf Life Of Canned Goods

You may share the same concerns over the shelf life of canned goods as I did when I first began to put aside food storage many years ago. Because my decision was to provide for a total of 23 people, and a portion of that food included canned meat, fish, vegetables, fruits, broths, soups and sauces, I struggled over juggling the shelf life of canned goods while trying to avoid having to toss it out when the sell by date expired.

Many food storage-related sites recommend that canned goods be rotated (consumed and replaced) before they reach their "sell by", "use by", or "best by" date, which is the date a manufacturer stamps on canned foods. This a workable plan for families living under the same roof, where consuming and replacing canned food only requires keeping on top of "expiration" dates. But what about preppers who have added to their food storage to provide for extended family members that don't live with them?

The answer to the dilemma isn't as readily available as it should be, therefore it took some digging to learn that the FDA does not regulate these dates, rather it is the manufacturers who use them for inventory purposes. Additionally, this is the date deemed optimal for the flavor and nutritional value of canned food. Even so, canned food still retains much of its nutritional value long after the sell by date expires provided it is stored away from excessive moisture where the cans can rust, or excessive heat or freezing conditions that will damage cans.

In the midst of ongoing drought and skyrocketing food prices, Americans throw out an astounding 40% of the food they buy, and annually $165 billion of edible food finds its way to land fills! That would not be the case if the public was informed that canned seafood has a shelf life of at least 5 years, canned meat for 2 years, canned vegetables for 5 years, and fruit for 18 months.

And frankly, that is a conservative estimate. *The Canning Process: Old Preservation Techniques Goes Modern*, written by Dale Blumenthal, is a Food and Drug Administration article that includes the results of a shelf life test preformed on 100-year old canned goods that were retrieved from the swamped steamboat Bertrand. Canned goods such as brandied peaches, oysters, plum tomatoes honey, and mixed vegetables were analyzed in 1968 after the swamped Bertrand was found a century later under 30 feet of silt. The tests were preformed by chemists at the National Food Processors Association who tested for bacterial contamination and nutrient value. Their findings were that although the food had lost its fresh smell and appearance, they did not find microbial growth and it was determined that the food was as safe to eat as it had been when it was canned more than 100 years earlier. The nutrient values varied depending upon the product and significant amounts of vitamins C and A were lost, but protein levels remained high, and all calcium values were found to be comparable to today's products.

The article also included the study of 40-year-old can of corn that was discovered in the basement of a California home. The corn was deemed safe to consume, containing no contaminates, and the nutrient loss was not significant. In fact, the study mentioned that the corn kernels looked and smelled like recently canned corn.

The study was published in FDA Consumer magazine, but is no longer being maintained. However, you can read the article in its entirety at the following link:

http://web.archive.org/web/20070509153848/
http://www.fda.gov/bbs/topics/CONSUMER/CON00043.html

We will have enough to worry about when a crisis hits. Consuming canned goods, whether slightly outdated or not (as long as the can is not bulging or has a compromised seal), should not be one of them!

The following are the warning signs of canned goods, glass jars, flexible pouches, and paperboard containers often included with long term food storage that should be watched for:

Canned Goods: Warning Signs

- Any opening under the double seam of the can
- A fracture in the seam of the can
- A side seam that has become unwelded
- A leaking can
- A bulging can

- Any hole or puncture in the can (**never** include obviously dented cans with your food storage)

Glass Jars: Warning Signs

- A damaged seal
- A pop-top that does not pop when opened indicates that the vacuum seal has been broken
- A broken or chipped glass jar–including the rim

Flexible Pouches: Warning Signs

- A break in the plastic
- A loose seal
- A fractured lid
- A swollen package
- Leaking of the container, including at notches intended for easy opening that has begun to leak

Paperboard Containers: Warning Signs

- A broken seal
- Any swelling of the package
- A tearing away of the adhesive bonding
- A slice through the paperboard container
- A leak

Reminder: Always store canned goods, glass jars, flexible pouches and paperboard containers away from moisture, extreme temperatures, temperature fluctuations, and direct sunlight.

## Food Storage Myths & The Shelf Life Of Food Storage Foods
The shelf life of food storage can be extremely confusing to understand. If we were to take to heart what nutritional experts

advise, dry bulk good like oats, flour, rice, corn and pastas have a fairly short shelf life. In all fairness, they likely base their advice on the consumer's storing dry goods in the original packaging, which exposes it to oxygen, and figure in the possibility it was exposed to direct sunlight, or moisture, or heat, which will greatly shorten the shelf life of bulk foods.

The reality is, the shelf life of bulk goods can be greatly extended by doing the following:

- Store bulk foods in a dark, moisture-free location. Direct sunlight must be avoided.
- Temperatures of 40-70 degrees is the optimal temperature range for long-term food storage (but never below freezing). Storing food in the coolest temperatures possible helps retain vitamin content and reduces germination rates. Conversely, higher temperatures and temperature fluctuations denigrates shelf life.
- Oxygen is the enemy of shelf life. Follow the storage instructions in Chapter 8, *Bulk Food Recommendations & Long-Term Storage* to extend the shelf life of bulk foods.

If your goal is to put aside food storage until it's needed, rather than to rotate it, storing longer shelf life food is the best approach.

The following is a detailed list of food storage shelf life when stored under optimal conditions:

<u>Indefinite Shelf Life</u>

- Baking Powder
- Baking Soda
- Cornstarch
- Honey
- Salt
- Sugar

## 30 Year Shelf Life

- Apple Slices, Freeze-Dried
- Corn, Dry
- Gamut
- Oats, Hulled
- Oats, Rolled
- Pasta
- Pink Beans
- Pinto Beans
- Potatoes (Dried); Sliced, Flaked, Diced
- Rice, White
- Wheat, Hard Red
- Wheat, Hard White
- Wheat, Soft White

## 25 Year Shelf Life

- Cracked Wheat

## 20 Year Shelf Life

- Adzuki Beans
- Black Turtle Beans
- Black-Eyed Beans (AKA Black-Eyed Peas)
- Cheese, Freeze-Dried
- Garbanzo Beans
- Great Northern
- Kidney Beans
- Lentils
- Lima Beans
- Milk, Powdered
- TVP

## 15 Year Shelf Life

- Buckwheat
- Butter, Powdered
- Cocoa Powder
- Fruit, Dehydrated & Freeze-Dried
- Margarine, Powdered
- Meat, Freeze-Dried
- Onion, Dehydrated & Freeze-Dried
- Vegetables, Dehydrated & Freeze-Dried
- Whey Powder

## 12 Year Shelf Life

- Durham Wheat
- Flax
- Millet
- Onions, Dehydrated
- Spelt
- Triticale

## 10 Year Shelf Life

- Barley
- Cheese, Powdered
- Flour, Wheat
- Flour, White
- Grouts
- Mung Beans
- Oats, Pearled
- Shortening, Powdered
- Small Red Beans
- Sour Cream, Powdered
- Soy Beans

## 8 Year Shelf Life

- Alfalfa Seed
- Quinoa
- Rye

## 5 Year Shelf Life

- Brown Sugar
- Bullion
- Coconut Oil
- Coffee
- Cornmeal
- Drink Mixes, Powdered
- Eggs, Powdered
- Fruits, Canned
- Gluten
- Granola
- Hot Cocoa
- Flour, Unbleached
- Meats, Canned
- Peanut Butter, Powdered
- Shortening
- Vegetables, Canned
- Wheat Flakes

## 3 Year Shelf Life

- Chocolate, Vacuum-Packed
- Nuts
- Peanut Butter

## 2 Year Shelf Life

- Baby Food
- Infant Formula, Powdered (shelf life varies–keep an eye on the "use by" date of formula)
- Vegetable Oil
- Yeast

## 6 Month Shelf Life

- Rice, Brown
- *Eggs, Fresh

*Refer to Chapter 8, *Bulk Food Recommendations & Long-Term Storage,* under A Basic Pantry List for information to preserve fresh eggs, unrefrigerated, for up to 9 months.

*Powdered infant formula is an important addition to food storage for those who are expecting or want to plan ahead should it be needed. Formula must be consumed by the use by date due to nutritional loss that an infant requires, and that date varies with each manufacturer, so it is important to keep on eye on the sell by date and replenish as needed.

# Chapter 8

## BULK FOOD RECOMMENDATIONS
## & LONG-TERM STORAGE

There is no mystery to bulk food storage. You already know what meals your family enjoys eating, now all you need to do is adapt it to food storage.

Practice cooking the meals you've modified for food storage by using the alternative cooking device you've chosen. Doing so is worthwhile for several reasons: it allows you to adapt to cooking with your chosen device, and if you experience problems, they can be corrected before a crisis. Just as important is being able to acclimate to the subtle differences at mealtime when adapting favorite recipes to long-term food storage.

Consider adding comfort foods to your food storage. Being able to enjoy an occasional treat like popcorn, or a boxed pizza (Chef Boyardee sells pizza kits that store well), or cake, trail mix or raisins will bring a little normalcy to daily life during a difficult time and it will give your family something to look forward to.

A fully stocked food storage plan doesn't need to happen overnight and it needn't put you in debt. A good approach is to make a list of the basics you need and purchase items as they go on sale. Once the basics have been put aside, begin to layer your food storage with a variety of spices and commercially canned or home canned beef, ham, chicken and fish that will add flavor and protein to meals.

The following lists are recommendations only. Pick and choose what makes sense for you and build from there, so in the end you will have food storage that you and your loved ones will enjoy eating.

Items with an asterisk found in the following lists require special consideration. Please refer to notations at the conclusion of each list.

## Food Storage Categories & Lists

## The Pantry

A basic pantry consists of items you will want to keep within easy reach. The list will be different for everyone, but the following basic pantry list includes what most would consider essentials.

<u>Basic Pantry List</u>

*Baby Food (if applicable)
*Baby Formula (if applicable)
Beef Broth
*Butter, (powdered/canned)
Cereal, both hot cereal and boxed cereal
Chicken Broth
*Cooking Oil
Corn
Corn Meal
Corn Starch
*Eggs, Powdered
*Flour
Honey
*Jam/Jelly

Milk, Powdered
Milk, Evaporated
*Wheat
Oatmeal
Pancake Mix
Peanut Butter
*Rice
Spaghetti Sauce
Stewed Tomatoes
Sugar, Granulated
Sugar, Brown
Sugar, Powdered
Tomato Paste
Tomato Sauce
Vinegar

* Baby Food is an important consideration when planning food storage. If you know there will be an infant or toddler among

those you will be providing for, or are just want to prepare for the unexpected, know that baby food has a shelf life of up to two years. Over time, you will be able to introduce storage foods to a toddlers diet which will be made easier by having a manual food grinder on hand.

*Baby Formula: Due to the possibility of a grid-down scenario that does not allow for refrigerating liquid formula, it is best to store powdered formula. Formula should be stored in a dark, moisture free location and must be consumed by the sell-by date, as formula contains vital nutrients that newborns require that deteriorates past the date stamped on the container. Consider storing Lactofree made by Mead Johnson, or Similac Lactose Free. There is no way to know if an newborn infant will be able to tolerate milk products, so erring on the side of caution is the best approach. When possible, breast feeding is best as it provides the most nutrients for infants.

*Butter: Powdered butter can be purchased online in #10 cans and has a shelf life of up to fifteen years. My recommendation is to make a cost-comparison before purchasing. One of my favorite sites is Honeyville Grain. They have an excellent reputation, their prices are fair, and their shipping is incredibly cheap. If you're interested in canned butter which has not been dehydrated, Red Feather makes an excellent product–but be forewarned–the price is much higher than butter sold at the grocers. Red Feather canned butter has a shelf life of two years or more, depending upon storage conditions. If you are on a tight budget, consider home canning butter. There are YouTube videos available offering step-by-step instructions, but beware! There are novices on YouTube who may have good intentions, but share poor advice. My recommendation is to visit katzcradul YouTube videos, *How To Can Butter-Part 1 & How To Can Butter-Part 2* to safely home can butter using the pressure canning method.

*Coconut Oil's shelf life is up for debate. Some claim its shelf life is 5 years or longer while others insist that its shelf life is closer to 2 years. Because there is no concrete information to base a consensus on, expecting a 2 year shelf life is prudent.

*Cooking Oil: Most cooking oils have a fairly short shelf life of from one to two years which can be improved upon by purchasing small containers (once opened, cooking oil is exposed to oxygen, decreasing shelf life) and by storing it in a refrigerator, or in a cool, dark location.

*Eggs: Powdered egg in #10 cans has a shelf life of up to five years. Contrary to popular belief, eggs straight from the chicken can be stored safely for up to nine months. Our forefathers stored eggs, unrefrigerated, over the long winter months when darkness reduced the egg production of hens.

Eggs can be preserved for up to nine months by coating them with mineral oil. For instructions, check YouTube tutorials. To test an egg for freshness, simply put it in a bowl of water that is twice the height of the egg. If the egg is very fresh, it will sink to the bottom of the bowl and lie on its side. A less fresh egg, although still safe to eat, will stand upright with its smaller, pointed end near or touching the bottom of the bowl and its broader end will point towards the surface of the water. A spoiled egg will float near the surface of the water. You can also test an egg for freshness with a "sniff test". Crack a questionable egg into a separate bowl and check it for an off-putting sulfur odor. Trust me, if the egg is spoiled you will know!

* Flour can be stored for up to ten years by extending its shelf life by following the guidelines found under *Storing Bulk Food Long-Term* later in this chapter.

*Jam and Jelly do not have to be refrigerated after opening.  It will last for over a week on your pantry shelf.  Store smaller jars of jam and jelly so that it can be consumed within a one-week time frame.  Use clean utensils to remove jam or jelly from the container to avoid cross contamination.  If you are uncertain if you would consume even a small container of jam or jelly in the course of one week, individual packets of jams and jelly's can be found online at restaurant suppliers and sometimes Costco and Sam's Club.

* Wheat: Hard red and hard white wheat will store for up to thirty years.  Both hard white and hard red wheat are popular with preppers, as they provide the elasticity to make excellent bread.  However, a sudden heavy diet of wheat may be difficult for the some to digest.

Whole Soft Wheat is often used for baking cookies, cakes, pastry, pie crusts, and biscuits, as it yields a lighter baked product than does hard wheat.  Whole soft wheat has better nutritional value than does white flour, but it is lower in protein and gluten than hard wheat.

Durum Wheat is the hardest of the wheat family and is often used for making pasta's.  Durum wheat is also known as semolina.

You can sprout wheat for fresh greens, which is easier for the body to digest.  Simply rinse the wheat kernels and then soak them in three times the amount of water as the wheat kernels in a lidded bin overnight;  (example; 1 cup of wheat berries requires 3 cups of water).  The next morning, drain off the water, re-rinse the wheat kernels, and place them back in the bin–a Tupperware-style bin with a lid will do.  Set in a dark location.  Re-rinse after 24 hours, then return the bin to its storage location.  Within approximately 36 hours, the wheat kernels will begin to sprout and can be eaten, or if you prefer longer sprouts, allow more time.

\* Olive Oil has a shelf life of 2 years when stored out of sunlight in a cool location. Once a can or jar is opened, the olive oil is exposed to oxygen, which will shorten its shelf life. Consider storing small containers of olive oil for extended shelf life.

\*Rice: The benefits of storing white rice is its impressive 30-year shelf life. Brown rice has the benefit of twice the amount of manganese and phosphorus of white rice, two and a half times the iron content, three times the vitamin B3, four times the vitamin B1 and 10 times the Vitim B6. However, brown rice has a disappointing shelf life of a short six months due to the oil that is stored in its bran layer. A solution for added shelf life is storing it in a refrigerator or freezer if you have the extra room. A steady diet of brown rice cannot be tolerated by some. Studies have shown that abruptly changing a person's diet to a high fiber content can lead to constipation and stomach pain.

Note: If your food storage plan includes cooking with wheat and brown rice, consider gradually increasing the amounts of brown rice and wheat served at mealtimes *before* a crisis happens, so if a family member experiences an adverse reaction from eating a high fiber diet, or develops an allergy (wheat allergies can occur when intake is increased) there will be time to make any necessary adjustments to your food storage.

Buying wheat directly from the grower or in bulk at a grocers can drastically reduce the cost. You will need a dependable manual grain mill to grind wheat as needed. Personally, I recommend the Country Living Grain Mill. They aren't cheap, as they retail for around $429.00, but they are extremely dependable for grinding wheat, corn and other grains. If you plan on grinding corn and beans, you will need a larger auger, which is sold separately. Whatever grain mill you decide on, make sure to buy replacement parts so you won't end up with buckets of wheat with no way to grind it if a part fails.

## Baking Supplies

If your alternate cooking method is a camp stove or an open fire pit, baking is possible with a cast iron dutch oven. Doing an online search for dutch oven cooking will yield a wealth of free, delicious recipes.

Baking Supply List

Baking Powder
Baking Soda
Chocolate Chips
Cocoa Powder
Corn Syrup
Extracts: Vanilla, Maple & Assorted as needed
Molasses
*Shortening
*Yeast

*Shortening: Crisco claims the shelf life of their shortening is a disappointing two years. However, if you check on various preparedness sites, you will notice people mention that Crisco that was stored for five years was perfectly good. I can testify to that myself with personal experience. It has to do with how shortening is stored. Store shortening and cooking oil in a cool, dark, moisture free location. In a pinch, butter flavored Crisco can be used in place of butter for baked goods.

*Yeast is a must for bread-making and many other baked goods. Because yeast has a fairly short shelf life of up to two years, it's important to keep a sourdough starter recipe handy that can be used in place of yeast if it's needed.

## Beans/Legumes

Beans are a member of legume family. Storing a generous selection of dry or canned beans will offer a variety of flavors to basic recipes. Beans provide healthy complex carbohy-drates and are an excellent source of protein, fiber, iron, cal-cium, zinc, B vitamin and folic acid. Beans can be cooked in a pressure cooker, greatly reducing cook time and fuel consumption.

Beans/Legumes List

Alfalfa Seed
Black-Eyed Peas
Black Turtle Beans
Dry Soup Mix (a mixture of beans)
Garbanzo Beans
Great Northern Beans
Kidney Beans
Lentils

Lima Beans
Mung Beans
Navy Beans
Pink Beans
Pinto Beans
Small Red Beans
Soy Beans
Split Pea

**Condiments**
Condiments are another way to add a variety of flavors to the most basic of meals.

Condiment List

Barbeque Sauce
Ketchup
Chili Sauce
*Mayonnaise
Mustard
Relish
Salad Dressing, Bottled or Dry Packets
Salsa
Soy Sauce
Syrup
Tabasco

Teriyaki Sauce
Worcestershire Sauce

\* Mayonnaise is a thorn in the side for many pepper's because of concerns that once a jar has been opened, and if refrigeration isn't available, the next step is food poisoning. It is a myth that commercially made mayonnaise must be kept refrigerated. The eggs used in commercially made mayonnaise is pasteurized, which kills bad bacteria (unlike homemade mayonnaise, which must be kept refrigerated). Commercially made mayonnaise also has lemon and vinegar added to it, which makes it inhospitable for bad bacteria. Many boaters who do not have the benefit of refrigeration, some who spend weeks at a time at sea, have already tested the theory of unrefrigerated mayonnaise and lived to tell about it. The only precaution is using a clean utensil each time mayonnaise is removed from the jar. However, if you're wary of testing this theory yourself, mayonnaise can be purchased in individual packets from restaurant supply stores and can sometimes be found at big warehouse stores like Costco and Sam's Club.

## Comfort Foods

We all have favorite comfort foods. If you were to ask someone who has lived through a long-term emergency, they will likely tell you they missed comfort foods the most. Something as simple as a bowl of popcorn, or a handful of trail mix can help alleviate the stress of a crisis because of the normalcy it offers.

Comfort Food List

Cake Mixes
Candy (chocolates have a fairly short shelf life. For long-term storage, consider hard candy)
Cookie Mix, Boxed
Brownie Mixes

Fruit Roll-Ups
Granola Bars
Jell-O, Boxed
Nuts, Canned or Vacuum Sealed
Pizza (Boxed Kit)
Pudding, Boxed or Containerized
Popcorn
Raisins
Trail Mix

## Convenience Foods

Convenience foods will get you through the onset of a crisis when your attention will be better spent on more important matters. They are also an important back-up when a short-term illness makes cooking from scratch difficult. Even if your diet may not normally include convenience foods, it is a good approach to put aside one to two weeks worth of easy to prepare foods.

<u>Convenience Food List</u>

Boxed Pizza Kits
Chili
Macaroni and Cheese
Pork & Beans
Ravioli
Soups-Assorted
Spaghetti
Stew
Top Ramen

## Dairy

Dairy is something most of us wouldn't want to be without. The good news is that it's not all that difficult to store. Non-fat powdered milk has a shelf life of up to 20 years when stored correctly.

As already mentioned in the pantry section, powdered eggs are available in # 10 cans that have a shelf life of up to five years, or you may choose to preserve fresh eggs by coating them in mineral oil, which will store for months. Our forefathers preserved eggs over the long winter to no ill effects. Refer to notes on preserving eggs under the pantry section.

Dairy List

Milk, Dry Non-Fat
Milk, Evaporated
Cheese, Powdered
*Cheese, Preserved in Wax
Sour Cream, Powdered

* Cheese: It's possible to keep hard cheese such as cheddar unrefrigerated for years by coating it with cheese wax. Years ago I heard about using the wax method to preserve cheese and I couldn't wait to try it. Finally, a way to avoid powdered cheese or settling for Velveeta cheese. I tried the suggested directions immediately, then tucked the waxed cheese out of sight for the next 6 months. That was the hardest part of the process, waiting to see if I'd just wasted 20 lbs. of pricey cheddar cheese. Happily, when I peeled away the wax to reveal the cheddar, it was free of mold and more delicious than when it was preserved because it had continued to age. This is a good news for lovers of sharp cheddar. It means that you can start out with medium cheddar (much cheaper) and it will age into sharp cheddar cheese. The trick is to make certain the wax is not cracked, where exposure to oxygen will begin the dreaded molding process. To view how to preserve your own cheese, visit katzcradul YouTube titled *Waxing Cheese*. Yum!

**Fruit**
Whether canned, freeze dried or dehydrated, fruit is a nutritious addition to long-term food storage. Fruits like bananas that can't

be canned can be dehydrated at home or purchased in #10 cans which has a shelf life of up to 15 years.

Fruit List (Canned/Dehydrated/Freeze Dried)

| | |
|---|---|
| Apples | Grapefruit |
| Applesauce | Mandarin Oranges |
| Apricots | Peaches |
| Banana, Dehydrated | Pears |
| Berries, Assorted | Pineapple |
| Fruit Cocktail | Plums |
| Fruit Pie Filling | Prunes |

**Grains**

Grains have an incredible shelf life, which is why they are a preference of preppers for long-term food storage. At the end of this chapter, refer to the instructions to store grains for optimal shelf life.

Grain List

Barley
*Brown Rice
Buckwheat
Corn
Corn Meal
Flax Seed
Millet
Oats
Quinoa
Rye
Spelt
Triticale
Wheat Flour
White Flour
White Rice

## Meat & Seafood Commercially Canned & Home Canned

Although canned meats and seafood can be pricey, they will add protein and a variety of flavor and textures to meals. Until recently, canned beef chunks and hamburger were difficult to find at a grocery stores or online, but that's begun to change as more and more people are investing in long-term food storage.

### Meat & Seafood List (Canned/Dehydrated/Freeze Dried)

| | |
|---|---|
| Bacon | Oysters |
| Bacon Bits (real bacon | Pork |
| bits, jars) | Spam |
| Beef Chunks | Salmon |
| Chicken | Sardines |
| Clams | Shrimp |
| Corned Beef | Steak |
| Crab | Tuna Fish |
| Ham | Turkey |
| Hamburger | *TVP (Assorted Flavors) |

*TVP is a low fat meat substitute made from either vegetable protein or wheat gluttons. TVP has a shelf life of up to 20 years and is available in a variety of flavors. It can be purchased in #10 cans or in bulk.

## Pasta

Pasta is inexpensive, has a shelf life of up to 30 years when stored properly, and adds filler and texture to meals. In other words, pasta is excellent for long-term food storage. Pasta provides carbohydrates, protein, fiber and a range of vitamins and minerals.

### Pasta List

Egg Noodles
Spaghetti Noodles

Fettuccine
Linguine
Macaroni

## Spices

Store a good supply of spices to provide meals with a variety of flavors. Purchasing spices in bulk and storing them in labeled canning jars will save money, and all you really give up is the fancy packaging.

<u>Spice List</u>

| | |
|---|---|
| Allspice | Liquid Smoke-Bottled |
| Alum | Mace |
| Basil | Marjoram |
| Beef Bullion | Mint |
| Caraway | Mustard-Dry |
| Cardamom | Nutmeg |
| Cayenne | Onion Powder |
| Celery seed | Oregano |
| Chicken Bullion | Paprika |
| Chili powder | Parsley |
| Chili Seasoning Mix | *Pepper |
| Chives | Poppy seeds |
| Cinnamon | Rosemary |
| Coriander | *Salt |
| Cloves | Saffron |
| Cumin | Sage |
| Curry | Savory |
| Dill | Sesame Seed |
| *Garlic Powder | Taco Seasoning Mix-Dry |
| Ginger | Tarragon |
| Kitchen Bouquet-Bottled | Thyme |
| Lemon Pepper | Turmeric |

*Salt, pepper and garlic powder are basic spices that carry wonderful bartering potential. For more about bartering, refer to Chapter 13, *Long-Term Survival*.

## Vegetables

Vegetables are a staple of food storage. Commercially canned and home canned vegetables have the benefit of being packed in water, which will cut down on the water you will need for cooking. This may seem like a small thing while water still flows from the kitchen faucet, but if an emergency ever involves grid-down that precious water contained in commercially canned or home canned vegetables will be a bonanza! Dehydrated and freeze-dried vegetables have a long shelf life of 15 years or more and come with the added benefit of light weight portability for anyone who plans to relocate in the event of a disaster.

### Vegetable List (Canned/Dehydrated/Freeze Dried)

| | |
|---|---|
| Artichoke | Mushrooms |
| Asparagus | Onions |
| Beets | Peas |
| Bell Peppers | Potato |
| Carrots | Potato Flakes |
| Celery | Pumpkin |
| Corn | Spinach |
| Green Beans | Tomato |
| Green Chili Peppers | Turnip Greens |
| Hominy | Water Chestnuts |
| Jalapeno Peppers | Wax Beans |
| Mixed Vegetables | |

## About Dehydrated and Freeze-Dried Food

Dehydrated and freeze-dried foods are a popular choice for preppers for its long shelf life. One of the discrepancies of shelf life quoted by manufacturers has to do with how much oxygen is left remaining in the food when packaged or canned, as oxygen shortens shelf life. Another factor is manufacturers have no way of knowing *how* the purchaser will store dehydrated and freeze-dried food, therefore some manufacturers give a more conservative estimate for shelf life. Without exception, oxygen, direct sunlight, heat, moisture and temperature fluctuations are the enemies of shelf life.

If you are preparing for a large family or group, and are struggling with an affordable way to put aside food storage, consider a combination of longer shelf life bulk foods such as beans, rice, wheat, canned food and dehydrated or freeze-dried foods.

Typically, commercially dehydrated and freeze-dried foods are packed in number 10 cans which has had the oxygen purged and nitrogen added for long shelf life. Another method used is adding an oxygen absorber packet during the canning process.

## Dehydrated vs. Freeze-Dried food Preparation

Manufacturers prepare dehydrated foods with heat from a commercial dehydrator, removing moisture to 2% to 3% for the longest shelf life possible. Do-it-yourself food dehydration is possible with an electric food dehydrator, an oven, or from the heat of the sun. As it's difficult to attain uniform drying without the aid of a commercial dryer, the shelf life of home-dehydrated food is typically shorter–approximately 12 months for home dehydrated fruit and six months for vegetables when stored in a cool temperature of 60 degrees. Dehydrated foods take time to re-hydrate (up to 45 minutes).

If you are interested in dehydrating your own fruits and vegetables, going to a pick-your-own farm will greatly reduce the cost. Dehydrating foods has become popular with gardeners and preppers alike and you will have no trouble finding websites devoted to preserving foods through dehydration that offer step-by-step instructions.

Freeze-Dried foods are prepared by first freezing the food and then removing almost all of the moisture in a vacuum chamber before sealing it in an airtight container. Freeze-dried foods re-hydrate within minutes and more closely retain the taste and texture of fresh fruits and vegetables. The commercial freeze drying process requires sophisticated machinery and is more costly to produce, which drives up the price of freeze-dried foods when compared to dehydrated foods. Freeze-dried foods are light weight, but remain similar in size as before the freeze-drying process, thus it is bulkier in size than is dehydrated food, which may be a consideration for those who have limited storage space or will be packing in food to another location.

## Storing Bulk Food: Buckets & Containers

Bulk food is typically stored in 5-gallon opaque buckets. Food storage buckets purchased at preparedness sites often have gamma seal lids, designed to keep bugs and moisture out. That's the good news. The bad news is they will cost from between $7.00 to $12.00 each.

There are a couple outside-the-box solutions that will save your budget and it starts with understanding that when lining buckets with Mylar bags, purchasing expensive buckets with gamma lids is not necessary. To keep costs down, go to your local bakery or deli and get buckets for free. Bakery's and delis go through a huge amount of food grade buckets and are usually more than happy to give them away. You will have to scrub them of the food they held, but the savings makes a little elbow grease worth the effort.

Another solution is the one I used. Remember, I was storing enough bulk food for 23 people for one year, therefore I had more buckets to purchase and fill than I care to remember. Purchasing traditional food storage buckets would have taken a huge bite out of my preparedness budget. I discovered the answer to my dilemma at Home Depot–orange paint buckets that are food grade for just a little over $3.00 each, including the lids which are sold separately. Problem solved!

The only issue with the buckets was discovered a few months later when I attempted to open one of the buckets to "borrow" flour, which I had forgotten to buy on my last trip to the grocery store. When I tried opening the lid, I'm quite certain I must have looked like a contender at a woman's wrestling competition. The bucket nearly won. The next trip to town (there aren't many, seeing as how "town" is over 90 miles away), I solved the problem with a $4.00 tool, which is a plastic lid opener designed for weaklings like me.

Without this little device, I pity the person who is forced to open a bucket of beans, another of rice, and yet another of flour to make a meal!

To double-check that a bucket is food grade, inspect the bottom of the bucket. It should have a #2 inside the stamped triangle with the words HDPE or Poly Ethylene. If you are unsure, contact the manufacturer. Never use a bucket that held chemicals or other harmful materials.

Boxed goods such as potato flakes, baking soda, boxed cake mixes, Jell-O, pudding and the like can be stored in stackable opaque tubs. But a word to the wise: use rubberized tubs rather than the cheaper, brittle plastic tubs that have a tendency to crack. Be sure to note the contents (when stored in a Mylar bag) and the purchase date on each item with indelible pen before storing them in the tub.

Do not stack tubs more than two high to avoid the bottom tub collapsing unless you are storing light weight items.

Use Duct tape to secure the lids to the tub to keep out insects and rodents. Mark the contents on the outside of each tub with indelible marker. If you will be stacking the tubs, don't write the contents on the lid, or you will find yourself in a frustrating search when you need a specific item. In fact, it doesn't hurt to note the contents on the side *and* the front of tubs, so if they're moved, you won't be clueless as to where the cocoa went.

## Mylar & Glad Bags
Bulk food needs to be protected from moisture, oxygen and bugs. Mylar bags and tight fitting bucket lids will offer that barrier. They are sold on Amazon and preparedness sites in 20" X 30" sizes which are designed to be used for 5-gallon food storage buckets. They cost around $1.50 each when you purchase them in gross. Mylar bags come in a variety of sizes, so if you will be packaging smaller items like hard candy, or nuts that can be stored in a tub in individual packages, check on smaller sizes as well. Typically, a Mylar bag heat sealer is used to seal the bags. Sounds reasonable until you price them, which starts at around $60.00 and can be as pricey as $160.00 or more. Not to worry, there's a solution. A hot iron will seal the Mylar bag just as effectively.

If your budget is tight and time is short, Glad Trash Bags can be used in an emergency. Glad bags are not treated with insecticides which makes them safe for food storage, but what Glad bags *don't* do is offer a bug, oxygen and moisture barrier that Mylar bags do.

## Storing Bulk Food For Long-Term Storage
Before you start filling buckets, it's important to prepare a location for their long-term storage. If this location will be a basement, it's best to keep the buckets off of the floor to protect them from moisture that can wick from cement or dirt floors onto storage buckets. Wood pallets work well for this and they can often be found for free at building sites and lumber yards.

You will be adding an oxygen absorber to the Mylar lined bucket, so before you get started, we need to discuss how oxygen absorbers work. This may be seem like way too much information, but you need to be able to tell the difference between a spent oxygen absorber and a viable one. So here goes . . .

Store oxygen absorbers in an airtight container to extend the shelf life. Oxygen absorbers are made of iron oxide powder that chemically reacts to the environment and removes the oxygen from the Mylar bag, which will greatly prolong the shelf life of bulk food. Oxygen absorbers come in different sizes, but for the purpose of bulk food storage, one 2000 cc size is used per 5-gallon bucket.

Once you have stored a package of oxygen absorbers for a period of time, it's possible their shelf life may have expired. The easiest way to be sure is to pinch the packet. If it feels soft, that is the iron oxide powder and the packet should be good to go. If it is hard, that indicates that the packet is past its shelf life. Another way to tell is when the packet gets warm to the touch when activated. However, once activated, there is approximately 30 minutes before the activation of the iron oxide is spent, which means activating the oxygen absorber and placing it in the Mylar bag is the final thing you will do before sealing the bag. This requires that the iron or Mylar heat sealer iron you will be using is plugged in, hot, and ready to go.

For your first few practice runs, it's easiest to use beans or rice. That way, the end result of the miracle of oxygen absorbers will be easier to see when your first try is successful. And it will be. When you fill the bucket, leave 1 to 2 inches of head room for the top of the Mylar bag.

There's only one more step before filling that first bucket if you will be using a hot iron. You will need a flat, stout piece of wood that is longer than the bucket which will be used to seal the bag. The piece of wood can be as simple as an old piece of trim wood, as long as it's flat, not rounded. After smoothing out any wrinkles of the top of the Mylar bag, it's time to create a seal with the hot iron or a Mylar bag heat sealer. You will need to leave an opening of a few inches in the middle of the Mylar bag–just enough space to toss the oxygen absorber in. Place the piece of wood across the bucket and lay the top of the Mylar bag across it and create a seal a little less than half of the width of the bag with the hot iron, starting at the end and working towards the middle. It only takes a few seconds for the heat of the iron to achieve a seal. Next, seal the other side, but remember to leave a gap where you will deposit the 2000 cc oxygen absorber. Next, toss in the oxygen absorber, depressing as much air from the Mylar bag as possible and seal the bag the rest of the way with the iron.

You're done! Leave the lid off of the bucket for 24 hours to allow the oxygen absorber to work its magic before putting on the lid. If you are successful, and I imagine you will be, you will be able to see small indentations in the Mylar bag of the rice or beans contained in the bag (provided that's what you packaged) and it will slightly resemble a shrink-wrapped bag.

After 24 hours, once the oxygen absorber is finished removing the oxygen from the Mylar bag, it's safe to use a pair of scissors to trim off the excess top portion of the bag, if any, being careful to not snip the seal. The final step is securing the lid of the bucket with a rubber mallet; although I will admit to using a hammer to no ill effects. If you are using a bucket with a gamma seal, all you need to do is twist it shut.

If the Mylar bag didn't achieve a tight seal, try again. In no time, you will be comfortable with the process.

Just as with marking the tubs, use an indelible marker to write the date and the contents on the outside of the bucket, not the lid. You can safely stack buckets three high, but any higher, and the weight can crack the lid of the lower buckets.

Visuals are always helpful. Before you make your first attempt, check YouTube for tutorials on filling storage buckets using Mylar bags and oxygen absorbers.

Review:

- Line a food grade bucket with a Mylar bag.
- Fill the bag with bulk food, leaving a 1" to 2" head space for the top of the Mylar bag.
- Place a wood scrap across the top of the bucket if you will not be using a Mylar bag heat sealer. It needs to be stout, 3 to 4 inches wide and longer than the bucket.

- Smooth out any wrinkles from the Mylar bag and lay it across the wood scrap.
- Iron one side of the of the Mylar bag from the edge towards the middle (leaving a gap in the middle to deposit the oxygen absorber).
- Smooth the other side of the bag and iron, leaving a gap in the middle.
- Activate and deposit one 2000-cc Oxygen absorber in the Mylar bag.
- Express the excess air out of the bag and iron the gap closed.
- Leave the lid off the bucket for 24 hours.
- Provided the bag achieved a tight seal, within 24 hours the oxygen absorbers will have removed the oxygen from the Mylar bag and it will resemble a shrink-wrap package. Secure the lid on the bucket and write the date and the contents on the outside (not the lid) of the bucket.

Note: There are other methods to preserve bulk food such as using dry ice, but the combination of Mylar bags and oxygen absorbers is the most popular because it is the simple and it's effective.

Sprinkling rock sulfur around any cracks or openings of your food storage area will help to control rodents.

# Chapter 9

## 72-HOUR EMERGENCY KITS, DECOYS & CACHING SUPPLIES

You may have heard them called 72-Hour Emergency Kits, Grab-And-Go Bags, Go-Bags, Bug-Out Bags, or Emergency Bags, but the principle remains the same: They are backpacks that have been filled with essential, can't-live-without-them supplies you will need to get you from point A to point B in an emergency. Each person in the family should have one. They should be kept in your vehicle, so whether you're at work, or out running errands, you will have the essentials to get home safely. If you commute by bus or train, or if you ride-share to work, keep a 72-Hour Emergency Kit at work. It's possible that transportation may be down, forcing you to walk home and each item in your 72-hour emergency kit will help get you home safely.

The following is a list of supplies typically packed in a 72-Hour Emergency Kit. You will notice a second advanced list of supplies that can be stored in a vehicle. The "extras" on the second list are worth consideration for anyone who works out-side easy walking distance from home and for those who live in an urban location where safety concerns may force you to flee without advanced notice.

What you choose to include in a 72-Hour Kit should always take into consideration your specific circumstances.

## 72-Hour Emergency Kit Recommendations

- Baby Food, *Cloth Diapers, Diaper Pins, Rubber Pants (if applicable)
- Batteries & Solar Charger
- Battery Run, Wind-Up, or Solar Powered Emergency Radio
- Body Soap/Antibacterial Soap
- Boots, Hiking
- Camp-Size Water Purifier
- Canteen/Water Bottle
- Clothing
- Compass
- Duct Tape
- Edible Plants Reference Book
- Feminine Products (if applicable)
- First Aid Manual
- Hatchet/Ax
- Headlamp
- Hunting Knife
- *Important Documents
- Lighting: Flashlight, LED/ Shaker-Style, Emergency Long-Burning Candles
- Magnesium Flint & Steel Fire Starter
- Maps: Street & Topographical
- Matches/Waterproof Matches/Lighters
- *Medical Supplies/ First Aid Kit & Prescription Medicines
- MRE'S
- Nylon Rope
- Poncho, Rain
- Replacement Water Filters
- Rope
- Shovel, Folding
- Sleeping Bag
- Swiss Army Knife
- Tarp
- Tent
- Toilet Paper
- Toothbrush
- Toothpaste
- Two-Way Radios
- Water
- Weapon & Ammo
- Wire

*Cloth Diapers, diaper pins and rubber pants are a necessity for those with infants unless you have the storage space and the budget for an estimated 5,000 disposable diapers per year to diaper an infant.

\*Important documents should be kept in duplicate at home, a get-away cabin (if applicable), or your vehicle. A widespread disaster that takes out the electrical grid will likely take down banking, the stock market and the Internet. Basic documents to keep on hand are: birth certificates, last will & testament, health insurance documentation, health records, inoculation records, marriage certificate, DMV information, Social Security documentation, school records, tax paperwork, automobile title, mortgage information, automobile and homeowners insurance documentation, property tax information, banking and all other financial documentation such as annuities, 401K and other retirement plans, and stock and bond investment documentation. For safety reasons, mark out your account numbers with indelible marker and keep those account numbers in your wallet that only you have access to.

\* If you take prescription medicine, it is important to have extra medicine stored in your 72-Hour Emergency Kit that will get you through a crisis when medical services may be unavailable. Have a talk with your doctor about extra prescriptions. If your doctor is unable to fulfill your request, don't stop there. Do an online search for an alternative.

**Advanced Supplies**

The following list suggests additional items you may want to store in your vehicle if the distance between work and home is greater than 20 miles, or if you plan to relocate to another location in the event of a crisis, or if you suspect your area may experience heavy looting, forcing you to flee with little to no notice. Keep in mind that it may take days longer than you expect to reach your destination if roadways become grid-locked or are unnavigable.

- Animal Snares/Traps
- Bucket, With Handle (Water & Edible Food Collection)
- Camp Cookware
- Portable Camp Stove & Fuel
- Can Opener

- Canned Milk or Powdered Milk
- Canned/Dehydrated/ Freeze-Dried Food
- *Cash
- Clothespins & Clothesline
- Clothing: Socks, Underwear & Cold Weather Gear, If Applicable
- Cooking Utensils
- Cooler
- Dish & Laundry Soap

- Dishes (metal)/ Paper Plates
- Duffel Bag
- Fishing Supplies
- Lantern, Lantern Fuel & Lantern Socks
- Newspaper & Lint/ Vaseline-Coated Cotton Balls (Fire Starters)
- Oven Mitt
- Replacement Water Filters
- Shampoo
- Towel & Washcloth
- Water (Extra) & Water Jug
- Wet Towelettes

* Because ATM transactions and banking will be disrupted in a power grid failure, keep cash with you in small denominations in case it's needed.

## Setting Up a Decoy

Setting up a decoy is a form of insurance that in a worst-case scenario, you may be able to save critical goods for ongoing survival. Looting will begin in earnest when people run out of food and water, heat and lights and realize the help they expected to arrive probably isn't coming. It's likely that dense urban areas will be the hardest hit by looters, simply because of the sheer number of desperate people, but suburbs and rural locations won't be immune to looting either. Storing a decoy of expendable canned goods and miscellaneous supplies in plain sight may satisfy an intruder enough that they grab what's there and leave. There are no guarantees, of course, but the average person isn't likely to continue rifling through your home looking for more once their immediate needs are met.

This same meager decoy stash can be used for charity should you decide to help strangers who show up on your doorstep to ask for help. Should they happen to see you grabbing a few items from a paltry decoy supply, they aren't as likely to be compelled to help others they encounter by pointing strangers in your direction. And don't think it won't happen. Even when people are desperate for food and water and medical supplies, some will want to help others. Those sent in your direction may be trustworthy, there only to ask for help, or they may be mercenary, willing to take whatever they can through force. Never tip your hand that you have a well stocked pantry! This is why it's advisable to make arrangements to share what you are able to with a community food bank or a Church at the onset of a crisis. You can then send anyone in need to that location while maintaining a safe buffer zone.

## Caching Supplies

Caching is a way to re-supply survival goods that breaks away form an "all or nothing" mindset. Even when your intentions are to survive in place, caching supplies can be a life saver for the unexpected. When burying a cache, the location you chose to bury it should have identifiable landmarks to make it's retrieval easier. When burying a cache on your property, it should be hidden out of the line of sight of your home. If looters are the reason you've had to vacate your home, the worst possible scenario would be for them to get wind that you have buried additional supplies.

The following are some of the top reasons why you would want to cache critical supplies:

- Preparing for a natural disaster such as floods, earthquakes, tornadoes and hurricanes requires preparing for the unexpected. If your home takes a direct hit during a natural disaster, you may be separated from your preps temporarily or long-term. Caching supplies in a retrievable location away from a home or bug-out cabin will allow you to restock critical supplies when they're needed the most.

- In the first few months following a nationwide or a widespread disaster, looting will be rampant in dense urban areas, and problematic in more rural ones. If you must flee to safety, having buried caches available that are filled with must-have prep goods will buy you time until it's safe to return home.

- If you have a bug-out cabin that you are unable to live in full-time, caching a portion of your critical supplies on the property will ensure that you'll have something to fall back on in case of looting while you are away.

- If your back-up plan includes fleeing to a safer location, caching supplies along the route you plan to use will help to insure safe passage. If your plan is to drive to an alternative location, there is no guarantee that the roads will be passable. Strategically placing a cache every 20 miles along the route–the distance a person can reasonably walk in one days time–stored with extra drinking water, food, clothing, emergency medical supplies, batteries, water purification tablets, and other critical goods represents survival.

- If your work is a long distance from your home, caching supplies along the route will allow you to resupply for survival.

Items you may want to include in a cache will likely mirror what you carry in a 72-hour emergency kit: Medical supplies, water, a hikers water purifier and replacement filters, MRE's, canned goods, dehydrated and freeze-dried food, medical supplies, replacement hiking boots, batteries, clothing, a flashlight, a headlamp, replacement 2-way radios, matches, lighters, fishing gear, traps, weapons, ammo and the like.

Before burying a cache, all items must be protected from moisture. Smaller items can be vacuum sealed and larger items can be wrapped tightly with heavy duty aluminum foil. For an extra layer of protection, they can then be placed in a double layer of zip-lock bags.

Line a plastic food grade bucket or PVC pipe with a Mylar bag before packing protected items–burying items in the ground means they *will* be exposed to moisture, so the objective is to take steps to protect your cache in every way possible. Pack the items in as tightly as possible. Seal off the Mylar bag, just as you would bulk food storage, adding oxygen absorbers before sealing. Let it rest for 24 hours before putting on the lid (or lids in the case of PVC pipe) and seal with 100% silicon caulking to waterproof.

Be sure to add a folding shovel with your 72-hour emergency kit to make digging up a cache easier.

Caches aren't restricted to being buried in the ground. They can also be hidden in walls. This can be done by removing the drywall, filling the space between studs with supplies, and re-installing it. Anything metal against the cached wall like a refrigerator, a washer and dryer or a bakers rack may throw a determined looter with a metal detector off track. Other places to cache supplies are between floorboards, or by building out or installing false walls for extra hidden storage space. PVC pipes installed to look like water lines can cache smaller valuables.

Hiding prep goods in plain sight can also be effective. Boxes stacked in a basement, marked "IRS", or "Tax Records" or jumbled boxes marked "Books" or "Christmas Decorations" may fool a looter. Just make sure the top layer of the box actually contains what you've noted, and you may be able to stay under the radar. Building a false bottom in a couch or bed or other furniture may also go unnoticed.

Look around your home and property to brainstorm creative hiding places you may already have that will thwart a looter. The results may surprise you.

# Chapter 10

## MEDICAL SUPPLIES

We live in an age of technology, where help is just a phone call away. During a crisis, all that we take for granted may change and it may be up to each of us to handle medical emergencies. That's why having a good store of medical supplies is critical, but it's no more important than having a solid understanding of how to handle a medical emergency. The Red Cross offers training courses, and if you check with community colleges in your area you may be able to find a non-credited class offering medical training or a CPR course that is affordable. If you have the time and are willing to make the commitment, many towns and cities welcome volunteer emergency responders where emergency training is offered.

Medical supplies may be difficult or impossible to find once a crisis strikes. If you take prescription medication, it is important to discuss extra prescriptions with your doctor. They should be kept in your 72-Hour Emergency Kit, so that you will have them available at the onset of an emergency. If you are unable to get extra prescriptions, research naturopathic medications that may substitute what you are currently taking.

The following medical supply lists begins with just the basics, followed by a more advanced list, and culminates with a third list that requires emergency medical training. If you plan to join forces with other preppers, I highly recommend joining forces with someone who has medical training. Cross-training should be a part of a medical emergency plan, so should the main caregiver of your family or group be incapacitated, emergency medical treatment can continue to be administered.

<u>Level 1 Basic Medical Supply List</u>

- Ace Bandages
- Aloe Gel
- Antacid Medicine
- Antibacterial Soap
- Antibiotic Ointment
- Anti-Diarrhea Medicine
- Anti fungal Ointment
- Aspirin
- Baby Powder (if applicable)
- Band Aids (assorted)
- Benadryl
- Body Lotion
- Butt Paste*
- Children's Fever Reducer
- Calamine Lotion
- Cold Packs
- Condoms
- Contacts Lenses (replacements)
- Contact Solution
- Dental Floss
- Diaper Rash Ointment (if applicable)
- Disposable Latex Gloves
- Epsom Salts
- Eye Wash
- Feminine Pads*
- Glasses (replacement)
- Gold Bond
- Hydrocortisone Cream
- Hydrogen Peroxide
- Ibuprofen
- Isopropyl Alcohol
- Lip Balm
- Mentholated Cough Drops
- Mosquito Repellant
- Mucinex
- Nasal Spray
- Non-latex Examination Gloves*
- Penlight*
- Pepto Bismol Chewable Tablets
- Pregnancy Test
- Petroleum Jelly
- Reading Glasses
- Rolled Gauze
- Splinter Removal Kit
- Surgical Tape
- Sterile Gauze Pads & Non-Sterile Gauze Pads*

- Sunscreen
- Thermometer (Adult and Children's)

- Tylenol
- VagiCare
- Vicks VapoRub

\* Butt Paste helps control chafing during heavy outdoor activity and for those on bed rest.

\* Feminine pads are sterile and can be used for larger wounds when sterile medical pads are unavailable.

\* Non-Latex Surgical Gloves are used when treating open wounds and will avoid cross-contamination.

\* A Penlight will help with examinations when it's necessary to check someone's pupils.

\* Having a good supply of sterile and non-sterile gauze pads is a must. They come in various sizes and they are affordable.

### Level 2 Medical Supply List

- Acidophilus (to help with digestion)
- Air Cast
- Ankle Brace
- AZO Standard (for urinary tract infection)
- AZO Yeast (for yeast infections)
- Castor Oil\*
- Clove Oil (for tooth sensitivity)
- Cohesive Bandages

- CPR Mask (avoids cross-contamination when administering CPR: available at the Red Cross)
- Crutches
- Dental Mirror
- Dental Probe
- Dental Wax
- Dermoplast
- Dramamine (for nausea)
- Elastic Gauze Bandages

- Eye Solution
- Finger Splints
- Israeli Bandages*
- Kerlix Gauze Bandage Rolls* (absorbent and will hold sterile bandages in place)
- Knee Brace
- Mole Foam (helps avoid blisters when hiking long distances)
- N-95 / N-100 Particulate Respirator / Face Mask*
- New Skin for treatment of cuts
- Potassium Iodide*
- Saline Solution (used to irrigate wounds)
- Sterile Swabs
- Steri-strips (used for deep, smaller cuts that do not require stitches)
- Surgical Masks
- Tea Tree Oil
- Tongue Depressors
- Tourniquet
- QuikClot*

* Castor Oil helps with constipation, however pregnant women and small children may have an adverse reaction to castor oil.

* Israeli Bandages, also known as battle dressing, provides compression for severe wounds.

* Potassium Iodide protects the thyroid from radiation exposure, which can later lead to cancer of the thyroid. Potassium Iodide should not be given to those who are allergic to iodine, and should not be given to pregnant women, children or infants without doctor approval.

* QuickClot helps stop the flow of blood from a wound.

### Level 3 Medical Supply List

- Ambu Bag to assist breathing–Infant, Child & Adult sizes
- Arm & Leg Splints
- Bandage Scissors
- Blood Pressure Cuff

- Central Venous Catheter Kit
- Extensive Dental Kit
- Fetal Doppler Monitor
- Kelly Forceps
- Lap Sponges
- Ringers Lactate Sterile
- Surgical Gloves
- Surgical Kit
- Sutures
- Stethoscope
- LMA Mask (for blocked airway)
- Olsen Hegar Needle Holder/Scissor Combination Forceps
- Orthopedic Casting Tape (to set broken bones)
- Pulse Oximeter (to measure oxygen in the blood)

Note: Chapter 11, *Protecting Yourself & Your Loved Ones From Pandemic* supplies a detailed list of pandemic-related medical supplies and Personal Protection Equipment.

# Chapter 11

## PROTECTING YOURSELF & YOUR
## LOVED ONES FROM PANDEMIC

Illegal immigrants account for nearly $11 billion of our nation's annual healthcare costs and with it comes Chagas disease, MRSA, Chikungunya, tuberculosis (including drug-resistant TB), dengue fever, hepatitis, chicken pox, measles, and malaria. Should the healthcare system fail during a protracted crisis, and the control of these diseases cease, the risk of pandemic increases.

However, the potential spread of these diseases hasn't drawn the attention that Ebola has since several U.S. medical workers contracted the disease in 2014.

Soon after a second Dallas nurse contracted the virus, question began to be asked about what constituted sufficient personal protection equipment (PPE) while healthcare workers came forward with complaints that they had not received sufficient training to treat Ebola patients while protecting themselves from contracting the virus.

Some in the medical and scientific fields voiced concerns over the possibility of this latest strain of Ebola being contagious *before* symptoms appear, and at the same time, doctors battling Ebola in West Africa reported that hemorrhaging wasn't as prevalent with the patients they were treating as it had been with previous outbreaks. Speculative red flags were raised that the Ebola virus may have become airborne, or could become airborne. Others warned that even if Ebola was not airborne, droplets from a cough or sneeze *was* infectious.

There were many valid questions and concerns being voiced, but it seemed that no one had the answers. During that same time frame, public outcry that requested flights from West African hot-spots be stopped was flat-out refused. The situation took its toll, leaving Americans to feel at risk and vulnerable.

Researchers from the National Centre for Foreign Animal Disease, the University of Manitoba and the Public Health Agency of Canada documented transmission of Ebola from pigs to monkeys, which led to speculation that the Ebola virus had gone airborne. However, the studies findings were that droplets from a sneeze or cough from infected pigs that were inhaled into the lungs of the monkeys was the transmission vector that led to their becoming infected.

A recent MIT study found that a sneeze, which can travel at speeds of up to 100 miles an hour, could spread a virus throughout a room and was capable of traveling through ventilation systems, dispersing the virus much further throughout a structure than was previously thought possible.

Warning bells were being sounded that the 21 day ceiling for the incubation period of Ebola may actually be longer.

Some experts claimed that the Ebola virus could not live outside a host for more than a few minutes or hours while others warned that the virus could live on surfaces for up to 21 days. Other conflicting advice was that the Ebola virus in the semen of male Ebola survivors could live in the testes for up to 30 days, while others claimed that 90 days was possible.

Soon after the two Dallas nurses contracted Ebola, the CDC announced new protocols for personal protection equipment (PPE). Surgical masks were replaced with N-95 particulate respirators, and suddenly, entering an isolation room with exposed skin must be avoided. It was sound advice, but the fact that it was offered after healthcare workers were infected led many to believe they were on their own should a full-blown epidemic occur.

The suggestions contained in this chapter were gleaned from careful study, but they are only suggestions. I do not hold a medical degree, nor do I have inside information. What I share with you here is what I will do, personally, should it become necessary to care for a loved one who contracts the Ebola virus or another life-threatening communicable disease at a time when medical help is unavailable. The suggestions err on the side of caution simply because not enough is understood about the transmission of the Ebola virus and its ability to mutate.

It is known that bodily fluids such as saliva, sweat, vomit, feces, urine, semen, mucus, and blood can transmit the virus. Currently, there is no cure for Ebola. When caring for someone with Ebola it is important to encourage them to drink plenty of water to stay hydrated, as diarrhea and vomiting can quickly lead to dehydration. For pain management, over-the-counter analgesics such as Advil or Tylenol is advised by medical professionals. It is reported that this current strain of Ebola has a fatality rate of between 50% to 70%.

If an outbreak occurs during a time of crisis when medical help is unavailable, the best way to protect yourself and your loved ones is to stay at home and maintain a "no one in, no one out" policy. In other words, isolate yourself and your loved ones.

It's the only way to ensure against contracting disease. But, is it realistic to expect to remain isolated for a long stretch of time? For some, the answer may be a resounding yes! But what if a family member arrives at your doorstep during an outbreak? If you invite them to stay, you could run the risk of exposure.

There's an answer, but it's not an easy one. At a time when medical help is unavailable, and you choose to allow someone to enter your home, the only way to protect yourself and your loved ones from contracting a disease is to place that person in quarantine until the incubation period has passed (at least 21 days for Ebola).

This may seem harsh, until you ask yourself how you would want the situation to be handled if it was you on the other side of the threshold. My guess is that most people would choose to isolate themselves to avoid infecting others.

This chapter concentrates on the Ebola virus, but because influenza is of great concern in the U.S. and elsewhere, I've included information on Influenza's incubation period and symptoms as well. Protocol for personal protection equipment (PPE) and setting up an isolation room described here for dealing with Ebola can be applied for most life-threatening diseases.

## Influenza: Death Rate, Incubation & Symptoms

Although influenza doesn't generate the same level of fear as Ebola does, it infects 200,000 people annually in the United States, leading to 37,000 deaths. Now consider what the death rate might be if medical help was unavailable and untrained civilians were responsible for the care-giving of loved ones who contract influenza and it suddenly becomes clear why taking extra precaution is the best approach.

The incubation period of Influenza is short; from 24 to 36 hours. An Influenza sufferer can be contagious one day **before** symptoms appear. Due to influenza's short incubation period, and the fact that it is possible for a sufferer to be contagious before symptoms appear, quarantining anyone who may have been exposed to the virus is mandatory.

Symptoms of influenza

- Fever
- Chills
- Cough
- Sore Throat
- Runny Nose
- Body Aches

- Headache
- Fatigue
- Diarrhea and vomiting–more common in children

## The Incubation Period For Ebola

The incubation period of Ebola can be as short as 2 days, or as long as 21 days. However it needs to be noted that some in the medical field have questioned if the incubation period of Ebola might be longer with this most current outbreak. At this point in time, officials are assuring the public that an Ebola sufferer is not contagious until the following symptoms appear:

Symptoms of Ebola

- *Fever greater than 101.5 degrees
- Severe Headache
- Muscle pain
- Weakness
- Diarrhea
- Vomiting
- Abdominal pain
- Bleeding or bruising

*Note: There have been reports by healthcare workers caring for victims of this latest Ebola outbreak that infected patients do not always present with a high fever.

## Caring For Someone With Ebola or Influenza

Some viruses are airborne, while others can mutate and become airborne. If you are not certain whether or not an outbreak is airborne, treat it as if it were.

A virus can enter through the mucous membranes of the eyes, nose and mouth. Touching someone who is ill or coming in contact with their bodily fluids, and then touching the eyes, mouth or nose can transmit the virus.

Without proper medical testing, it may be impossible to know if a person has a life-threatening disease, or something that will more easily run its course. The safest approach is to err on the side of caution and treat illness as if it were life-threatening, especially when medical help is unavailable.

The disinfecting of walls, floors, surfaces and certain items of PPE such as rubber boots or a full face respirator can be done with a solution made from <u>One Cup of Bleach per One Gallon of Water.</u>

## Setting Up An Isolation Room

Keep anyone who may have been exposed to the Ebola virus isolated from others for at least a precautionary 21 day incubation period. The best barrier is a separate room. The door should remain closed except when a designated caregiver enters or exits the room.

Always remember that droplets from spit, a cough or a sneeze *are* infectious. If you do not have a separate room available to care for someone with Ebola, cordon off an area as far away from others as possible with heavy mill plastic that has been securely taped closed with duct tape, taking care that there are no gaps to allow the virus to travel outside of the isolation area.

The isolation room should include bathroom facilities–which during grid-down would require a camp-style toilet. Under no circumstances should someone who is contagious, or thought to be contagious, share a bathroom with others–this includes an outhouse. Remember, bodily fluids will transmit the disease. Surfaces can also carry live virus; some say for as long as 21 days.

Because the feces and urine of someone infected with Ebola will contain the virus, the patient should use a lined camp-style toilet. Solid waste and urine must be neutralized with approximately 1/2 cup bleach and left to sit for an hour or more before being removed outdoors to be burned.

The isolation room should be free of soft surfaces such as curtains or upholstered furniture which can hold the virus. The mattress should be covered in heavy mill plastic and carefully sealed with duct tape to protect it from bodily fluids. An upholstered headboard or dust ruffle should be removed from the room.

Close off any ventilation vents that could allow the virus to spread to other parts of the home.

Keep a lined garbage receptacle in the isolation room for the disposal of medical refuse and discarded personal protection equipment (PPE). A second garbage receptacle will be needed in the doffing area. As needed, medical refuse should be transferred outdoors to be burned safely away from the home or other living quarters.

Disinfectant wipes and alcohol based handrub must be available in the isolation room and the doffing area, which is explained in more detail later in this chapter under donning and doffing PPE.

## Setting up an Undressing (Doffing) Area

It is necessary to set up a separate area from the isolation room to doff PPE. This separation is necessary because once PPE is removed, the caregiver has no defense against contracting the virus. In a perfect world, a bathroom with a separate exit will be available–this set up doesn't require the caregiver to exit back through the isolation room and chance infection once PPE is removed. As we don't live in a perfect world, it's more likely that an area will need to be set up for doffing PPE. The doffing area can be cordoned off with heavy mill plastic and carefully sealed off with duct tape. Because exposure to the isolation room while removing PPE can lead to the caregiver contracting Ebola, the best location for the doffing area is just outside the isolation room door. Keeping the isolation door closed while the caregiver doffs PPE will create a buffer zone. This serves the purpose of containment of the virus between the caregiver and patient while lessening the chance of spreading the virus to living areas.

The doffing area should have a full-length mirror (an inexpensive, utilitarian full-length wall mirror will suffice) to make it easier and safer to remove PPE. This will be made clearer once you've reviewed the donning and doffing steps later in this chapter and you have had the chance to practice the technique.

The doffing area will need to have enough room for the caregiver to doff PPE, the space for a large garbage can to dispose discarded PPE, and a table with a surface area that is large enough to hold disinfectant wipes, alcohol handrub, nitrile gloves and a supply of garbage bags. Space requirements also include a tub large enough to step into when disinfecting rubber boots, as well as a step-off mat, which is described in the doffing PPE section later in this chapter. If there is room for a small, hard-surface chair, having one available in the doffing area will make removing rubber boots easier.

## Personal Protection Equipment (PPE) List & Estimated Costs
The PPE listed below are specific to Ebola, but will also offer protection from other communicable infectious diseases like influenza.

Note: Until this current Ebola strain has been studied in more detail, N-100 particulate respirators are recommended, rather than N-95 particulate respirators. Although pricier, they will filter out smaller particulates.

- Alcohol Based Handrub (such as Purell)

*Purell alcohol-based handrub cost approximately $5.00 per 12 ounce bottle. You will need a generous supply of alcohol handrub which will become clear when viewing the video that is suggested later in this chapter.

- Disinfectant Wipes

* Protex disinfectant wipes are available at Amazon for $23.40 per canister of 120 wipes. You will need several containers.

- Nitrile Gloves– both regular length and longer12-inch length

*Nitrile gloves are currently sold on Amazon for $9.00 per 100 pair, which amounts to .09¢ per pair. Purchase both regular length and longer, 12-inch length nitrile gloves. The shorter pair of gloves are worn under the cuff area of Tyvek coveralls, and the longer length nitrile gloves are worn over the cuff. Doubling up on protective nitrile gloves provides necessary protection against contracting the Ebola virus.

- N-100 Particulate Respirators or Full-Face Respirators

*N-100 particulate respirators cost approximately $7.75 each. Because a particulate respirator can only be worn once per visit to the isolation room, it will be necessary to have plenty on hand.
*The cost of a full face respirators start at $135.00. Full face respirators do not need to be disposed of after each visit to the isolation room as particulate respirators do, but they must be scrupulously cleaned after each visit to the isolation room. A cleaning solution of one cup of household bleach per one gallon of water can be used to disinfect full face respirators.
* Filters for a full-face respirator typically cost $15.00, and they must be disposed of and replaced after each visit to the isolation room.

Note: The video that is suggested later in this chapter, *Donning and Doffing of PPE for Ebola Isolation Units* recommends N-95 particulate respirators. However, N-100 masks are capable of filtering out smaller particulates. They are pricier, but until further study of the Ebola virus concludes that N-95 particulate respirators are sufficient, a more stringent approach may be called for.

Due to cost, it's likely that most will choose disposable N-100 particulate masks over full face respirators *unless* future research of the Ebola virus indicates the necessity to wear a full-face respirator which is capable of filtering out smaller particulates than N-100 particulate respirators.

- Tyvek Zippered One-Piece Coveralls

*Disposable Tyvek coveralls typically cost $5.60 each when purchasing them in a gross of 25. You will need plenty, as they must be disposed of after each visit to the isolation room.

- Disposable Full Face Shields

*Full Face Shields are relatively inexpensive, around $2.30 each when purchased in a gross of 24. Full face shields do not have to be worn if wearing a full face respirator. Full face shields must be disposed of after each visit to the isolation room, therefore you will need a generous supply.

- Surgical Hood/Bio Safety Hood

*Amazon sells both surgical hoods and bio safety hoods, and the principle is the same. They are made to protect the wearer from contamination of bodily fluids. Bio safety hoods can be purchased for $1.64 each when purchasing a gross of 50. It's advisable to buy a good supply of bio safety hoods, as they must be disposed of after each visit to the isolation room.

- Disposable Impermeable Surgical Apron

*Disposable surgical aprons do not need to be heavy-duty to work as a barrier, protecting the wearer from contaminants. Long sleeve styles that have thumb holes to keep the apron sleeves from sliding up while working is preferable. They cost approximately .80¢ each when purchased in a bulk of 75. Surgical aprons must be disposed of after each visit to the isolation room, so it's best to buy them in quantity.

- Rubber Pull-On Boots (one-piece style without snaps, laces or openings)

*The cost of rubber pull-on boots will vary. For the purpose of PPE, an inexpensive, no-frills pair will do. It is important to choose rubber boots that are one piece that protect from bodily fluids getting inside the boot. Because rubber boots must be thoroughly disinfected with bleach solution between use, it is more efficient to have several pairs available for caregivers.

- Rubber Tub and Step-Off Mat

* The rubber tub is filled with disinfecting bleach solution and must be large enough to comfortably step into while wearing rubber boots. Its use is to disinfect the boots as thoroughly as possible after leaving the isolation room and entering the doffing area. The cost of both the tub and step-off mat are minimal one-time expenditures. Amazon has 6-gallon Fortifex feed tubs for $22.00 and slip-resistant mats for $13.00.

- Duct Tape

*Duct Tape typically costs between $4.00 to $5.00 per roll unless purchased on sale. It will be necessary to purchase a generous supply of duct tape to set up a makeshift isolation room and doffing area. In certain circumstances, it will be necessary to use duct tape to secure PPE, which is described later in this chapter.

- Household Bleach

* It will be necessary to have a generous supply of household bleach on hand to disinfect PPE and surfaces in isolation and doffing areas and to neutralize the waste of an Ebola sufferer.

## Estimated Cost Of Full PPE & Limiting Visits to the Isolation Room

The estimated cost of each change off PPE is approximately $18.27. This is exclusive of a boot disinfecting tub, step-off mat, pull-on rubber boots, alcohol handrub, disinfectant wipes, duct tape, and household bleach that will be needed in quantity.

Because it may be difficult to afford a generous supply of PPE, limiting visits to the isolation room may be necessary. I realize this is easier said than done, for it's impossible to put a price tag on the welfare and support of a loved one. However, without a generous supply of PPE, and if supplies run out, the caregiver then risks exposure and exposing other family members if visits to the isolation room continue. Such an outcome is a worst-case scenario.

A solution to this dilemma, especially when children are involved, is for the caregiver to remain in the isolation room for longer periods of time rather than making frequent visits which can quickly exhaust PPE supplies.

## Practice Donning and Doffing PPE

It is extremely important for caregivers to practice putting on (donning) and taking off (doffing) PPE before caring for someone stricken with Ebola or another life-threatening communicable disease. If done incorrectly, it can lead to caregivers becoming infected.

I urge you to watch the following YouTube video: Donning and Doffing of PPE for Ebola Isolation Units, provided by the North Carolina Division of Public Health. Of all the YouTube videos (and trust me, I have watched them all), this was the most thorough. The following is the YouTube URL:

https://www.youtube.com/watch?v=N6F61J93FvE

## When Water Is In Short Supply

Keep in mind that the hospital personnel simulating the donning and doffing seen on the YouTube video are in an environment that may not exist if a pandemic outbreak occurs during grid-down. In the video, the healthcare worker simulates washing his hands approximately 17 times. This may seem excessive, but when dealing with a deadly virus like Ebola, there is no such thing as excessive precaution.

From a preparedness standpoint, we should take into consideration that in grid-down, water will not flow from faucets once municipalities run out of emergency back-up power.

The solution is to trade washing hands with soap and water for washing them with alcohol handrub. The WHO has recommended it over soap and water for caregivers battling Ebola in West Africa where clean water is in short supply and sinks with running water are not always available where patients are cared for.

If you are like me and need confirmation of the facts before adopting an out-of-the-box solution, go to the WHO article, *Clean Care Is Safer Care: System change - changing hand hygiene behavior at point of care* at the following URL:

http://www.who.int/gpsc/tools/faqs/system_change/en/

## What You Should Know Before Donning PPE

PPE should be donned **before** entering the isolation room. Putting PPE on after entering the isolation room can lead to the caregiver contracting the virus. .

Tyvek coveralls are not one-size-fits-all. They should be purchased based upon the size of the wearer and should take into consideration any street clothes that will be worn beneath the coveralls. The Tyvek coveralls should be tested for a proper fit by the wearer reaching, stretching and bending before entering the isolation room to be certain the fit is not too tight, which can lead to tears in the Tyvek fabric that could expose the wearer to the virus.

## Step-By-Step: Donning PPE

Step 1. Remove jewelery and any personal items from pockets. Long hair should be pulled away from the face and secured with a rubber band. Make sure to hydrate before donning PPE, as extended stays in the isolation room does not allow for hydrating.

Step 2. Disinfect hands with alcohol-based handrub such as Purell. This step protects the caregiver and the patient.

Step 3. Put on the inner pair of nitrile gloves (there are two pair that will be worn). The inner gloves remain under the sleeve of Tyvek coveralls.

Step 4. Put on Tyvek coveralls and add a zip-tie to the zipper tab. This will make it easier to locate the zipper when doffing the Tyvek coveralls.

Step 5. Pull on rubber boots, then pull the legs of the Tyvek coveralls over the boots. This will stop bodily fluids from entering boots. If uncertain if movement may expose the top of the boot, secure the bottom of the Tyvek coverall legs to the boots with duct tape while allowing room for normal movement.

Step 6. Put on an N-100 particulate respirator by holding it against the nose and mouth with one hand and pulling the elastic bands around the head with the other. The bottom band should be placed around the back of the neck, and the top band should be placed above ear level around the back of the head. Make sure that the bands are not twisted. Next, press down on the metal bands that are incorporated in the particulate respirator, including the bridge of the nose, to ensure a tight, secure fit.

**Warning**: Facial hair, even stubble, can stop the wearer of a particulate respirator or a full face respirator from achieving a tight seal, which can lead to exposure.

Step 7. Put the surgical/biosafety hood on, making sure that no hair is exposed and the ears and neck are covered. The hood should drape over the front, shoulder and back of the Tyvek coverall.

Step 8. Put on the disposable surgical apron, placing thumbs through the thumb holes of the apron, if applicable.

Step 9. Put the second, outer pair of nitrile gloves on, which are pulled over the cuff of the Tyvek coveralls. If you do not have longer, 12 inch nitrile gloves, secure the second outer pair of nitrile gloves with duct tape over the cuff area to hold them in place.

Step 10. Put the disposable face shield on over the surgical hood. The face shield must cover the entire face, leaving no exposed skin.

Step 11. Wash gloved hands with alcohol handrub before entering the isolation area.

### Use The Buddy Method
It's best to have a designated person inspect the caregiver for exposed skin or hair before entering the isolation room. If no one is available, the caregiver should us a mirror to make sure PPE was put on properly. Exposed skin or hair can lead to a caregiver contracting the virus through bodily fluids or droplets from a sneeze or cough from the patient.

### What You Should Know Before Doffing PPE
It is extremely important that a caregiver follow extreme safety measures to properly remove PPE, or they risk becoming infected and infecting others. Doffing PPE is less forgiving than donning them because it is likely gloves and other PPE have been contaminated while caring for an Ebola patient. It is doable, even for a novice, but it requires plenty of practice before caring for someone with a potentially deadly virus. This is why practicing donning and doffing PPE is just critical as having the proper PPE available.

As previously mentioned, PPE it should be doffed away from the patient in a separate, cordoned off doffing area.

The following step-by-step instruction assumes that the caregiver is wearing a particulate respirator, rather than a full face respirator.

### Step-By-Step Doffing PPE
Step 1. Wash gloved hands with alcohol handrub before leaving the isolation room.

Step 2. Before leaving the isolation room, check PPE, including rubber boots, for contamination. If contamination is found, wipe it off with a disinfectant wipe and discard. If a wipe was used to remove contaminants, wash gloved hands with alcohol handrub.

Step 3. Move to the doffing area, stepping into the tub of bleach solution while wearing rubber boots–the tub should be placed just inside the doffing area. Remain standing in the tub of bleach solution for one minute to allow the boots to be disinfected and then step out onto the step-off mat.

Step 4. Wash gloved hands.

Step 5. Inspect PPE for contaminants a second time, and if found, wipe off the contaminant with a disinfectant wipe and discard, then wash gloved hands.

Step 6. Remove outer gloves using the glove in glove technique. Using one hand, grasp the outside of the opposite gloved hand near the wrist. Peel glove inside out and once removed, hold the glove in the other gloved hand. Still grasping the removed glove, remove the second other outer glove by sliding the index and middle fingers of the single gloved hand under the remaining gloved hand and peel it away, rolling inside out. Once removed, discard the gloves.

Step 7. Inspect the remaining gloves for contaminates. If found, remove the contaminate with a disinfectant wipe. Discard wipe and wash gloved hands.

Step 8. Carefully remove the disposable apron by untying it (if applicable) and pulling it forward, away from the body, and roll it from the inside out to avoid coming in contact with the outside of the apron, which should be assumed to be contaminated.

Always doff PPE slowly, as contact with exposed skin may lead to contracting the virus.

Step 9. Wash gloved hands.

Step 10. Inspect PPE for a third time. If contaminants are found, wipe it off with a disinfectant wipe and discard. Next, wash gloved hands.

Step 11. Follow the zipper of the Tyke coveralls from the waist area up to locate the zipper and then unzip. This is easiest done when a zip tie has been added to the zipper. Be careful not to let the gloved hand come in contact with exposed skin.

Grabbing the coveralls from the outside with gloved hands, pull the coveralls away from the body and down, turning the coveralls inside out as they are removed. Avoid touching street clothes beneath the Tyvek coveralls as they are being doffed, as gloves should be assumed to be contaminated.

Note: Caregivers are not likely to have an extra person suited up in PPE to help with the doffing of PPE, therefore anything that makes the doffing process easier and safer is the best approach. As previously mentioned, the doffing area should have a full-length mirror available to make locating the zipper easier, thus making it less likely that the caregiver will accidentally touch the exposed skin of the neck or face while doing so.

Step 12. Wash gloved hands after removing the Tyvek coveralls.

Step 13. Remove the face shield while leaning forward and grasping the band at the back, and pull forward. Do not touch the front of the face shield. Once removed, discard the face shield.

Step 14. Wash gloved hands.

Step 15.  Lean forward and remove the bio safety hood by grasping the top of the hood and slowly pulling it off the head.

Step 16.  Wash gloved hands.

Step 17.  Again, inspect boots for contaminants.  If contaminates are found, remove with a disinfectant wipe and discard, followed by washing gloved hands.

Step 18.  Remove the second, inner pair of gloves using the glove in glove technique.

Step 19.  Wash ungloved hands.

Step# 20.  Put on a clean pair of nitrile gloves.

Step 21.  Remove the N-100 particulate respirator while tilting the head forward and grasping first the bottom strap and then the top strap and remove without touching the front of the respirator or the exposed skin of the face or neck.

Step 22.  Wash gloved hands.

Step 23.  Remove gloves using the glove in glove technique.

Step 24.  Wash ungloved hands.

Step 25.  Sit down to remove rubber boots.  Do not touch the exterior of the boots while removing them.  Use a plastic bag to cover them as they rest on the floor and then flip the bag right-side up and tie off without touching the exterior of the boots–they must be fully sanitized with bleach solution.

Step 26.  Wash ungloved hands.

Step 27. Put on the street shoes and spray the bottoms of the shoes and the floor of the doffing area with bleach solution before exiting.

Step 28. If there is sufficient water available, shower upon exiting the doffing area.

## Disinfecting Surfaces & Disposal of Medical Waste

Disinfecting walls and the surfaces of the isolation and doffing area can be done with bleach solution of <u>one cup bleach per one gallon of water</u> using an atomizer bottle. Spray walls and surfaces and let air dry. Medical waste should be burned outdoors, away from living areas.

# *Chapter 12*

## SAFETY

Stories of heroism during a disaster are always heartwarming. They shine a light of hope on an otherwise dismal time. Many times, it isn't just individuals willing to help others, but entire communities. During a national disaster, there will be new and returning heroes and communities reaching out to those in need. It is one true thing we can hold on to while we face the challenges that arrive with sudden calamity.

Conversely, a full-blown crisis will bring forward those who are willing to use whatever means necessary to ensure their survival. It is this second group that you must protect yourself from.

### Staying Under The Radar

Keeping a low profile in the midst of a crisis will be more challenging for those who are prepared than for those who aren't. I realize this may seem like an odd statement when the whole point of *Get Prepared Now!* is to help you prepare for a disaster. But remember, you will have food and supplies that others will want. The way to keep from becoming a victim is fairly simple: do not advertise your preparedness.

<u>Cooking Odors:</u> As already mentioned, cooking odors should be avoided during a time of looting and social unrest, as this will draw people to your doorstep, particularly when living in a dense population. When planning for food storage, make sure

to include meals such as MRE's or prepared canned food for times of heavy unrest. If necessary, canned food can be eaten straight from the can without heating.

<u>Lighting, Motorized Tools and Vehicles</u>: Driving a vehicle when everyone else around you is on foot advertises the fact that you have fuel. Running a generator or a chainsaw screams that you are prepared and have what others are seeking. If you were to do so, expect a visit either from someone curious about your preparedness, or from a looter.

To get a better idea of the need for stealth during a grid-down disaster, all you have to do is to think back to a camping trip, or a hike in the woods, or a country drive. What might stand out in your mind is the quiet. Grid-down will blanket neighborhoods in quiet when electronics, tools and traffic noise disappear. If you must run a generator, consider building a soundproof enclosure now, before a crisis strikes, to cut down on the noise it generates. Along those same lines, when collecting wood, consider using an ax instead of a chainsaw.

Lighting would be difficult to live without, but if you're not careful, it can serve as a beacon for looters. Most of the population will have to cope with darkness after nightfall during a crisis that takes down the grid, therefore light spilling from a window will advertise your preparedness. Make sure to set aside blackout curtains or blackout fabric and duct tape to carefully cover windows when lighting your home.

## Telling Others About Your Preparedness

It's possible to draw people to you well before a disaster hits! All it takes is sharing the fact that you have put aside food storage and supplies with neighbors, co-workers, friends and extended family members.

Ask any prepper who has made that mistake, and most will tell you that the feedback went something like this: "I know where *I'm* going if things get bad!" But is this really just a joke shared between friends, or is it more likely that this person will expect help when an emergency outlasts their food and water supply?

Unless you are able to put aside an equal portion of provisions for each person who is likely to come to you for help during a crisis, it may be the prudent thing to keep preparedness efforts between immediate family members. This is one of the most difficult decisions preppers must make because our natural inclination is to help others in need. But, you must consider that while helping others, your provisions will disappear rapidly and can jeopardize the security of your loved ones.

## Helping Strangers

Offering charity to strangers in need is something many of us will feel compelled to do when we see others suffering. However, if charity isn't offered carefully it could expose you to danger.

Instead of handing out food to strangers, it's a safer approach to get involved with your community leaders, churches, or local food banks. Make arrangements to deliver what you are able to share at the onset of a crisis to that location. This approach will reduce your exposure to opportunists, or worse.

Keep in mind that most people will not have an alternate cooking device or cooking fuel to cook something like beans or rice. For this reason, canned milk, vegetables, fruit and prepared meals such as canned chili and stew will be the most appreciated foods for those in need. Inexpensive can openers can be purchased in quantity, which will be needed, as will books of matches.

## Keep A Watchful Eye & Beef Up Those Doors and Windows

The onset of a crisis may draw people together, but the goodwill extended at the beginning of a crisis might not last. Desperation can be a strong motivator and even the kindest of people may be driven to acts they never thought possible should they be without food and water.

This is not the time to let your guard down. Continue to make yourself as small a target as possible. Keep supplies such as firewood, ATV's, bicycles, garden tools, and building materials as far out of sight as possible where they're not as likely to be seen by passersby. These items will be in huge demand during a time of crisis.

Beef up all locks and door jams to make doors as impenetrable as possible to would-be intruders. Start with an inspection of your doorjambs. If they were installed with today's standard building practices, one swift kick could splinter them and offer easy access to an intruder. There are doorjambs available made to withstand a battering ram, and for the protection they offer, they're an inexpensive solution. At the very least, doors should have a strike plate with as many screw holes as possible--three at least. Install 3-inch screws to the strike plate that will make it harder for a swift kick to break through. Door hinges should have three screw holes and should be installed inside exterior doors. If you don't have an ANSI level 1 deadbolt on exteriors doors now, it would be wise to install them.

The doors themselves should be sturdy, which excludes a hollow-core door. A solid wood, steel, aluminum or fiberglass door is a huge improvement over a hollow-core door.

Windows offer easy access to a wood-be intruder. A door with panes of glass to allow extra light in is a benefit in good times and a risk in bad! If your exterior doors has a window that would allow an intruder to punch through to unlock the door, it should be replaced with a solid door that has a peephole, which offers the added security of being able to view who is on the other side of the door before opening it. Home invasion is already on the rise. Consider how much worse the problem will become after a disaster.

Plate glass windows offer yet another opportunity for an intruder. In fact, the lack of proper window security accounts for more than 30% of residential break-ins. The following are ways you can reduce the risk windows pose to home security:

- Storm windows are made to survive 100 mile per hour impacts. They are typically made with a layer of PVB (polyvinyl butyral) sandwiched between a layer of glass on either side. Although the glass may break with impact, the middle layer of PVB can stop an intruder from gaining entrance.
- Lexan sheets are available in various strengths, from impact-resistant to bulletproof. The negatives of Lexan sheeting is that it's pricy and it should be installed by a professional, which adds to the cost. Anyone planning on using passive solar to heat their living spaces should know that Lexan can negatively impact the effectiveness of passive solar heating.
- Storm shutters are available in many styles: accordion-opening, swing-opening, and the most popular for security, shutters that roll into place. It is likely that all but the most determined looter will avoid the hassle of breaking through this added safety measure.
- Security film is made of a transparent, thin sheet of resilient polyester that is designed to be applied over the entire windowpane. If the window is shattered, the film is designed to hold the glass fragments together, making it more difficult for an intruder to gain entrance.

Note: Pre-cut plywood to the dimensions of your windows for protection should a window be broken.

### Fencing and Watch Dogs

A dog will alert you to an intruder long before you are aware of their presence. Police officers will be the first to tell you that the serious bark of a large dog, willing to back up their bark, will usually stop an intruder. Although most preps can be hidden out of site, something like a garden or chicken coop can't be. A large dog and fencing can help protect your family and your property from opportunists.

Note: If you choose to have a dog, be sure to put aside a generous amount of dog food.

## Physical Fitness
Physical fitness can't be obtained by anything but sweat-equity. Getting in shape, enough to meet the demands of life without conveniences, only requires movement, which can be achieved at a gym or by walking, swimming or bicycling. If you feel you have room for improvement, now is a good time to grab a friend or a family member and hit the pavement.

## Self Defense
Self defense courses are, in my opinion, a must. It is a troubling reality that in the midst of a crisis, when people should be helping one-another, there will be some willing to do whatever it takes to get what they want at another's expense. They *will* be out there and knowing how to disarm or deflect an attacker will allow you to get away safely. Self-defense training is not typically expensive, so check around your vicinity to find out what's available.

## Home Defense
How you choose to defend yourself and your loved ones is personal to each individual and it's a subject worth several books on its own. If your plan includes a gun for self-defense, it is imperative to take a gun safety class, where you and family members can become familiar with the principles of gun safety. Owning a gun and knowing how to defend yourself with one are two different things. Reading about shooting, or watching videos isn't enough. A firearms class will give you the skills to properly

defend yourself against intruders. Practicing these skills is necessary to develop better hand-eye coordination and reflexive skills necessary for accurate shooting, especially when under stress.

No matter what your self-defensive preference is, it is extremely important to agree upon a plan of action with other adults in your family or group ahead of a crisis. There should be an agreed upon plan of action regarding how an intruder will be dealt with and this plan should be carried out. Waiting to have that talk while an intruder is crawling over your fence, or breaking into an outbuilding, or kicking down your front door is a recipe for disaster! Have a plan in place, and practice it. That way you can react as a cohesive group without hesitation, which will greatly increase your chance of survival.

Children will be the most vulnerable should an intruder gain entrance into your home. A designated person should be assigned to their care and a safe place to retreat should be agreed upon, well before an actual event occurs.

## Banding Together With Others For Safety & Pooling Skill-Sets

Chapter 2, *Keeping It Simple & Must-Have Skills*, describes the challenges that come with a protracted crisis. If you have never been interested in old westerns, or a watching a series like *Little House On The Prairie*, now is a good time to change that around--at least until you can get a feel for the workload involved with surviving a lifestyle free of the conveniences we take for granted today.

There will be water to gather and purify, wood to be chopped for those living in a cold climate, laundry that will need to be hand washed and hung dry and meals will need to be cooked from scratch on cooking devices that are not as efficient as what we're used to. Water will need to be heated for dish washing, bathing and cleanup. Hunting and fishing and gathering wild edible plants may be part of a survival plan, and each of these require skill-sets and the work it will take to preserve this food. Gardening is a must to survive a long-term disaster, and requires sweat-equity and the work it takes to preserve the overflow from the garden by storing it in a root cellar, or by home canning, or through food dehydration.

This was not said to overwhelm you. It is simply a reality that must be faced. For a husband and wife to perform all of these necessary chores while caring for children, and have the time and energy left over to patrol a property during times of unrest and out of control looting will be extremely difficult.

Joining forces with other like-minded people is a direction that some preppers choose. Doing so will enable you to combine skill-sets, food supplies, preparedness goods and it will go a long way towards increasing personal safety.

Many band together with friends or family members. It makes perfect sense; you already know if you can trust them, and you are familiar with their personality traits; their strengths and weaknesses.

Conversely, approaching a stranger must be done carefully or not at all. There are preparedness and survival sites where you can meet up with others in your vicinity who are looking to join forces with other like-minded preppers. Setting up a meeting place in a neutral location is preferable and information you share should be kept to a minimum until you get to know them. They do not need to know what town you live in, or your phone number, or your address. At first, e-mails will suffice to communicate back and forth.

Never hand over a laundry list of what you've managed to put aside. It's sufficient for them to know that you are prepared. After all, those first baby steps should be centered upon compatibility and skill-sets. For instance, if it's discovered the person you've just met is obsessed with guns and ammunition and the subject of food storage, or lighting, or heating, or water procurement, or communications is never brought up, it's probably time to walk away with no harm done.

You should be looking for someone who is involved in all aspects of preparedness. Combining skill-sets is one of the main reasons why seasoned preppers seek others to band with. No one person can possibly be trained in every skill-set needed for ongoing survival. Finding someone who has medical training, and another who has carpentry skills, and another with hunting, mechanical or gardening skills will greatly increase the chances of long-term survival.

Approaching those in your neighborhood or community can be risky. Once you've revealed an interest in self-sufficiency, the door has been opened for conjecture on their part. However, if you tread lightly, you may be able to get a feel for their receptiveness. Many preppers I know have opened the subject up by mentioning they have decided to put aside a few days food supply for a natural disaster most common to their area. It may open the door for a conversation where you discover they, too, have an interest in preparedness. If not, at least you haven't left yourself vulnerable.

## Travel During A Disaster

Be sure to keep a compass, street maps and topographical maps in your vehicle or 72-hour emergency kit or vehicle that covers your immediate location to your destination point, no matter how many maps this may entail.

Never depend upon a GPS device or a cell phone directional app, as these conveniences may be disrupted in a full-blown crisis.

When traveling during or directly after a crisis, be especially careful of downed power lines. In the case of an earthquake or flood, be cautious when crossing a bridge, as the foundation may have been weakened with the movement of the earth. Watch for roads that may be crumbling or otherwise weakened.

## Vehicle Must-Haves

Vehicle and tire maintenance should be a top priority. Keeping your gas tank topped off will ensure that you are able to reach home. If you will be traveling farther than a tankful of gas during a crisis, it will be necessary to bring extra fuel with you. It is highly unlikely that gas stations will be able to pump gas during a wide-scale emergency for the simple reason they don't have emergency back-up power to pump gas. However, if a miracle happens, and you find an operational gas station, you will need cash because it's even less likely that they will be able to accept credit or ATM cards.

<u>Vehicle List</u>

- Air Pump (battery run)
- Tire Jack
- Fix-a-Flat
- Jumper Cables
- Lug Wrench
- Motor Oil
- Spare tire
- Tool Kit

**Have a Family Plan**

Find out what the emergency plan for your child's school or daycare is. You need to know if your child will be relocated to another location in an emergency and where that location will be. You will need to know if you will be allowed to pick your child up during an emergency and whether or not it would be permissible for a designated person to pick up your child if you are unable to. If they will allow a designated person to pick up your child, the school or daycare will likely require your signed consent and your alternate's pertinent information. Give another signed consent form to the designated person to avoid confusion.

Choose an alternate contact person who lives outside your area and have all family members keep this person's contact number with them. If a disaster is localized, family members may be able to get messages to one-another through this alternate contact should you become separated.

Make sure the phone number is written down and in the possession of each member of your family or group. Storing the number on a cell phone contact list can backfire if the battery dies or the phone is lost or damaged. Although cell phone calls may not get through when phone lines are jammed, it's possible that a short text will.

Old-school clip-in land line phones may still work during an emergency that takes the grid down–at least while your provider's emergency back-up power lasts. Add one to your preparedness list instead of relying on a portable land line phone that is dependent upon electricity to operate

It is possible that an emergency may place neighborhoods under evacuation orders. Have an alternate meeting place where all family members can meet up should you become separated during an emergency. Practice dry runs with your children to familiarize them with the meeting location.

## Know Your Homes Breakers & Shut-Offs

Keep a flashlight at your bedside. Disasters can lead to broken natural gas or propane lines. To light a match or a candle instead of grabbing a flashlight to make an inspection could cause an explosion. Both natural gas and propane are highly explosive. If you discover a leak, get everyone out of the house and leave the door open so that fresh air can circulate. Do not attempt to turn on any lights when you have a gas or propane leak. A spark can ignite built up fumes. Propane is heavier than natural gas, so it tends to settle closer to the ground and is harder to air out of a space. Propane will have a service valve on the tank where natural gas shutoffs are located on the meter, which is typically installed outdoors against the foundation of the house, but this can vary. In the event of a leak, turn the valve to the off position. There may be cases where a gas leak cannot be controlled at your homes shut-off and it will be necessary to evacuate.

Some emergencies require turning off the power to your home at the circuit breaker. Electrical breakers are typically behind an easily identifiable panel.  Every member of the family old enough to be of help in a crisis should be taught about utility shutoffs to your home.

Water main shut-offs aren't always as easy to find, especially in older homes where they can be buried in an obscure corner of a basement or crawlspace.  I speak from experience.  Learn where your water shut-off is located now, before an emergency, so you won't be floundering in the dark wondering if you will ever find it.

## When You're the Fireman *and* the EMT

When lighting involves candles, lanterns and oil lamps and cooking most be done over an open flame,  the chance of fire increases Add several ABC fire extinguishers to your preparedness list.  ABC extinguishers contain monoammonium phosphate and are designed to put out liquid fires, combustible material fires and electrical fires. Your local fire department may not be able to reach you in the case of fire or other emergencies during a full-blown crisis.

If you will be heating with a wood-burning stove or a fireplace, it's important to keep chimney fire retardant on hand. The chimney flue should be checked for creosote buildup. Make sure your wood heat stove or wood cook stove has a protective, non-flammable barrier installed behind and under it such as cement board, sheet metal, or ceramic tile.

In an emergency that disrupts communications or causes grid-lock or power outages, ambulances may not be running, leaving you to handle a medical emergency.  Emergency medical training courses and a thorough first aid manual will enable you to administer aide when you are the EMT.

## Keep Cash On Hand

The ability to make cash withdrawals from ATM's and banks may be interrupted indefinitely in a crisis.  Keep as much cash on hand as possible for last minute items you may need.  Keep small denominations: $1's, $5's, and $10's in case change is not available.

## What to Do in a Nuclear Attack

Radioactive fallout cannot be seen or detected by our sense of smell or taste. In the event of a nuclear attack, wearing an N95 or N100 mask will help protect against breathing in radioactive particulates, but they are not as effective as a mask with an NBC rating. It is important to remain indoors until you are certain it's safe to venture outside—and why storing between 2 to 4 weeks of food and water in your home, rather than an outbuilding, is advisable. The absorption of radiation is cumulative and long exposure to radiation, or continued on and off exposure, can build up in the body and cause illness or death.

To combat the effects of radioactive fallout, which has been known to cause thyroid cancer, either Potassium Iodide (K1) or Potassium Iodate (K103) can be taken to coat the thyroid to protect it from the absorption of radiation. Potassium Iodide (K1) is safer to take and has fewer side-effects, but Potassium Iodate (K103) is more effective.

It's advisable to seek a physicians advise before taking either Potassium Iodide (K1) or Potassium Iodate (K103), especially for infants, children and pregnant or breastfeeding women. The signs of allergic reaction after ingesting iodine are nausea, flushing of the skin, labored breathing and fever.

If a nuclear attack occurs while you are traveling, drive directly to the nearest fallout shelter if possible. Otherwise, seek a culvert or location where you are sheltered by earth which will absorb at least a portion of the radiation.

If you are home, cover doors and windows with heavy-mill plastic sheeting and attach it securely with duct tape. Move to a basement if possible—being below ground level will protect you from the worst of the fallout. If you don't have a basement, move to the center of your home, staying as far away from windows and doors as possible.

If you believe you've been exposed to radioactive fallout, take off your clothing and secure them in a bag, storing them away from your immediate area. Rinse your hair and skin thoroughly with water, but avoid scrubbing, as this can rub fallout particles into your skin.

The following are the different levels of protection against radiation, starting with the least effective to the most effective.

Outdoors – Very little Protection
Home or Office – Medium Protection
Basement – Better Protection
Fallout Shelter –Optimal Protection

A root cellar can serve as a fallout shelter. Additionally, shelters can be constructed in a basement or dug into the ground or a hillside. The following building methods can filter out some or all radiation fallout, depending upon the strength of the blast and its proximity to you:

16 inches of solid brick
16 inches of hollow concrete blocks filled with mortar or sand
2 feet of packed earth, or 3 feet if loose earth
5 inches of steel
3 inches of led
3 feet of water

It's impossible to predict the full impact of a nuclear attack without an expert who can calculate and measure fallout and its trajectory. The spread of fallout depends upon the bombs yield and if the explosion was at ground level or detonated above ground level (an above ground level blast will spread radioactive fallout further).

Wind plays a role in the spread of fallout as well; its direction, and the velocity of prevailing winds that carry the plume. It's possible for radioactive fallout to spread for hundreds or thousands of miles and have long-lasting health ramifications for anyone exposed. On the other hand, it's possible for the majority of damage from a blast to be contained within a 15-mile radius. Rain and snowfall will spread fallout by collecting radioactive particles from the atmosphere and depositing it on the ground, which can create hotspots.

If an announcement is made of an impending nuclear blast, and if there is time, bring food, water, clothing, hygiene supplies, medical supplies– including prescription medicine–bedding, a camp toilet, a flashlight, extra batteries and an emergency radio to your safe location. An emergency radio will keep you apprised of breaking news and alert you when it's safe to go outdoors. The exact length of time you will need to remain inside is impossible to predict, but a general rule of thumb is 2 weeks, or longer. Time-lines will vary depending upon the magnitude of the blast and your proximity to the blast.

Pets should be kept indoors. Air conditioning and heating systems should be turned off to avoid drawing outside air into your home that could contain radioactive particulates.

After the blast, it's okay to consume canned or boxed food and food that has been stored in buckets with protective lids. Wipe cans off before opening them and be sure to keep your hands and the area under your fingernails clean to avoid transferring fallout material to the food. Fruits with an outer protection like bananas or oranges can be consumed, but wipe them clean and carefully peel before eating.

Water is safe to drink as long as it was kept covered. Water from a covered well should be safe to drink, but if you are unsure whether or not well water was contaminated with fallout, refer to Chapter 4, *Water: Gathering, Storing & Purification* under Fallout Purification. If you rely on municipal water, listen for Emergency Broadcasts that will inform you if the water in your area is safe to drink, or if it must be purified. Never rely upon a water purifier to rid water of fallout. Open bodies of water like a lake, stream or a pond should be assumed to be unsafe and must be purified as described in Chapter 4, *Water: Gathering, Storing & Purification* under *Fallout Purification*.

Contact with radioactive particles may lead to burning of the skin within a few hours. You cannot spread radiation to others except through vomiting soon after exposure. The signs of serious radiation illness is sore throat, loss of appetite, hair loss, paleness, bleeding gums, diarrhea, and bruising. If you have any of these symptoms, seek medical attention if possible.

## If You Must Flee

When people grow desperate for food, water and medical supplies, when there is no way to heat homes, or fill the tanks of vehicles, or purchase goods or services, some areas will become powder kegs, where staying under the radar will be the best option. But if for any reason staying under the radar isn't enough, leaving may be your only choice.

It's possible that you may need to vacate your home, if only for a short period of time. Looters and vandals will likely comb an area, grab what they can, and move on.

Choosing a get-away location should be done well before it's needed. Becoming familiar with the area; the routes in and out, whether is has a water source (which should be within easy walking distance to your chosen location), fishing, wild game and wild edible food will tell you if has survival potential.

Consider burying caches at this location if it meets your criteria. It will buy you time until you're able to return to your home.

If you're not used to camping, now is an excellent time to develop those skills, including cooking with a camp stove or over a fire pit.

Many of the extra items suggested in Chapter 9, *72-Hour Emergency Kits, Decoys & Caching Supplies* will be needed if you must flee. Items like an animal snare, a water bucket, a camp stove, cooking supplies, extra food, hygiene products, a towel and washcloth, extra clothing, clothesline and clothespins to hang laundry and alternative lighting may seem like overkill if you're simply thinking in terms of a 72-Hour Kit to get you from work to home, but it represents a lifeline should you be forced to vacate your home for safety reasons.

## Wild, Edible Food

Wild edible plants, grasses, weeds, and flowers abound in the city, the country, and forests, but most people are unaware that much of what we may view as landscaping eye candy or unappealing blights in yards and abandoned city lots is edible. Today we view dandelions and clover as a nuisance weed that we must rip out of the lawns with frustrating regularity, but during the Great Depression dandelions and clover were sometimes served as a meal while people struggled to put food on the table. Long before there were drug stores, wild plants and herbs served as life-saving medicines, poultices, and tonics. Tea made from willow bark was used to reduce fevers, and the leaves of yarrow were gathered to control blood loss. These natural medicinal cures will regain popularity if ever pharmacies are forced to close their doors.

A thorough book on wild edible plants specific to your region should be packed in your 72-Hour Emergency Kit. It should include a color photograph of edible plants, weeds and herbs as well as a color photograph and a description of any poisonous look-alike that may exist.

Practice identifying edible plants that grow in your area until you are confident you can identify edible plants, berries and mushrooms from possible poisonous look-alikes.

## Gardening Is Possible, Even If You Must Flee To The Wilderness

The Native Americans used a method called the Three Sisters to grow corn, beans and squash. The brilliance of planting this way is that it took little room to grow, and the plants did most of the work as each plant provided something unique to the other: the climbing beans utilized the corn stalk to wrap itself around to gain sunlight; the beans captured nitrogen from the air, which enriched the corn after the first years harvest; squash, which sends long vines, remains close to the ground, providing natural weed control, and the shade provided by the large squash leaves helps keep the ground moist.

Nutritionally, these three foods; corn, beans and squash provide protein, carbohydrates and vitamins and enabled the Native Americans to survive while eating the lean meat of wild game. This is critical in more ways than you might expect, as eating too much lean meat can be deadly, which we'll discuss in Chapter 13, *Long-Term Survival.*

## How To Grow A Three Sisters Garden

Build several flat-topped mounds close together, with each mound approximately 12 inches high and 20 inches around. In the center of each of the mounds plant several maze seeds close together. Once the maze has grown approximately 6 inches tall it's time to plant beans and squash–altering them: beans, then squash, then beans and squash . . . and so on.

## How to Survive Animal Attacks

Spending time in a wilderness setting increases the odds of coming into close proximity with wild animals. There may be times when you are able to avoid confrontation, and times when an animal's aggression will force you to defend yourself. It is likely that should food resources dwindle, animals who typically avoid humans may become more aggressive.

Learn what predators live in your area, and know how to recognize their tracks and their spore, so if you were to spot any telltale signs, you can avoid an encounter by retreating.

**Feral Dogs:** Personally, I view feral dogs as being one of the biggest problems that we are likely to encounter post-disaster as pet owners are forced to turn their pets loose when they can no longer feed them. This problem will be experienced in urban, rural and wilderness settings alike. Although there are no hard numbers available on the feral dog problem in the U.S., it is estimated there are approximately 200 million feral dogs in the world. Already in the U.S. animal control is unable to stay on top of the feral dog population due to a lack of funds and manpower.

Dog repellant or a weapon is the best defense against a feral dog attack. A weapon can be something as simple as a baseball bat. You are more likely to encounter a feral dog after dusk and early morning. If you encounter a feral dog, turn to the side. Facing a dog head-on puts you in the position to attack in their eyes, and they may react to that threat aggressively. Remain as calm as possible. Do not wave your arms in an attempt to ward off an attack, as this can have the opposite effect.

Look for higher ground, such as a tree that can be climbed, but do not turn your back as you make your way to safety. If you are unable to get to higher ground, and the dog attacks, defend yourself by going for the eyes with your thumbs, or land a hard blow to the throat or ribs to incapacitate it long enough for you to get away.

**Bear:** The smell of food will attract a bear. Never leave food near a campsite or in a tent. When storing food, cache it in a tree away from your location, or cache it in the ground, away from your immediate area until it's needed. A bear's sense of smell is over 2,000 times greater than a humans. They will detect the smell of food if buried or cached in a tree, but it's better to lose food than to risk being seriously injured.

If you are in an area that's known to have bears, make noise. Most bears will retreat from the sound of humans. Getting near or between a cub and a sow, or coming in close proximity to a kill are the two most dangerous situations to be in.

If you encounter a bear, never run. Running makes you prey in their eyes and can trigger an attack. Back up slowly and remove yourself from the area. Do not make eye contact with the bear, as this will be interpreted as a challenge.

The best defense against a bear attack is a gun. If all you have is pepper spray, aim at the bears face inside the range of 25 feet.

If you encounter an aggressive brown bear and have nowhere to run, drop to the ground and play dead while protecting your head with your hands and your stomach by tucking your legs against your torso. Stay in this position for up to 20 minutes after the bear leaves before getting up, as brown bear are known to lie in wait for signs of movement.

If you encounter a black bear, the rules are far different. Make yourself look as big as possible. Wave your arms and shout. If the bear charges, fight back, just as you would a large dog. Aim for its sensitive snout, using whatever has the potential to inflict pain like a large rock or a stick and stand your ground.

**Coyote:** There have only been two reported deaths in the U.S. caused by a coyote attack. Both of the victims were adults. However, there have been numerous attacks on small children by coyotes which involved their being bitten, and in several reported cases, a coyote attempted to drag a child off, but was stopped by a parent or another adult. While hiking, keep children near you, and do not allow them to lag behind or get ahead. There have been cases where a coyote has entered a tent or a backyard and attacked an adult while they slept. Keep food away from your campsite and tent to avoid drawing a coyote's attention.

Coyotes are usually no larger than 35 pounds, so a hard kick to the ribs should put an end to the attack–it only takes 75 pounds of pressure for a kick to crack the ribs of a coyote.

If the coyotes natural prey were to be hunted into scarcity during a prolonged crisis, be prepared for coyotes to become bolder with regard to attacks on humans.

**Moose:** Of all the dangerous animals you may encounter in the wild, moose come in at number five, so don't be fooled by their slow, lumbering appearance–Moose can charge at 35 miles an hour! Never come between a calf and a cow. If you encounter a moose, and you don't have a gun to defend yourself with, climb a tree or get behind something large enough to avoid being trampled such a large boulder or a thicket of trees.

Don't bother puffing yourself up to look larger, or waving your arms, yelling, or stomping because these actions will not intimidate a moose. Moose are unpredictable and they are easily startled. Either shoot or climb a tree, and if you must back up to get to a tree, do so slowly, avoiding direct eye contact.

**Mountain Lion/Cougar:** When hiking in lion country, the bigger the group the better. Make noise as you travel. Cougars will usually choose to slip away when they hear humans. Here is an animal that you *do* want to make eye contact with. Make yourself appear as large and intimidating as possible. Wave your arms, speaking as loud and as firmly as possible.

Cougars are known to attack children. If you are hiking with children keep them close to you and if an attack is imminent, make sure they do not run, as it will trigger an attack. Never turn your back on a cougar.

If attacked, fight back while protecting your head and neck-this is the region where they typically attack their prey.

**Wild Boar:** Attacks from wild boars are fairly rare, but the male boar's razor sharp tusks, their sharp teeth and the fact that they can charge from the bush without warning has gained the respect of many who share their territory. Expert advice gives two options; shoot them or climb out of their reach as quickly as possible. Avoid making eye contact with a wild boar and forget about trying to make yourself look larger, or yelling, as these actions will not intimidate them. Wild boars have an ornery disposition, can run up to 30 miles an hour, and can weigh as much as 300 pounds.

As with most wild animals, getting too near their young is often what spurs an attack. When attacking, a boar will raise its head, and once it connects with its victim, it jerks its head down and then back up, using its tusks (four in all) to inflict maximum damage. A sow charges with mouth open and uses its sharp teeth.

If attacked by a wild boar, wounds can include broken bones and deep lacerations that may require extensive stitches. Wounds must be treated with antibiotics.

**Wolf:** Wolf attacks are rare. One of the best ways to avoid attracting a wolf is by keeping your camp site and tent free of food. Wolves are not particularly afraid of humans and have been known to wander into a camp site to help themselves to whatever food they can find. If a wolf is spotted nearby your campsite keep a fire going as wolves are wary of fire.

Wolves are more likely to attack a child, so never let children walk ahead or behind the adults in the group. If you are approached by a wolf do not make eye contact or show your teeth, as either will be viewed as a challenge. Do not run or turn your back on a wolf. If there is a tree nearby, climb it.

Make yourself appear as large as possible, waving your arms and opening your coat. If you have a backpack, hoist it over your head to make yourself appear larger. If you are attacked, and do not have a gun available to defend yourself, stand your ground, fighting back with whatever you have available; a rock, a stick, or a knife, taking advantage of their sensitive snout by striking it with whatever is on hand to inflict pain.

# Chapter 13

## LONG-TERM SURVIVAL

Once you have put aside basic preparedness goods and food storage, you may discover you enjoy living a more self-sufficient lifestyle. The stress of having only a few days food in the pantry will be a distant memory. In its place is the peace of mind of knowing, no matter what, your family will get by. Instead of having to run to the grocery store for something as simple as a can of corn or a spice you've run out of, it can be "borrowed" from food storage and replaced on your next trip to the grocers. Not only will this save gas money and valuable time, but the freedom it represents is incredible!

If you find yourself wanting to climb the next rung of self-sufficiency like many preppers do, you may decide to continue your preparedness efforts. In reality, there is no way to know how long a crisis may last. An economic collapse could easily last for a decade like the Great Depression did. It's for certain that many in the financial world have been sounding the alarm that what's coming could make the crash of 2008 seem tame in comparison.

Preparing for a protracted crisis requires thinking in terms of one year or more of food storage and the supplies to grow and tend a garden. You will also need a way to preserve the overflow from the garden. The importance of gardening and preserving the bounty will become clearer with the following subjects: *Understanding Protein Poisoning* and *Wild Game Scarcity*, which may not be popular with those planning to hunt for a substantial portion of their food needs, but it's better to go into preparedness knowing all of the facts.

## Understanding Protein Poisoning (Also Known As Rabbit Starvation)

Protein Poisoning can occur when a large portion of a person's diet consists of lean meat like that of a rabbit or caribou, although any wild game can yield lean meat when a sufficient food supply isn't available and the animal's body begins to cannibalize fat and muscle for survival.

Today, we don't hear about this condition because American diets are balanced. However, if the nation is ever thrown into a long-term crisis, and people turn to wild edible foods to survive, wild game will suffer a shortage of the food they depend upon. This could easily lead to lean muscle mass of wild game.

Although fat-free diets are currently in vogue, the fact is our bodies need 60 Grams of fat per day. This is why many many preparedness sites recommend items like tuna fish and sardines packed in oil rather than water, peanut butter, mayonnaise, olive oil, coconut oil, corn, whole grains, cheese, canned milk, eggs, chocolate, brown rice, nuts, and freeze-dried and canned meat like beef, ham and chicken. Simply put, they provide the fats and calories our bodies need to stay healthy. Caloric requirements go up with an increased workload, and that definitely applies to the added work we will be required to do during a long-term crisis.

A diet consisting predominately of lean meats will lead to malnutrition that exhibit with the following symptoms; fatigue, diarrhea, low blood pressure, low heart rate and headache and can lead to death.

The human liver can metabolize only 285 to 365 grams of protein each day and the kidneys cannot process large amounts of urea (a byproduct of protein cannibalism of the animal) from the bloodstream. To safely eat lean meats requires including a diet of fruits, vegetables and carbohydrates, along with eating the organs of the animal that supplies fat, which Native Americans and Eskimos have practiced for centuries.

## Wild Game Scarcity

There is another reason why depending upon wild game as a main food source could backfire, which I have never seen discussed on survival or preparedness sites, but it's an extremely important part of the puzzle that you should be aware of.

Years ago, I asked a seasoned Alaskan Fish and Game Warden about the number of wild game versus the human population. Specifically, I asked him if the number of wild game could support the protein demands of the U.S. population during a collapse. Unfortunately, he didn't hesitate when he stated that the game would be hunted out for the most part within six months to a year. The larger game that survives the onslaught of hunters will have remained on mountain ranges and deep in the wilderness–game that will be extremely difficult to locate and pack in once hunted.

Unfortunately, hard numbers were not kept on wildlife population and their possible depletion during the Great Depression, but many individual accounts described game like deer and wild turkeys to have been nearly hunted out.

Today, ATV's, night vision goggles, and sophisticated weaponry will likely lead to hunting on a much larger scale and some who will be hunting game will have zero education about gun safety.

The U.S. population totals 311 million people, yet the deer population in the U.S. is estimated to be between 24 to 30 million. For elk, the estimated population is 1 million, for black bear the estimate is 300,000 and 30,000 for brown bear, which are predominantly dispersed between Canada and Alaska. Caribou range throughout Alaska and Canada, numbering approximately 300,000. Moose are distributed throughout the northern portion of the U.S., and Canada, which total 300,000 and the mountain goat population is estimated to be around 100,000, with their habitat spread between

Washington, Idaho, Colorado, Montana, Utah, Nevada, Oregon, Texas, South Dakota and Canada. Wild boar are concentrated in Alabama, California, Florida and Texas and their numbers are estimated to be approximately 5 million. Wild turkey numbers are approximately 7 million throughout the U.S.

Clearly, the demographics of popular game found in the U.S. will not support the protein needs of the population, and it can be assumed that within six months to one year, larger wild game could be hunted out as was reported during The Great Depression. If you plan to hunt for survival, be sure to put aside plenty of bulk food or MRE's and store garden seed for continued survival.

There remains smaller game we haven't covered yet. The beaver population in the U.S. is estimated to be around 6 to 12 million, and a "guesstimate" of the squirrel population throughout the U.S. is 1.12 trillion. The number of wild rabbit and hare, raccoon and opossum in the U.S. is not known, but clearly their ability to adapt to rural and urban environments make them good candidates for snaring in a survival situation.

## Gardening

Garden seed is nothing short of an insurance policy against hunger. Should a crisis be long-lasting, growing a garden will allow you to avoid going hungry, but garden seed isn't created equally, so it's important to understand the differences.

Hybrid seed is the result of cross-pollinating plants to produce high yeild crops, but the seed from these crops are not dependable as they have a disappointing failure rate. Although hybrid seed has been used in agriculture for decades, hybrids tend to produce bland fruits and vegetables with little of the flavor and distinctness that fruits and vegetables once offered. Although hybrid seed is available at many hardware, feed and seed, grocers, and nurseries, they are meant to be purchased each growing season. That's not a workable plan if ever there comes a time when retailers are forced to close their doors.

Heirloom seed produces true to type crop because they are open-pollinated. In other words, they haven't been altered from what the Good Lord intended. Heirloom seed is what our grand-parents and great-grandparents planted, and the fruits and veg-etables grown from the seed yields the distinct flavor of each fruit and vegetable. If you doubt this, I challenge you to a taste test. Go to a farmer's market and purchase an heirloom tomato. On your way home, pick up a store-bought hot-house tomato. Slice into each and take your own taste test. The difference will astound you. And to think that since the industrial revolution we've been denied the hardiness and flavor of heirloom fruits and vegetables!

Another positive of heirloom seed is that you will have a much better selection of plants to choose from. That same heir-loom tomato sold at a farmers market has dozens of "cousins" and here's where a little homework will pay off. Be sure to buy heirloom seed that grows best in your specific climate zone. Yes, it's convenient to order one-size-fits-all heirloom seed that come in a handy tube. But your garden will reward you if you do the research and buy what's happiest growing in your region.

Certain fruits, vegetables and beans grow better in a hot cli-mate zone. Others do better in a milder climate zone. If you live in a northern climate zone, where the growing season may be short, it's important to do your homework on which type of seed will produce the best fruits, vegetables, beans and grain in a short growing season. There are many heirloom seed com-panies that offer individual seed which will allow you to choose varieties that will thrive in whatever climate zone you live in.

A frequently asked question on prepper sites is whether or not it's okay to freeze garden seed. The answer is no. Freezing can damage garden seed. Instead, store them in a cool, dark, moisture free location.

The down side of heirloom seed is that although many heir-looms have adapted to disease, pests and weather conditions for various climate zones, the seed may not be as hardy as hybrid vari-eties. This is something you can ask about when purchasing seed.

It is important to know what garden pests and diseases are prevalent in your area, so you can put aside the tools to combat them. If you have never grown a garden, you may be surprised to discover the many home remedies that will rid the garden of pests while avoiding pesticides. Check with local gardeners, or community gardens, or purchase a book specific to your climate zone to learn how to control garden pests and disease.

Gardening can be done in several ways: Square foot and containerized for those who have limited space, and garden plots for those who have yards. You may be surprised how much food you can grow in a small space! But to be successful may take a book on the type of gardening that fits best with your circumstances.

No matter if your search leads you to containerized, or square foot, or garden plot gardening, it's worthwhile buying a how-to book on seed saving, so you will be assured to have the ability to grow fruits and vegetables season after season.

Before we move on to storing the overflow from a garden, a warning about GMO seed. GMO seed is seed that has been genetically altered using recombinant DNA technology. You may have heard it refereed to as Frankenseed because it alters the DNA molecules while in vitro into a single molecule, creating a new gene that was generated from other species of plants or animals. In the end, this DNA that is transferred into an organism causes various traits that would never naturally occur in nature. Food grown with GMO seed come with a host of health concerns, not the least of which is that GMO seed is treated to resist the affects of the herbicide Round Up. Growers can then spray Round Up as liberally as they like on GMO crop that kills everything *but* plants grown from GMO seed. But at what cost to the consumer? The main ingredient in Round up is Glyphosate. Glyphosate interferes with CYP pathways and receptors that are responsible for the bodies ability to fight off infection and disease. Some researches are warning that consuming food grown from GMO seed lowers testosterone and vitamin D levels and interrupts the bodies ability to control cholesterol.

Although scientific studies link GMO seed to tumors, low birth rate, infertility, high mortality rate, and failure to thrive in mammals and amphibians, the results of these studies are not being reported to the public by mainstream media. Today, over 90% of corn, canola, cottonseed, soy and sugar beet crops are grown from GMO seed. Alfalfa, papaya, zucchini and yellow summer squash are increasingly being grown from GMO seed as well.

## Storing The Overflow From The Garden

There are a number of ways to preserve the overflow from the garden, which has been broken down here, because just as with garden seed, preserving food is never a one-size-fits-all. Have a look to see what might work best for you.

Root Cellars have become popular again as people look for a way to economically grow and preserve fruits, vegetables and grain. A root cellar is usually dug into the side of a hill, which insulates it on the top and sides, using the ambient temperature of the earth to keep foods cooler, thus protecting it from summer heat and punishing cold. You can go online in search of Do-It-Yourself root cellars that can be built from used lumber which will drastically cut the cost of building one. The food stored in root cellars must be monitored for spoilage. Root cellars work best when food is stored on floor-to-ceiling shelving, as some fruits and vegetables do better in cooler conditions while others do better stored higher, where temperature fluctuations can be as great as 10 degrees warmer. If you have a yard, root cellars can be dug straight into the ground if you don't happen to have a hillside or slope to take advantage of. Because the proper storing of fruits and vegetables is a book on its own, consider purchasing one or checking one out at your local library.

Note: If you live in a hot climate zone, check first before digging a root cellar. In certain hot climate zones, root cellars will not stay cool enough for effective food storage, and the best solution is food dehydration. If you live in an extremely cold climate zone, caution must be taken to protect foods from freezing in a root cellar. Often, digging deeper into the earth, or covering the top of the root cellar with straw, or insulating it will help avoid freezing conditions. Some homesteaders use manure in the root cellar because as manure breaks down during the decomposition process, it creates enough heat to keep the root cellar from freezing.

Food Dehydration has been utilized to preserve wild game, fish, fruits and vegetables since early man. The benefit of dehydrating food is its light-weight portability, and when dehydrating your own food, it will drastically reduce the overall cost of food storage.

Surprisingly, the dehydrating process does not reduce caloric intake, and there is no change in the fiber content. Vitamin A is mostly retained, but vitamin C is greatly reduced when drying vegetables. Thiamin, riboflavin, and niacin and minerals can be retained if the water used for re-hydration is consumed. Iron is not destroyed in the drying process.

Generally, dehydrated foods should not contain more than 5% moisture to avoid its molding, thus leading to spoilage. Whether to dehydrate meat or not must be left to the reader, for sun-drying meats is not recommended by experts due to concerns of E. coli and the possible contamination of meats when sunlight alone does not provide the heat required to kill harmful bacteria. However, the USDA advises that cooking meat to 160 degrees before dehydrating will kill E. coli.

A book on food dehydration will detail how to dehydrate food, but you can also find valuable information on the Internet. One of my favorite online sites is BackingChef.com.

This is where that saying "practice makes perfect" has never been so true. Dehydrating food is easy, but it is not without its pitfalls when you're just getting started. It's best to try it now to learn the ins and outs of proper food dehydration while it doesn't represent hunger should your first couple of attempts be unsuccessful.

Check the Internet for DIY instructions to build a food dehydrator that isn't dependent upon electricity to run so you will have the means to dehydrate food, even in grid-down.

Home Canning is another way to preserve food, but safety guidelines must be followed carefully to avoid botulism, which can be deadly. An inexpensive home canning manual such as the Ball Complete Book of Home Preserving offers guidelines to safely home can low-acidic foods such as meats and vegetables using the pressure canning method (there is an important difference between a pressure cooker and a pressure caner) and the boiling water method for foods that are acidic such as fruit.

The challenge for home canning foods during grid-down is the need to maintain temperature for the boiling method, or PSI (pounds per pressure) for the pressure caner method. However, if you are fortunate enough to own a wood cook stove, with practice and a decent supply of firewood, home canning is possible, just as our forefathers did.

Under no circumstances should improvisation be used when home canning. Using manufactured jars like that of a pickle jar doesn't allow for a proper seal to keep the food safe.

Glass canning jars can be re-used as long as they don't have cracks or chips along the rim that won't allow a proper seal. Lids are one time use only, so it is important to make sure to stock plenty of them. When you feel you have enough set aside, consider adding more, because in a long-term crisis, canning may be necessary season after season. Tattler reusable lids are a solution that many preppers turn to for home canning.

Note: Toss any home canned food that looks spoiled when opened, or gives off an odor or foams when heated.

## Alternate Modes Of Transportation

If a crisis takes down the grid for a protracted period of time, fuel will be difficult or impossible to find, and if you are able to find it, the cost will likely be astronomical. This is why having an alternate mode of transportation that is not dependent upon fuel is important.

A sturdy mountain bike or a road bike is a worthwhile consideration to lighten the load of having to walk long distances. Used bikes in good condition can be found at moving and garage sales, secondhand stores and craigslist. If you go this route, be sure to pick up extra parts such as replacement tubes, tires, chains, brakes, pedals, wheels and cables, along with the tools to keep up with necessary repairs.

If you live on or near a waterway, a non-motorized boat such as a rowboat or a canoe may be a solution. The smaller, the better, as portability will be key to avoid theft while opportunists are on the lookout for alternative transportation.

If you live on property where keeping a horse is possible, and you are willing and able to care for one–including growing their feed–the problem of transportation can be solved. It would take an incredible commitment, but if you live on acreage and have been flirting with the idea of a horse, it may be worth another look.

If you live in a rural location where storing a quantity of gasoline or diesel is possible, investing in a motorcycle or 4-wheeler can be a temporary solution. The downside is the expense and the fact that once fuel storage has been exhausted you will be on foot unless you have provided for a back-up.

## Extending The Shelf Life Of Fuel

Gasoline that has a quality stabilizer like PRI-G added to it can last up to two years. However, this varies depending upon weather conditions–gas deteriorates quickly in heat. Gasoline and diesel should be stored in a cool, dark location. Diesel has a much longer shelf life of around 10 years when a stabilizer like PRI-D is added.

If you plan to store a large quantity of gasoline or diesel fuel, a long-term option is to store it in a 55-gallon steel drum in the ground. Before filling the barrel, it should be treated with a rust inhibitor or with a liberal layer of roofing tar to protect it from corrosion. Lower the barrel into the ground below the frost line--a shaded area will protect it from sunlight which will speed oxidation, shortening the shelf life of fuel. Fill the barrel to the top to reduce condensation and make sure the lid is on tight before covering the hole with a board. If you want to camouflage its location from potential looters, the board can be covered with leaves, twigs, or yard clippings.

## Navigation

As mentioned previously, GPS may not be operational during a nationwide emergency. GPS satellites are owned, maintained and controlled by the U.S. Department of Defense. In a national emergency the public use of GPS can come under the umbrella of "Selective Availability" and be made unavailable when national defense must remain a top priority.

A strong CME or EMP has the potential to disable GPS. Logistically, heavily treed areas, or being inside a building can block GPS signals in all but the more expensive, multi-channel GPS systems, but even then, there are no guarantees they will work.

As a country, we have become heavily dependent upon technology, but a crisis that lasts for an extended period of time will have the nation turning to old-school staples like a compass, street maps, and topographical maps which should cover points A to B, no matter how many maps this entails. If you find yourself having to travel a long distance on foot, you will thank yourself for planning ahead.

## Communications

Talking on the phone is so basic that it's hard to imagine a time when we won't be able to pick up the phone to make a call.

In a disaster that impacts the electrical grid, communications will be possible with the use of two-way radios. Coverage varies, so check before purchasing them, but even a basic 2-way radio will offer around two miles of coverage. Topography plays a part in coverage, however. Mountainous areas and valleys can disrupt line-of-sight capabilities, as can an operators being inside a building that blocks the signal.

Where 2-way radios will allow you to communicate between family members or groups, Ham radio is capable of keeping you informed locally, across the nation, and even globally. However, operating a Ham Radio requires taking the Amateur Radio License Exam. To continue to use a Ham Radio during a blackout, solar or battery back-up or a combination of both will be necessary. For advise on how to get started, get in touch with a ham operators group near you, or go online.

## Hygiene

If ever a long-term crisis involves a downed electrical grid, it will impact the utilities we rely upon. Water delivery will cease once municipal water facilities exceed their emergency power back up– generally between three days to one week. This must be planned ahead for because life without running water and flushing toilets would be extremely difficult without having a back-up plan in place.

Sanitary and storm sewage controls will also cease to function after municipality emergency power back-up is exhausted, which generally means you can expect to experience evidence of system failure within a short period of time. Once sanitary and storm sewage processing becomes non-operational, it is possible that homes will experience sewage back-up, which can be a health risk. Personally, I would place the issue of dealing with foul odors associated with a sewer back-up side by side with the health risks!

Because of the importance of avoiding a sewage back-up into the home, the step-by-step instructions to plug a sewage line was posted below for a second time:

http://www.rentonwa.gov/uploadedFiles/Emergencies/AJLS/ How_To_plug_A_Sewer_Line.pdf

Unlike municipal sewer systems, septic tanks are set up for individual homes and are not dependent upon the electrical grid. Septic tanks generally need to be emptied every year to three years, depending upon the capacity and usage. It helps to use toilet paper designed for septic tanks that dissolves in water, but it's wise to have septic tanks drained regularly. Keep a back-up like a simple, $20 camp toilet, just in case. Using gravity to empty a toilet into a septic (pouring 1 gallon of water into the bowl is usually sufficient) will place a drain on your water supply.

Some who live off-grid or in rural cabins use a gray water system. It's a simple method of diverting water draining from bathtubs, sinks and sometimes a washing machine to empty onto the ground or held in water containment barrels. The gray water can then be used to water a garden or other secondary uses. When storing gray water for re-use, it's important to avoid releasing strong chemicals or harsh detergents down drains that will end up in gray water barrels.

Unfortunately, many areas in the U.S. don't allow gray water systems. However, in the midst of a crisis it doesn't take a stretch of the imagination to believe that rules against gray water drainage and collection would be forgiven when the re-use of gray water will reduce the strain placed upon fresh drinking water supplies. If setting up for gray water interests you, talk to a plumber who can instruct you on how it's done and what supplies and manual tools you would need to have on hand to make the conversion.

Being without a flushing toilet can be overcome if you plan ahead. Here are a few solutions:

Camp Toilets are inexpensive (around $20) and are workable solutions for those who live in the city or the country. Their use has few requirements; heavy plastic bags to line them and a shovel to dig a hole to dispose of the contents as needed. For sanitary reasons, even a deep hole should be covered with a layer of dirt after depositing the contents of the liners to stop disease from being spread by fly's and other insects.

Look for a camp toilet with a seat for comfort of use and a collapsible lid to cut down on odors. It's worth having several camp toilets set aside for larger families or groups.

Compost Toilets that don't require electric power or water are available. The cost starts at around $1,500 and goes up from there, depending upon the capacity you will need. Some compost toilet models use small wind turbine ventilators for power, others can be hooked to solar power, some work without power and are vented to the outdoors, some require the use of mulch, or sawdust and so on. As you can see, there are any number of configurations available for compost toilets, but the major drawback is the cost and restrictions for those who live in condos, or apartments, where their installations would be impractical.

Outhouses are fairly inexpensive to build. They are suitable for rural areas and suburban locations (basically, anywhere there is a yard available). Most areas prohibit outhouses, but regulations may be lifted when the alternative is unsanitary conditions that can lead to disease. If you are concerned about becoming the neighborhood "pit stop," an outhouse can always be disguised as a shed or a playhouse. Go online for building ideas and set aside the materials that will be needed to build one, including 2 X 4's, plywood, nails, screws, and roofing materials. It is important to keep an outhouse hole protected from fly's to control the spread of disease, so be sure to pick up the materials to build a contained sitting area and a toilet seat that can be closed when the outhouse is not in use.

Note: For those planning to build an outhouse, it's worthwhile keeping a camp toilet or two on hand for middle-of-the-night nature calls and for children who may have to adjust to using an outhouse.

Bathing, laundry & general clean-up will require a work-around. Tuff Stuff tubs are an excellent choice for bathing and laundry. They can be stored outdoors and can withstand freezing weather and summer heat without cracking. A 50-gallon Tuff Stuff tub that measures 41" X 30" X 15" costs approximately $89 on Amazon.

Hand washing laundry is easier to do with the aid of a hand agitator or washboard. They are available at Amazon and Lehman's. You will also need clothesline and clothespins. To express the water from laundry, an old-school wringer style mop works well.

For a recipe to make laundry soap that will save money and won't take up a ton of storage (you can make it as you go), go to the Duggar Family website and look up Michelle Duggar's liquid laundry soap recipe.

Stock up on a generous supply of body soap, shampoo, conditioner, body lotion, shave cream, razors and the like. And, don't forget to include dish soap to the list!

## Bartering

There may come a time when bartering becomes the medium of exchange for goods and services. Skill-sets and simple tangibles like a bucket for water collection or a pair of magnified reading glasses could easily eclipse designer labels if life as we know it suddenly requires function over bling.

The following skills-sets will be in high demand during a protracted crisis:

- Animal Husbandry
- Blacksmith
- Candle-making
- Carpenter
- Childcare
- Cook
- Dentist
- Fisherman
- Gardner/Grower
- Glazier
- Home Canning/Food Dehydration
- Hunter
- Holistic Healing
- Knitting
- Mechanic
- Midwife
- Physician
- Welder
- Well Digger
- Seamstress/Mending
- Soap making
- Tree-Felling/ Wood Gathering
- Weaving

The leverage of having the right bartering goods will be enormous during a protracted crisis. Many basic goods can be purchased in gross at dollar stores. Buying high-ticket items like generators or weapons might not be the best strategy because of the risk involved. Once you've revealed that you have prep goods of value, it could open the door to theft.

Bartering Goods

- Ammunition
- Axes
- Batteries
- Blade Sharpener, All
- Bleach
- Body Lotion
- Body Soap
- Bolts, Assorted Sizes
- Bungee Cords
- Camp Stoves
- Candles
- Can Openers
- Carbon Monoxide Detectors

- Cast Iron Cookware
- Cold Weather Clothing: Children & Adult–All
- Clothesline
- Clothespins
- Color Pencils
- Cooking Oil
- Coolers
- Crayons
- Dental Floss
- Dental Emergencies Manual
- Dental Supplies, All
- Diapers, Cloth
- Diaper Pins
- Diaper Rash Ointment
- Dish Soap
- Duct Tape
- Egg Beater, Manual
- Egg Timer, Manual
- Fire Alarms
- Fire Extinguishers
- First Aid Manual
- Flour
- Food Storage Buckets
- Food Storage Containers
- Fuel, All
- Games–Boardgames, Card Games & Dice
- Garbage Bags
- Garden Gloves
- Garden Seed
- Garden Tools
- Hand Carts
- Hatchets
- Lamp Wicks
- Lanterns
- Lantern Mantles
- Laundry Agitator, Manual
- Laundry Soap
- Lighters
- Lumber, All
- Matches
- Medical Supplies, All
- Medicine–All
- Milk, Canned
- Milk, Powdered
- Nails, Assorted Sizes
- Notepads
- Nylon Rope
- Oil Lamps
- Pencils
- Pens
- Pepper
- Plastic Wrap
- Printer Paper
- Reading Glasses
- Rubber Pants, (Infant)
- Salt
- Screws, Assorted Sizes
- Scrub Pads
- Scrubbing Powder
- Shampoo
- Spice, All
- Sugar
- Tape
- Tarps

- Tin Foil
- Toilet Paper
- Toilets, Portable
- Tools (Manual), All
- Toothbrushes
- Toothpaste
- Twine
- Vaseline

- Washers, Assorted Sizes
- Washtubs–Any Size
- Water Jugs
- Wheelbarrows
- Work Gloves
- Yeast
- Zip Lock Bags

The above is only a partial list. I'm sure you can think of many items that weren't included. Going into debt when investing in bartering goods isn't necessary. Some of the simplest items like matches and bleach will be worth their weight in gold! If you are interested in venturing into larger investments, camping supplies like tents, backpacks and water purifiers will offer excellent bartering leverage.

Ammunition is a wild card. Although it's a popular item to stock for bartering because it will be in huge demand, it has the potential to invite theft. One rule of thought is to barter ammunition with locals who you know you can trust for safety reasons.

# Chapter 14

## A REVIEW OF PREPAREDNESS GOODS & MATERIALS

To get an idea of the preparedness goods and materials you may want to have on hand takes observation. Take just one 24-hour period and note what was essential to your everyday life. For instance, did you turn on lights, or cook, or pick up the phone to call a family member or a friend? Did you shower, or use the facilities, or wash your hands, or wash dishes or do laundry? Did you watch TV or listen to the radio to catch up on what was going on in your vicinity and the world?

Now consider what it would be like to be without those conveniences. When you plan ahead for the unexpected, you pave the way for a smoother transition for life without the conveniences we take for granted today.

Once basic food storage and preparedness goods are put aside, a luxury like a generator to run appliances, tools and miscellaneous devices will make life easier, but if a generator is pivotal to your preparedness plan for grid down, keep in mind that this convenience will be in place only as long as your fuel supply lasts- -or in the case of a solar generator, as long as sunlight is available.

The next several pages provide a quick overview of the goods you may want to have on hand. Please don't let it overwhelm you! Items can be purchased over time as money allows.

If you are on a tight budget, start with food and water storage, then begin to add medical and hygiene supplies, and go from there. Bartering goods like salt and reading glasses and household bleach can be purchased for next to nothing at Dollar Stores, but until you have the basics in place, they can wait.

There are no rules for preparedness. Each person will find a pace that works best for their needs and pocket book. Adding to critical goods one week or one month at a time, keeping in mind that each item you purchase, will bring you closer to your goal of preparedness.

## When Murphy's Law Calls

Murphy's Law applies to preparedness. Should there be just one can opener available to open hundreds of cans of food, it *will* fail, which would be extremely exasperating when for a few dollars, you could have had several spares on hand.

You may have heard the expression; Two is one and one is none, which simply means that without having a back-up for a critical item, and it breaks, you will be left with nothing. That may be okay for something like a can of hair spray, but it would make for untold hardship should it be a can opener or an ax that is critical for survival.

If ever retail establishments and services shut down for any length of time, I believe barterable goods and skill-sets will be the new currency. Whenever I'm asked about stockpiling gold or silver, I suggest first putting aside food and water, then critical preparedness goods, and after the basics have been provided for, bartering items should follow. With any remaining funds, investing in junk silver will make purchasing barter goods and services simpler. There's absolutely nothing wrong with protecting wealth, but you can't eat silver or gold, nor can you heat a home, or light a fire, or read by it.

The following preparedness lists were condensed from previous chapters and compiled in alphabetical order for a quick reference guide.

## 72-Hour Emergency Kit

- Baby Food, Formula, Cloth Diapers, Diaper Pins, Rubber Pants
- Batteries & Solar Charger
- Battery Run, Wind-Up, or Solar Powered Emergency Radio
- Body Soap
- Boots, Hiking
- Camp-Size Water Purifier
- Canteen/Water Bottle
- Cash
- Clothing
- Compass
- Duct Tape
- Edible Plants Reference Book
- Feminine Products
- First Aid Manual
- Fishing Supplies
- Hatchet/Ax
- Headlamp
- Hunting Knife
- Important Documents
- Lighting: Flashlight, LED/Shaker-Style, Emergency Long-Burning Candles
- Magnesium Flint & Steel Fire Starter
- Maps: Street & Topographical
- Matches/Waterproof Matches/Lighters
- Medical Supplies/ First Aid Kit & Prescription Medicines
- MRE'S
- Nylon Rope
- Poncho, Rain
- Prescription Medicine
- Rope
- Shovel, Folding
- Sleeping Bag
- Swiss Army Knife
- Tarp
- Tent
- Toilet Paper
- Toothbrush
- Toothpaste
- Two-Way Radios
- Water
- Water Purifier, Back-Up/ Replacement Filters
- Wire

## 72-Hour Emergency Kit, Advanced

- Animal Snares/Traps
- Bucket, With Handle
- Camp Cookware
- Portable Camp Stove & Fuel
- Can Opener
- Canned Milk or Powdered Milk
- Canned/Dehydrated/ Freeze-Dried Food
- Clothespins & Clothesline
- Clothing: Socks, Underwear & Cold Weather Gear, If Applicable
- Cooking Utensils
- Cooler
- Dish & Laundry Soap
- Dishes (metal)/ Paper Plates
- Duffel Bag
- Lantern, Lantern Fuel & Lantern Socks
- Newspaper & Lint/ Vaseline-Coated Cotton Balls (Fire Starters)
- Oven Mitt
- Shampoo
- Towel & Washcloth
- Water (Extra) & Water Jug
- Weapon/Ammo
- Wet Towelettes

## Bartering Goods

- Ammunition
- Axes
- Batteries
- Blade Sharpener
- Bleach
- Body Lotion
- Body Soap
- Bolts, Assorted Sizes
- Bungee Cords
- Camp Stoves
- Candles
- Can Openers
- Carbon Monoxide Detectors
- Cast Iron Cookware
- Cold Weather Clothing: Children & Adult–All
- Clothesline
- Clothespins
- Color Pencils
- Cooking Oil
- Coolers
- Crayons
- Dental Floss

- Dental Emergencies Manual
- Dental Supplies, All
- Diapers, Cloth
- Diaper Pins
- Diaper Rash Ointment
- Dish Soap
- Duct Tape
- Egg Beater, Manual
- Egg Timer, Manual
- Fire Alarms
- Fire Extinguishers
- First Aid Manual
- Flour
- Food Storage Buckets
- Food Storage Containers
- Fuel, All
- Games–Boardgames, Card Games & Dice
- Garbage Bags
- Garden Gloves
- Garden Seed
- Garden Tools
- Hand Carts
- Hatchets
- Lamp Wicks
- Lanterns
- Lantern Mantles
- Laundry Agitator, Manual
- Laundry Soap
- Lighters
- Lumber, All

- Matches
- Medical Supplies, All
- Medicine–All
- Milk, Canned
- Milk, Powdered
- Nails, Assorted Sizes
- Notepads
- Nylon Rope
- Oil Lamps
- Pencils
- Pens
- Pepper
- Plastic Wrap
- Printer Paper
- Reading Glasses
- Rubber Pants, (Infant)
- Salt
- Screws, Assorted Sizes
- Scrub Pads
- Scrubbing Powder
- Shampoo
- Spice, All
- Sugar
- Tape
- Tarps
- Tin Foil
- Toilet Paper
- Toilets, Portable
- Tools (Manual), All
- Toothbrushes
- Toothpaste
- Twine
- Vaseline
- Washers, Assorted Sizes

- Washtubs–Any Size
- Water Jugs
- Wheelbarrows

- Work Gloves
- Yeast
- Zip Lock Bags

## Bulk Food Storage Needs

- Food Storage Buckets
- Heat Sealer or Iron
- Mylar Bags
- Oxygen Absorbers
- Wood Pallets (if applicable)

## Camp Gear & Critical Goods

- Anti-Gravity Water Pump
- Ax
- Back Pack
- Batteries
- Canteens
- Coffee Pot-Camping/ Percolator Style
- Coleman Style Lanterns
- Compass
- Cooking Utensils
- Dutch Oven
- Eating Utensils
- Fire Pit Tripod
- First Aid Kit
- Fishing Pole
- Flashlight-Both Battery and Shake Style
- Flint Fire Starter
- Folding Chair

- Hatchet
- Head Lamp
- Hunting Knife
- Maps
- Matches-waterproof
- Mess Kit
- Nylon Rope
- Shovel, Folding
- Sleeping mat
- Solar Lanterns
- Swiss Army Knife
- Tarps
- Tent
- Two-Way radios
- Water Bottle
- Water Canteen
- Water Containers, Collapsible
- Water Purifier-Hiker Size

## Clothing

- Children's & Infant Clothing
- Coats
- Gloves
- Hats
- Hiking Boots
- Kerchiefs
- Long Johns
- Mittens
- Neck Scarves
- Rain Boots
- Rain Poncho
- Snow Boots
- Socks-Cotton & Wool
- Sweats
- Tennis Shoes
- Underwear

## Communications

- Ham Radio
- Radio, 2-Way
- Radio, Battery Run
- Radio, Solar
- Radio, Emergency Wind-Up

## Cooking Implements

- Can Openers
- Cast Iron Dutch Oven & Cookware
- Coffee Maker-Camping, Peculator Style
- Cooking Thermometer
- Egg Beater-Manual
- Egg Timer-Manual
- Fire Pit Tripod
- Food Grinder-Manual
- Pasta Maker-Manual
- Pressure Cooker
- Reflector Oven
- Wheat Grinder-Manual

Entertainment

- Board Games
- Books
- Card Games
- Coloring Books
- Colored Marking Pens
- Construction Paper
- Crayons
- Colored Pencils
- Dice
- Finger Paints
- Hobby Items
- Notebooks & Journals
- Musical Instruments
- Outdoor Activities: Horseshoes, Badminton, Volleyball, Tether Ball, Lawn Croquet, Basket Ball, Soccer
- Paper
- Pencils
- Pens
- Play Dough
- Sheet Music

Food Preservation

- Home Canning Supplies
- Food Dehydrator
- Root Cellar
- Wild Game Curing
- Wild Game Smoker

Food Storage

- Baby Food (if applicable)
- Bulk Food
- Canned Goods
- Condiments
- Dehydrated Food
- Formula (if applicable)
- Freeze-Dried Food
- MRE's
- Spices

## Fuel

- Alcohol / Alcohol Gel/Sterno
- Briquettes
- Coleman Fuel (White Gas)
- Diesel
- Fire Wood
- Gasoline
- Kerosene
- Lamp Oil
- Propane

## Gardening

- Heirloom Garden Seed-specific to your growing zone
- Digging Spade
- Garden Stakes
- Gardening Gloves
- Hoe
- Insect Pest Control
- Mulch
- Pruners
- Rake
- Sheers
- Shovel
- Spade Fork
- Trowel
- Twine
- Wheelbarrow

## Heating & Cooking Alternatives

- Barrel Stove
- Camp stove

- Cylinder Stove
- Propane Cook Stove
- Propane Heat Stove
- Rocket Stove
- Shepherd Stoves
- Solar Oven
- Tent Stove
- Volcano Stove
- Wood-Burning Cook Stove
- Wood-Burning Heat Stove
- Wood-Burning Fireplace Insert

Hygiene & General Clean-Up

- Bleach
- Body Lotion
- Body Soap
- Camp Toilet
- Cloth Diapers, Diaper Pins & Rubber Pants
- Clothes Agitator, Manual
- Clothes Line
- Clothespins
- Conditioner
- Dental Floss
- Deodorant
- Dish Drain
- Dish Soap
- Feminine Products
- Hand Sanitizer
- Laundry detergent
- Moisturizer
- Pot Scrubbers
- Razors
- Shampoo
- Shaving Cream
- Solar Shower
- Toothbrushes
- Toothpaste
- Wash Tub, Tough Stuff/Galvanized
- Wringer-Style Mop Bucket

Large Preparedness Goods

- Burning Barrel
- Chainsaw
- Generator

- Hand Cart
- Hand Dolly
- Two-Man Tree-Felling Saw
- Tree-Felling Ax
- Wringer Washer

Lighting Basics

- Candles
- Flashlights: Battery Run, Solar, or Shake Style
- Head Lamp
- Hurricane Lamp
- Kerosene Lamp
- Lanterns & Mantles
- Oil Lamp
- Solar Lighting

Medical Supplies, Basic

- Ace Bandages
- Aloe Gel
- Antacid Medicine
- Antibacterial Soap
- Antibiotic Ointment
- Anti-Diarrhea Medicine
- Anti fungal Ointment
- Aspirin
- Baby Powder
- Band Aids
- Benadryl
- Body Lotion
- Butt Paste
- Children's Fever Reducer
- Calamine Lotion
- Cold Packs
- Condoms
- Contacts Lenses
- Contact Solution
- Dental Floss
- Diaper Rash Ointment
- Disposable Latex Gloves
- Epsom Salts
- Eye Wash
- Feminine Pads
- Glasses, Reading
- Gold Bond
- Hydrocortisone Cream
- Hydrogen Peroxide
- Ibuprofen
- Isopropyl Alcohol

- Lip Balm
- Mentholated Cough Drops
- Mosquito Repellant
- Mucinex
- Nasal Spray
- Non-latex Examination Gloves
- Penlight
- Pepto Bismol Chewable Tablets
- Pregnancy Test

- Petroleum Jelly
- Rolled Gauze
- Splinter Removal Kit
- Surgical Tape
- Sterile Gauze Pads & Non-Sterile Gauze Pads
- Sunscreen
- Thermometer
- Tylenol
- VagiCare
- Vicks VapoRub

## Medical Supplies, Advanced

- Acidophiles
- Air Cast
- Ankle Brace
- AZO Standard
- AZO Yeast
- Castor Oil
- Clove Oil
- Cohesive Bandages
- CPR Mask
- Crutches
- Dental Mirror
- Dental Probe
- Dental Wax
- Dermoplast
- Dramamine
- Elastic Gauze Bandages
- Eye Solution
- Finger Splints

- Israeli Bandages
- Kerlix Gauze Bandage Rolls
- Knee Brace
- Mole Foam
- N-95 Respirator/ Face Mask
- New Skin
- Potassium Iodide
- Saline Solution
- Sterile Swabs
- Steri-strips
- Surgical Masks
- Tea Tree Oil
- Tongue Depressors
- Tourniquet
- QuikClot

## Medical Supplies, Expert

- Ambu Bag to assist breathing–Infant, Child & Adult sizes
- Arm & Leg Splints
- Bandage Scissors
- Blood Pressure Cuff
- Central Venous Catheter Kit
- Extensive Dental Kit
- Fetal Doppler Monitor
- Kelly Forceps
- Lap Sponges
- Ringers Lactate Sterile
- Surgical Gloves
- Surgical Kit
- Sutures
- Stethoscope
- LMA Mask
- Olsen Hegar Needle Holder/Scissor Combination Forceps
- Orthopedic Casting Tape
- Pulse Oximeter

## Medical Supplies, Pandemic Care

- Alcohol-Based Handrub
- Bleach
- Disinfectant Wipes
- Duct Tape
- Full-Face Respirators
- Full Face Shields
- N-95 / N-100 Particulate Respirators
- Nitrile Gloves– regular & 12-inch length
- Rubber Pull-On Boots
- Rubber Tub
- Step-Off Mat
- Surgical Apron
- Surgical Hood / Bio Safety Hood
- Tyvek Zippered One-Piece Coveralls

<u>Navigation</u>

- Compass
- Street Maps
- Topographical Maps

<u>Odds & Ends</u>

- Ash Pail
- Batteries
- Bungee Cords, Various Sizes
- Duct Tape
- Fireplace Grate
- Fireplace Set
- Heavy Mill Plastic
- Manual Food Grinder
- Maps-Both Street & Topographical
- Nylon Rope-Various Sizes & Strengths
- Pails-Various Sizes
- Twine
- Tubs-Various Sizes

<u>Paper & Storage</u>

- Aluminum Foil
- Paper Plates
- Paper Towels
- Plastic Cups
- Plastic Garbage Bags—Various Sizes
- Plastic Wrap
- Storage Food Keepers with Lids
- Toilet Paper
- Water Storage Containers
- Zip Lock Bags – Various Sizes

## Recommended Courses, Training & Hands-On Experience

- Gardening
- Medical Emergency Training
- Tactical/Self Defense Courses
- Training Pertaining To Barter-Friendly Skill-Sets

## Reference Books

- Curing Wild Game
- Gardening–specific to your climate zone
- Home Canning
- Emergency Medical / First Aid
- Emergency Dental
- Food Dehydration
- Food Storage Related Cook Book / Recipes
- Root Cellars; How to build one & food storage overview
- Seed Saving
- Wild Edible Foods–specific to your region

## Tools (Manual) & Critical Materials

- 2 X 4's
- 4 X 6's
- Allen Wrench
- Automotive Tools & Replacement Parts
- Bolts-Assorted Sizes
- Chicken Wire
- Crescent Wrench
- Flat head Screwdrivers-Assorted Sizes
- Hammer
- Heavy Mill Plastic-Blackout & Clear
- Monkey Wrench
- Nails-Assorted Sizes
- Nuts-Assorted Sizes

- Phillips Screwdrivers-Assorted Sizes
- Players
- Plywood
- Rope
- Saw
- Screws-Assorted Sizes
- Sharpening Stone
- Shovel
- Tarps
- Washers-Assorted Sizes
- Work Gloves

## Travel (Alternative Modes)

- Horse
- Bicycle
- 4-Wheeler
- Cross-Country Motorcycle
- Street Motorcycle
- Rowboat
- Canoe

## Water Storage & Purification

- Bleach
- Buckets With Handles
- Iodine
- Ion
- Manual Well Pump
- Purification Tablets
- Water Collection Cylinder
- Water Containment System
- Water Containers
- Water Purifier & Extra Filters
- Wheeled Hand Cart

—

We've covered a lot of ground, starting with the many reasons to prepare and on to the rudiments of preparedness, but when it comes to survival, the learning curve never stops.

I would like to invite you to visit http://prepperslifeline. com/ which provides information on preparedness, updates on the state of the world, and money-saving tips to help get you prepared as quickly as possible without breaking the bank.

Blessings,

Barbara Fix (AKA Survival Diva)

## THE MOST IMPORTANT PREPARATION
*By*
*Michael Snyder*

There are many people out there that are absolutely obsessed with physical preparation for the incredibly hard times that are coming, but they totally neglect spiritual preparation.

Personally, I have no idea how anyone is going to make it through what is coming without God. I know that I wouldn't want to face the years ahead without Him.

And it is a fact that this life does not go on indefinitely. There are some people that get insurance policies for just about anything that you can think of, but they don't even give a second thought to what will happen to them once they die.

I feel like I would be doing a disservice if I didn't explain to you the most important thing that you could take away from this book. If I had not given my life to the Lord Jesus Christ, I would probably be dead today. He has taken the broken pieces of my life and has made them into a beautiful thing, and He can do the same thing for you.

If you would like to know how you can become a Christian, I encourage you to keep reading. A lot of the time people find Christianity to be very confusing. In the following pages, I have tried to explain the core of the Christian faith in a way that hopefully just about everyone will be able to understand.

Fortunately, the Christian gospel is very, very simple to understand, and the stakes are incredibly high.

If Christianity is true, then it is possible to have eternal life.

I am not just talking about living for millions of years or billions of years.

I am talking about living for eternity.

If you had the opportunity to live forever, would you take it?

Many people would respond by saying that they are not sure if living forever in a world like ours would be desirable, but what if you could live forever in a world where everything had been set right?

What if you could live forever in a perfect world where there is no more evil or suffering or pain?

Would you want that?

The truth is that is exactly what God wants for you. He loves you very much and He wants to spend forever with you.

If you could, would you want to spend forever with Him?

If God is real, and there really is an afterlife, who wouldn't want to spend eternity with Him?

To be honest with you, if eternal life really exists, there is not a single issue of greater importance to every man, woman and child on the planet.

Who would not be willing to give up everything that they own to live forever in paradise surrounded by people that love them?

All over the world people perform all kinds of religious acts, desperately hoping that they will gain favor with God. Some religious nuts even blow themselves up during suicide attacks, hoping that their "sacrifices" will earn them favor with God. But are those really ways to get to heaven?

What does the Bible have to say?

The truth is that the plan of salvation described in the Bible is very simple.

It starts with God.

The Bible tells us that God created humanity and that He loves us very much.

In fact, God loves you more than you could possibly ever imagine. The Scriptures go on and on about how great the love of God is and about how deeply He cares for each one of us individually.

But there is a huge problem.

The problem is that humanity is in deep rebellion against God.

Humanity has rejected God and is continually breaking His laws.

Most people like to think of themselves as "good" people, but the truth is that none of us are truly "good". Each one of us has broken God's laws over and over again. We are lawbreakers and criminals in the sight of God. The Scriptures call us sinners.

Perhaps you think that you are a "good person" and that God should let you into heaven based on how good you are.

If that is what you believe, ask yourself this question...

Have you ever broken God's laws?

Posted below is a summary of the Ten Commandments. Are you guilty of violating His rules?...

#1) You shall have no other gods before Me. (There is only one true God – the Creator of all things. Have you ever served a different God? Have you ever expressed approval for a false religion just because you wanted to be polite? Have you ever participated in activities or ceremonies that honor other religions?)

#2) You shall not make any idols. You shall not bow down to them or serve them. (The Scriptures tell us that we are to love God with everything that we have inside of us. Even if you have never bowed down to an idol or a statue, you may have created a "god" in your own mind that you are more comfortable with. That is sin. In fact, we are not to have any "idols" in our lives that we love more than God.)

#3) You shall not take the name of the Lord your God in vain. (Have you ever used God's holy name as a profanity or as a curse word? Have you ever failed to give His holy name the honor that it deserves?)

#4) Remember the Sabbath Day, to keep it holy. (Is there anyone alive that has kept this commandment perfectly?)

#5) Honor your father and mother. (Have you ever been rebellious or disrespectful to your father or your mother even one time? If so, you have broken this commandment.)

#6) You shall not murder. (Even if you have never killed anyone, it is important to remember that Jesus considers hatred to be very similar to murder.)

#7) You shall not commit adultery. (Sexual promiscuity is absolutely rampant in our society today, but you don't even have to sleep with someone to break this commandment. In Matthew 5:27-28, Jesus said that "whosoever looketh on a woman to lust after her hath committed adultery with her already in his heart".)

#8) You shall not steal. (Have you ever stolen anything from someone else? It doesn't matter if it was valuable or not. If you stole something, you are a thief.)

#9) You shall not lie. (Have you ever told a lie? If so, you are guilty of breaking this commandment.)

#10) You shall not covet. (Have you ever jealously desired something that belongs to someone else? This sin is often the first step toward other sins.)

The first four commandments are about loving God. In the Scriptures, you are commanded to love God with all of your heart, all of your soul, all of your mind and all of your strength.

The final six commandments are about loving others. In the Scriptures, you are commanded to love others as you love yourself.

Have you always loved God and loved others like you should have?

Sadly, the truth is that we are all guilty of breaking God's laws.

In fact, if we took an honest look at how guilty we truly are we would be absolutely horrified.

Take a moment and imagine the following scenario...

One of the biggest television networks has decided to do a huge two hour prime time special all about your life. It is going to be heavily advertised, and tens of millions of people are going to watch it.

Doesn't that sound great?

But instead of a two hour documentary about how wonderful you are, the network has discovered all of the most evil and horrible things that you have ever thought, said or did and they are going to broadcast those things to tens of millions of people all over the world for two hours during prime time.

What would you do if that happened?

Sadly, the truth is that whoever that happened to would be utterly ashamed and would never want to be seen in public again.

Why?

Because we have all done, said and thought things that are unspeakably evil.

We are sinners in the eyes of God, just as the Scriptures tell us...

"For all have sinned, and come short of the glory of God" (Romans 3:23).

God created us to have fellowship with Him, but He also gave humanity the ability to choose. Unfortunately, humanity has chosen to be in deep rebellion against God and we have all repeatedly broken His laws. When we broke God's commandments, our fellowship with God was also broken. By breaking God's commandments, we decided that our will would be done instead of God's will. And if you look around the world today, you can see the results. Evil and suffering are everywhere. God hates all of this evil and suffering very much. In the Bible, our rebellion against God is called sin.

As a result of our sin, the Scriptures tell us that we are separated from God...

"The wages of sin is death" [spiritual separation from God] (Romans 6:23).

So what can be done about this separation from God?

Why doesn't God just forget about our sins?

Well, the truth is that God cannot just sweep our evil under the rug. If God did that, He would cease to be just.

For example, how would you feel about a judge that decided to issue a blanket pardon for Hitler and all of the other high level Nazis for the horrible things that they did?

Would that be a "good" judge? Of course not.

There is a penalty for evil, and because God is just, that penalty must be paid.

Fortunately, Jesus Christ paid the penalty for our sins by dying for us on the cross. He took the punishment that we deserved...

"But God commendeth his love toward us, in that, while we were yet sinners, Christ died for us." (Romans 5:8).

We were guilty, but the Son of God, Jesus Christ, died in our place.

Being fully man, Jesus could die for the sins of mankind.

Being fully God, Jesus could die for an infinite number of sins.

He was mocked, he was beaten, he was scourged ruthlessly and he was nailed to a wooden cross. He was totally innocent, but He was willing to suffer and die because He loved you that much.

Jesus paid the penalty for your sins and my sins so that fellowship with God could be restored.

Not only that, but Jesus proved that He is the Son of God by rising from the dead...

"Christ died for our sins...He was buried...He rose again the third day according to the Scriptures" (1 Corinthians 15:3-4).

You see, if there was any other way for us to be reconciled to God, Jesus would not have had to die on the cross. He could have just told us to follow one of the other ways to get to heaven. But there was no other way. The death of Jesus on the cross is the only payment for our sins and He is the only way that we are going to get to heaven. In the Scriptures, Jesus put it this way...

"I am the way, the truth, and the life: no man cometh unto the Father, but by me." (John 14:6).

But it is not enough just for you to intellectually know that Jesus is the Son of God and that He died on the cross for our sins.

The Scriptures tell us that we must individually commit our lives to Jesus Christ as Savior and Lord. When we give our lives to Jesus, He forgives our sins and He gives us eternal life...

"But as many as received him, to them gave he power to become the sons of God, even to them that believe on his name" (John 1:12).

"For God so loved the world, that he gave his only begotten Son, that whosoever believeth in him should not perish, but have everlasting life." (John 3:16).

"That if thou shalt confess with thy mouth the Lord Jesus, and shalt believe in thine heart that God hath raised him from the dead, thou shalt be saved." (Romans 10:9).

So exactly how does someone do this?

It is actually very simple.

The Scriptures tell us that it is through faith that we enter into a relationship with Jesus Christ...

"For by grace are ye saved through faith; and that not of yourselves: it is the gift of God: Not of works, lest any man should boast." (Ephesians 2:8,9).

If you are not a Christian yet, then Jesus is standing at the door of your heart and He is knocking. He is hoping that you will let Him come in. He loves you very much and He wants to have a relationship with you...

[Jesus speaking] "Behold, I stand at the door, and knock: if any man hear my voice, and open the door, I will come in to him" (Revelation 3:20).

Jesus asks that you give Him control of your life. That means renouncing all of the sin in your life and making Him your Savior and Lord. Just to know intellectually that Jesus died on the cross and that He rose from the dead is not enough to become a Christian. Having a wonderful emotional experience is not enough to become a Christian either. You become a Christian by faith. It is an act of your will.

Are you ready to make a commitment to Jesus Christ?

If you are ready to invite Jesus Christ into your life, it is very easy.

Just tell Him.

God is not really concerned if you say the right words. What He is concerned about is the attitude of your heart.

If you are ready to become a Christian, the following is a prayer that can help you express that desire to Him...

"Lord Jesus, I want to become a Christian. I know that I am a sinner, and I thank You for dying on the cross for my sins. I believe that you are the Son of God and that you rose from the dead. I repent of my sins and I open the door of my life and ask You to be my Savior and Lord. I commit my life to You. Thank You for forgiving all of my sins and giving me eternal life. Take control of my life and make me the kind of person that You want me to be. I will live my life for You. Amen."

If you are ready to enter into a personal relationship with Jesus Christ, then I invite you to pray this prayer right now. Jesus will come into your life, just as He has promised to do.

If you do invite Jesus Christ to come into your life, you can have 100 percent certainty that you have become a Christian and that you will go to heaven when you die. In 1 John 5:11-13, the Scriptures tell us the following...

"And this is the record, that God hath given to us eternal life, and this life is in his Son. He that hath the Son hath life; and he that hath not the Son of God hath not life. These things have I written unto you that believe on the name of the Son of God; that ye may know that ye have eternal life".

Do you understand what that means?

It means that you can know that you have eternal life.

The Bible says that if you have invited Jesus Christ into your life, your sins are forgiven and you now have eternal life.

What could be better than that?

But your journey is not done.

In fact, it is just beginning.

The Christian life is not easy - especially if you try to go it alone.

There are four keys to spiritual growth for any Christian...

#1) The Bible - If you do not have a Bible you will need to get one and read it every day. It is God's instruction book for your life.

#2) Prayer – Prayer does not have to be complicated. The truth is that prayer is just talking with God. God wants to hear from you every day, and He will fundamentally transform your life as you pray to Him with humility and sincerity.

#3) Fellowship - The Scriptures tell us that we all need each other. Find a fellowship of local Christians that believe the Bible and that sincerely love one another. They will help you grow.

#4) Witnessing - Tell others about the new life that you have found in Jesus Christ. Helping even one person find eternal life is of more value than anything else that you could ever accomplish in this world.

If you have invited Jesus Christ to come into your life, I would love to hear from you. You can write to me at the following email address...

TheEconomicCollapseBlog @ Hotmail.com

We are entering a period of time that the Bible refers to as the last days. It will be a period of great darkness and the world is going to become increasingly unstable. According to Jesus, there has never been a time like it before, and there will never be a time like it again. But in the middle of all of this, God is going to do great things. He is raising up a Remnant that will keep His commandments, that will boldly proclaim the gospel of salvation through faith in Jesus Christ, and that will see their message confirmed by the power of the Holy Spirit just like the very first believers in Jesus did. This is already happening all over the globe even though no organization is in charge of it. You can read about the Remnant in Revelation 12:17 and Revelation 14:12. God is starting to bring things full circle. The Remnant of the last days is going to do things the way that the Christians of the first century did things. Have you ever wondered why so many Christian churches of today do not resemble what you see in the Bible? Well, the sad truth is that over the centuries churches got away from what the Scriptures tell us to do, but now God is restoring all things. Without God we can do nothing, but with God all things are possible.

Today, we have an even greater opportunity than the first century Christians did in some ways. During the first century, there were only about 200 million people on earth. Today, there are more than 7 billion. That means that there are about 35 times as many people living on the planet today than there were back then.

The global population has experienced exponential growth over the past couple of centuries, and that means that we have the opportunity to impact more lives than anyone else ever has. I believe that the greatest move of God that the world has ever seen is coming, and I believe that millions upon millions of souls will be brought into the Kingdom. I encourage you to be a part of what is happening.

As the global economy collapses and unprecedented troubles break out around the globe, people are going to be looking for answers. Hundreds of millions of people will have their lives totally turned upside down and will be consumed with despair. Instead of giving in to fear like everyone else will be, it will be a great opportunity for the people of God to rise up and take the message of life to a lost and dying world.

Yes, there will be great persecution. The world system absolutely hates the gospel and the Bible tells us that eventually Christians will be hunted down and killed for what they believe.

But those that have read the last book of the Bible know that we win in the end. God loves you very much and He wants to make your life a greater adventure than you ever imagined that it possibly could be. Yes, there will be hardships in this world, but if you are willing to pursue God with a passion and become totally sold out to Him, you can make an eternal difference in countless lives.

When you get a chance, go read the book of Acts. Do you want your own life to look like that?

It can.

In these last days, those that have a passion for God and a passion for reaching the lost are going to turn this world upside down with the gospel of Jesus Christ.

The Scriptures tell us that "there is joy in the presence of the angels of God over one sinner that repents." When a single person makes a commitment to Jesus Christ, there is great celebration in heaven.

As millions upon millions of precious souls are brought into the Kingdom in the years ahead, what do you think the atmosphere in heaven is going to look like?

Yes, darkness and evil will also prosper in the days ahead. A one world government, a one world economy and a one world religion are coming. This world system will utterly hate the Remnant and will try to crush us with everything that they have got.

It is going to take great strength and great courage to stand against the world system in the times that are coming. You have the opportunity to be a part of a greater adventure than anything that Hollywood ever dreamed up, and in the end it may cost you your life.

But in Revelation chapter 2, Jesus tells us that if we are "faithful unto death" that He will give us "a crown of life".

Do you want that crown? I do.

For those of us that have a relationship with Jesus, we know that we have the ultimate happy ending. Jesus has forgiven our sins and has given us eternal life, and nobody can ever take that away from us.

Life is like a coin – you can spend it any way that you want, but you can only spend it once.

Spend your life on something that really matters.

God is raising up a Remnant that is going to shake the world. You do not want to miss out on the great move of God that is coming. It is going to be unlike anything that any of us have ever seen before.

If you enjoyed this book, I encourage you to also connect with me on the Internet. You can find my work at the following websites…

The Economic Collapse Blog: http://theeconomiccollapseblog.com/
The American Dream: http://endoftheamericandream.com/
The Most Important News: http://themostimportantnews.com/

Thank you for taking the time to read this book. I would love to hear any feedback that you may have.

My wife and I are praying for all those that visit our websites and for all those that will read this book.

May the Lord bless you and keep you.

May the Lord make His face shine upon you and be gracious to you.

May the Lord lift up His countenance upon you and give you His peace.

Michael Snyder

# ABOUT THE AUTHORS

## Michael T Snyder

Michael T. Snyder is a graduate of the University of Florida law school and he worked as an attorney in the heart of Washington D.C. for a number of years. Today, Michael is best known for his work as the publisher of The Economic Collapse Blog (http://theeconomiccollapseblog.com/). Michael and his wife, Meranda, believe that a great awakening is coming and are working hard to help bring renewal to America.

## Barbara Fix

Barbara Fix is the author of *Survival: Prepare Before Disaster Strikes* and hundreds of preparedness-related articles under the pen name Survival Diva. You are invited to visit Barbara's blog, http://prepperslifeline.com/ for current news impacting preparedness and common sense, budget-friendly tips designed to get you prepared without breaking the bank.

Made in the USA
San Bernardino, CA
24 November 2016